C000170727

BOYS OF '86

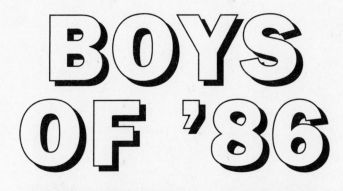

BOYS OF '86

THE UNTOLD STORY OF WEST HAM UNITED'S GREATEST-EVER SEASON

TONY McDONALD and DANNY FRANCIS

MAINSTREAM
PUBLISHING

EDINBURGH AND LONDON

Copyright © Tony McDonald and Danny Francis, 2001
All rights reserved
The moral rights of the authors have been asserted

First published in Great Britain in 2001 by
MAINSTREAM PUBLISHING COMPANY (EDINBURGH) LTD
7 Albany Street
Edinburgh EH1 3UG

ISBN 1 84018 474 4

No part of this book may be reproduced or transmitted in any form
or by any means without written permission from the publisher,
except by a reviewer who wishes to quote brief passages in connection
with a review written for insertion in a newspaper, magazine or broadcast

Copyright permissions cleared by the authors. The authors have tried to trace
all copyright details, but where this has not been possible and amendments are
required, the publisher will be pleased to make any necessary arrangements
at the earliest opportunity.

A catalogue record for this book is available from the British Library

Typeset in Berkeley Book and Helvetica
Printed and bound in Great Britain
by Butler and Tanner Ltd.

CONTENTS

This book is dedicated to the thousands of long-suffering Hammers fans all over the world who still dream of one day seeing their team make another strong challenge for the League Championship . . . just as the Boys of '86 did.

ACKNOWLEDGEMENTS

The authors would like to thank the following people, without whose help it would not have been possible to produce this book.

Firstly, and most importantly, to the players of 1985–86 who have contributed so candidly to this book. They have given up their time, racked their memories and made every effort to ensure no stone has been left unturned when covering the events of that record-breaking campaign.

Our good friend Steve Blowers, for his invaluable input, proofreading and the loan of his priceless scrapbooks and memorabilia from that year.

The fanatical autograph and memorabilia connoisseur Terry Connelly, also for the use of his scrapbooks containing helpful news cuttings from the season.

Young Jenni Ryder whose typesetting of the statistical section made her realise that there really was once a truly great West Ham United team to ruffle the feathers of the elite.

Roy Francis, for providing reminders and memories.

And finally, to John Lyall, for building a team that provided us all with excitement and entertainment . . . and memories that will last forever.

BOYS OF '86

Introduction

HISTORY – Mai Tai

Chart Position: Number 8, June 1985

West Ham United manager John Lyall was only halfway through his post-match inquest following the 3–1 pre-season friendly defeat at Leyton Orient on 11 August 1985, when the visitors' dressing-room door suddenly burst open.

Lyall's voice was drowned in a hail of abuse from an irate Hammers fan who proceeded to tear into the manager and the players who had just lost so humiliatingly to their humble neighbours from the Fourth Division.

Central defender Tony Gale didn't know the identity of the fan and thought he might be a member of the notorious Inter-City Firm (ICF), the hard group of fans who attached themselves to the East London club during football's dark days of the '70s and '80s.

'It's the one thing I remember about our pre-season build-up,' says Gale. 'Orient beat us – and beat us well – and, quite frankly, we were a shambles.

'I don't know how that geezer managed to get into our dressing-room but he made himself absolutely clear about what he thought of our performance, and the club overall.

'John just stood there, silent, as the fella laid into us like a nutter. He said: "What the fucking hell's going on here? We've gone right down the fucking pan, you bunch of tossers. We had a shit season last year and now we've lost to fucking Orient. Where do we go from here?"'

The intruder was finally ushered back out through the door and out onto Brisbane Road, no doubt still in a rage after seeing new signing Frank McAvennie open the scoring in the 20th minute, only for the O's to come from behind to win easily.

BOYS OF '86

The start of the new Canon League First Division season was only six days away and no one at Upton Park – including players and fans – were looking forward to it with too much optimism.

In fact the pessimism around Upton Park then mirrored the mood of a nation that was growing increasingly tired of football. The tragic events of the previous season, with deaths at Birmingham, Bradford and Heysel, had cast a large black shadow over the British game. Years of trouble on the terraces (and in the surrounding streets), in unsafe, decaying stadiums, were beginning to take their toll.

Sure, it was society's problem but football was so often the outlet for the mindless minority who thrived amidst the tribalism. The ICF may have been recognised as West Ham's menacing mob but every club had its own hooligan 'crew' who found their identity through their club's colours.

The far-reaching effects of the 1989 Hillsborough Disaster, and Lord Justice Taylor's report that followed it, were still in the future. In the summer of '85 football was a swearword to many and the clubs were very aware of the part they had to play in trying to revive the fortunes of our national sport.

The Bradford Fire Disaster, which had claimed the lives of 56 people who perished in the blaze at Bradford City's Valley Parade ground in May, precipitated demands under the Safety of Sports Grounds Act which forced clubs to make safe certain areas of their grounds. This basically meant replacing wooden structures with metal and it took the tragic events of Hillsborough – where 96 encaged Liverpool fans died after being crushed on the terraces and against crush barriers, prior to the FA Cup semi-final with Nottingham Forest four years later – to bring about the all-seater stadium revolution.

The ugly, metal fences in place at many grounds to keep the troublemakers off the pitch all came down in the immediate aftermath of Hillsborough but as the 1985–86 season dawned, Upton Park was one of only three London grounds – along with Highbury and QPR's Loftus Road – without pitchside fences.

Not that Prime Minister Margaret Thatcher and her Conservative government were going to leave football to police itself. A new Act was introduced banning the sale of alcohol inside grounds, although this of course did nothing to prevent the thirstier fans from getting well oiled in nearby pubs hours before kick-off.

West Ham United chairman Len Cearns, at the head of a family-dominated Board that included two of his brothers – Will (vice-chairman) and Brian, and his son Martin, with Jack Petchey the only 'outsider' – took his responsibilities very seriously.

In a progressive move, West Ham introduced a Family Seating Area within the East Stand, offering tickets at concessionary rates in the hope that fathers would bring their wives and children with them.

The club suspended its Irons Travel Club and further deterred supporters from attending away matches by also refusing to sell away tickets. They compromised at the end of the year by selling a limited number of tickets to season-ticket holders only.

West Ham installed closed-circuit television cameras around the Boleyn Ground to identify the law-breakers and Cearns – or 'Mr Len' as he was affectionately known to John Lyall and other club employees – set the tone for the start of the season when he issued a rare warning statement in the first home matchday programme.

He wrote: 'Keep the fences away, cut out the abuse and foul language, encourage both teams, and football could quickly regain what it has sadly lost. We've had some great times here – may they soon return.' The chairman's message may have been more in hope than expectation but some great times did, indeed, soon return.

But it still took until the second half of the season, when Hammers showed that they really weren't going to come down with the Christmas decorations after all, to fully convince a sceptical public that West Ham was a force to be reckoned with again.

The facts show that crowds were falling anyway well before the tragic events that stunned all of football in the spring of 1985. Hammers finished ninth in 1983–84, Trevor Brooking's last season at the club, but the average League attendance at Upton Park was down to 21,249. After Brooking retired, Alan Devonshire suffered his terrible injury and the team slumped to 16th place in 1984–85, crowds had dropped to an average of just 18,401.

Incredible though it seems now, the attendance for the home League match against Manchester United on Friday, 15 March 1985, was a meagre 16,674, even taking into account that the size of the crowd was clearly affected by the fact that the game was screened live on TV and played on a Friday evening.

The team's poor early season form in 1985–86 did nothing to win back the missing thousands. Things got worse before they got better, as Hammers pulled in an average of 16,686 up to the game against Everton on 2 November.

It was not as if the club could blame televised matches for the apathy among its traditional followers. The Football League and TV

BOYS OF '86

chiefs were at loggerheads all summer and the upshot was that live football remained off screen until the start of 1986, when, as it happened, West Ham would feature in the first match to be shown under the long-awaited new agreement.

But West Ham were suffering along with the rest. In fact, the disappointing gate of 15,034 for the visit of Aston Villa in October was the fifth highest in the top flight that day. By then, however, the club felt they had no option but to slash season-ticket prices in another effort to boost crowds and their own coffers. The Upton Park season was just three games old when the club announced that the top-priced seat in the West Stand had been reduced to £95 (yes, that's ninety-five pounds!), while the best seats in the newer East Stand were cut to £77, and the East Terrace (better known as the 'Chicken Run') to as little as £52 . . . for the season. Fans who today pay around £500–£600 for a standard season ticket will look back in disbelief at the prospect of paying £126 for the best season ticket in the West Stand upper tier at the start of 1985–86.

Not that a season ticket was even a necessity then, because sell-outs were a thing of the past. You could simply turn up just before 3 p.m. on a Saturday and pay at the turnstiles. Matchday prices were not exactly extortionate: the dearest seat cost £7.50 and the cheapest only £4.00. Kids could get in for just three quid.

It was not as if cash-strapped parents were under pressure from their children to buy replica kits and the hundred-and-one other souvenir items that have now become the accepted norm either. People wore the shirts but to nothing like the extent they do today. New shop manager Kate Bouchard and her staff worked from a glorified Portakabin on the main forecourt, off Green Street, but they were not deluged with orders for the new home and away shirts, which then ranged in price from £12.99 to £15.99. Shorts cost between £6.99 and £8.50 and socks between £3.50 and £3.99. Oh, and for an optional extra pound, they'd stick the name of the club's sponsor – AVCO Trust, a finance company from Reading – on the front of your shirt, so that it was pukka.

At that time, the only sportsmen's names to appear on the back of shirts were on strips worn by the heroes of American football, the giants of the Dallas Cowboys and Chicago Bears, who were part of the new gridiron craze sweeping the UK thanks to Channel 4's ground-breaking TV coverage that attracted an audience of millions at 6 p.m. on Sundays. So three-letter Neil Orr didn't win himself any new cost-conscious fans at the expense of 12-character David

Swindlehurst in the same way that, after forking out almost £50 for a replica shirt, a modern-day visitor to one of the club's nine prime site retail outlets spread around Essex might choose Joe Cole instead of, say, Nigel Winterburn.

Walk from Upton Park tube station to the redeveloped new Dr Martens West Stand today and you'll be spoiled for choice in your pre-match reading material. As well as the club's two official publications, the traditional matchday programme and the monthly *Hammers News Magazine*, you can also sample the more forthright views in fanzines like *Over Land And Sea*, *On The Terraces* and the semi-official *Ironworks Gazette*. But back in 1985, you had to make do with *Hammer*, the 60p club programme – a simple, 24-page mix of colour and black-and-white, largely written and edited by Colin Benson and carrying a page-three leader that bore the unmistakable mark of club historian Jack Helliar, who used to write and print those charming pocket-sized programmes himself from his Canning Town factory for many years before the high-speed, four-colour presses revolutionised the print industry in the early '80s.

Half-time entertainment consisted of announcer Bill Remfry's record requests – today's gyrating Hammerettes would have been arrested for their body language alone – and there was always the consolation that your hunger could be cured by the Percy Dalton peanut seller who scuttled noisily and freely around the touch-line catching coins and hurling bags of his wares high into the terraces with all the aplomb of a Test cricketer.

By the end of the 1985–86 season these terraces would be packed again, thronging with 30,000-plus expectant fans who, with their faith restored, were full of hope that they would be there to see history in the making.

In the end, after an astonishing marathon end-of-season schedule that no Premiership club would be expected to undertake today, it wasn't quite enough. Liverpool and Everton, the two Merseyside giants who had dominated English football for the previous decade, clung on to the major silverware. This time the Reds exceeded even their own very high standards by winning the First Division League and FA Cup double.

In the unlikely event that you have read the autobiographies of the Liverpool and Everton stars of that era, you will know that few of them gave the serious threat West Ham posed to their dominance the credit it deserved. To them, and the majority of their supporters, John Lyall's team were no more than crafty Cockney 'upstarts' who audaciously tried to wrest glory away from Anfield and Goodison and, having narrowly failed, never came back for another go.

The Boys of '86 is a detailed journey through West Ham United's greatest-ever season of League football. The year we finished third. The year we nearly won the League.

It might say something about the lack of silverware achieved at Upton Park (no major trophy since the 1980 FA Cup triumph and nothing better in the League either before or since 1985–86) that one third-place finish in the League should inspire a whole book in its memory. If so, then 15 years on, the level of performances and the stylish manner in which Lyall's side provided the most engrossing, entertaining football produced by any club that season, are well worthy of more detailed analysis.

And who better to take us through that memorable, exhilarating journey than the men who made it happen – the Boys of '86 themselves. With the exception of Tony Gale at Blackburn Rovers in 1995, none of the players used by West Ham that season went on to win a League Championship medal, so the 1985–86 campaign means even more to them today than it did then.

Unfortunately, John Lyall politely declined to be interviewed for this book. Now retired and living life in peace and tranquillity on his Suffolk farm with his loving wife Yvonne, the 61-year-old Lyall would prefer to let history tell of his achievements in 34 unblemished years at Upton Park. He returned our letters and phone calls with typical courtesy but, sadly, could not be persuaded to talk about the finest season in his long and distinguished career.

John doesn't subscribe to Sky and is content to watch the European games shown on terrestrial television. He claims not to be missing the game that consumed him for so many years and his happiness sounds genuine enough when he phones to say:

'I'm really enjoying myself out here on the farm, where we've lived for the past seven years. I've got 35 acres and my son, Murray, lives just 25 yards away with his wife and our grandchildren. I'll spend three hours mowing the lawn, digging molehills. We've got stables and a lake where I can fish, which I really enjoy. I'm doing things now that I'd never done before when I was so wrapped up in football. At weekends, sometimes we go to auctions where I look for bargains for our home, which is situated in a lovely valley. We're not far from civilisation – Ipswich is just ten minutes from here, Manningtree is just up the road and I can be back in the City of London in an hour and a half. But I like the countryside and even the prospect of moving back to our old place at Ongar wouldn't appeal to me now.'

John briefly enquires about circumstances surrounding the departure of Harry Redknapp and how West Ham have been doing in general but he just won't be persuaded to travel back through his time at Upton Park, not even his best-ever season in the Football League.

'I've done my bit, I've got other priorities now,' he says. 'I'm not being cruel but it's all in the past. It was work to me and now I've got my pleasure in life. I'm not turning my back on West Ham but I'd only say the same things to you now about that season as I've said before. By all means use those quotes if you wish.'

With that, John Lyall returned to life on the farm and so the story of the club's most successful League campaign ever is left to the men who became West Ham's history-makers. They provide a unique insight into how a team no one had tipped as title contenders recovered from a poor start, sorted out their problems internally and set off on an incredible run that only ended in tears on the final Saturday of a dramatic season.

But *Boys of '86* is not just about goals, games and Hammers' surge up the First Division table. The players talk very candidly about themselves and their teammates, the value of true team spirit and camaraderie and how problems were resolved.

We examine the personalities and traits of the players themselves; how they were viewed by each other, their off-the-field habits, the banter and the humour that made the training-ground and the dressing-room such a buzzing place to be that season.

Even the 'nutter' who went berserk in the dressing-room at Leyton Orient was smiling proudly by the end of it . . .

BOYS OF '86

Chapter 1

FRANKIE – Sister Sledge

Chart Position: Number 1, July 1985

Beautiful blondes and Frank McAvennie go hand in hand, but not even the former road digger from Glasgow could quite have imagined what was in store for him soon after he jetted into London to complete the formalities of his move from St Mirren in July 1985.

John Lyall had collected his new £340,000 signing from Heathrow Airport and as the Hammers' manager recalled in his autobiography, *Just Like My Dreams*:

'We drove back through the centre of London, because he wanted to look at the King's Road. I was to learn that he was a fashion-conscious lad, very concerned about his appearance. I could tell that he was thrilled to be in London.

'We drove through the city, where the traffic was particularly heavy. Passing us on the opposite side of the road was a convoy of black limousines with police motorcycle escort. Sitting in the back of one of the cars was Princess Diana. She passed within a few feet of us. Frank was impressed.

'"This is London, Frank," I said.'

In two separate spells at Upton Park covering a five-year period, McAvennie would come to know the capital like the back of his hand. On and off the field, he made big headlines and was one of the first footballers, since George Best almost two decades earlier, to be elevated to celebrity status. He came to enjoy the London nightlife as much as he loved scoring goals but in those first few weeks away from home, the West End club scene had still to be explored.

To West Ham supporters, McAvennie was a mystery, yet another in a long line of summer signings bought more in hope than expectation. Sure, the Scot had impressed often enough for St Mirren in the Scottish First Division, where he had scored 50 goals in 135 outings for the Buddies, but he was virtually unknown south of the border, having entered the professional game at the age of only 20.

As McAvennie admitted at the time of his move: 'Missing out on all that coaching as a young teenager, I am very much a novice really.'

While champions Everton were completing the transfer from Leicester City of England striker Gary Lineker for £800,000, and Liverpool were appointing Kenny Dalglish as player-manager to replace Joe Fagan, West Ham were paying less than half their club record fee (£800,000 for Paul Goddard five years earlier) for a player whose name most Hammers' fans had never heard of and could not even pronounce. There was no ballyhoo surrounding Hammers' biggest signing of that summer. The national papers gave the move scant coverage and it was very much a case of 'Frank who?'.

McAvennie himself could barely believe what was happening to him. He had had spells on the dole back home on the mean streets of Glasgow's East End and had scraped a living with a variety of jobs – as a painter and decorator, a road digger and a garage worker. He had even spent some weekends working for the Territorial Army.

Having agreed the deal with the player at an M1 service station, Lyall was, however, upbeat about McAvennie's ability to contribute to the goal threat already posed by his main strike pairing of Tony Cottee and Paul Goddard, who had scored 26 League goals between them the season before. Lyall said:

'Frank operated frequently in attack for St Mirren last season but midfield is his real position. Cottee and Goddard got a lot of goals for us last season but we did not score enough from midfield – and this is what we hope Frank will do for us. He netted 17 goals last season and has regularly been among the leading Scottish scorers.'

Lyall had snatched McAvennie from under the nose of Luton Town whose manager, David Pleat, was on first-name terms with Frank's parents, having pursued the 25 year old for some time. Luton were a respectable First Division outfit at the time, while Pleat was fast gaining a reputation as one of the most highly rated managers in the English game, poised for a big career move to Tottenham Hotspur within a year, but he was not persuasive enough to land McAvennie.

Frank explains:

'I went down to Luton for talks with Pleat but in the middle of our

BOYS OF '86

discussions the club chairman, David Evans MP, walked into the room and, with a slap of my back, said: "Hello Macca". I didn't like his style – only people I knew well called me that – and I decided there and then that I wasn't going to Luton.'

Not that McAvennie was head-over-heels about being in London either when he first arrived, and admits he came close to returning home to his working-class Glasgow roots before he had made his name in a claret-and-blue shirt:

'I felt very unsettled in the first couple of months down there. I said to John Lyall at the time that I wanted to go home but he told me to give it a go and if I still felt the same way in another couple of months, he would allow me to leave.'

McAvennie had always supported Celtic as a kid and was linked with a possible move to Parkhead, when David Hay was managing the green-and-white hoops, before West Ham got him.

'I had been warned that the people of London could be cold at times but I didn't expect that to bother me because it normally takes me only two seconds to settle in anywhere. I just thought that because no one was talking to me, they didn't like me. I did feel lonely at that point.

'The problem stemmed from the fact that the players didn't understand a word I was saying. Then Tony Gale explained to me that every time I shouted for the ball, the lads thought I wanted to fight them! It was my accent.

'I don't know what John said to the players but soon after my chat with him about feeling homesick, the boys had a big night out and that did the trick. We started off drinking at The Ship in Gidea Park, moved on to the Slater's Arms in Romford and ended up at Stringfellows in the West End. I remember thinking to myself that night that my new teammates were all poofters, because it was the first time I'd ever seen blokes dancing together. I was amazed and kept my back to the wall, but they were simply winding me up!'

McAvennie never had any worries about football, however. He was immediately impressed with the coaching sessions put on by Lyall and his assistants, Ronnie Boyce and Mick McGiven.

'It was a shock to my system, coming down from St Mirren, where you never even saw a ball for the first two weeks of pre-season training. It was all running up there. But on my first day at West Ham I thought it was a wind-up because they gave us a ball each. John would point to the ball and say: "That's the tool of your trade and you've got to learn how to use it."

'We still did a lot of running – in the afternoon!'

Club captain Alvin Martin was pleasantly surprised by the mystery-man from Glasgow:

'We'd had these reports of a bad boy coming down and I expected some lairy Jock to walk in, all mouth and trousers, but Frank wasn't like that. Quiet and unassuming, he wasn't the greatest trainer I've ever seen but at the beginning he was obviously trying to make an impression in training.

'Over the years, though, you see so many players come in who have two good sessions and then they can't reproduce it on the field. Frank could run with the ball, take people on and he had a bit of pace about him, too. I thought, yeah, he looks half decent.'

Martin had been a central figure in the last successful Hammers' team of the early '80s, when they beat Arsenal 1–0 in the 1980 FA Cup final and, a year later, romped to the Second Division Championship with a record points haul and also reached the League Cup final, as well as the quarter-finals of the European Cup Winners' cup when that competition still had credibility.

The big Scouser saw nothing in the pre-season preparations of 1985, however, to make him think that he would go even remotely close to lifting any silverware at the end of the season.

Hammers' fans were still unhappy about the sale earlier that summer of Paul Allen, the talented England Under-21 skipper, reigning Hammer of the Year and one of the brightest young prospects in the country. The tigerish midfielder, who made history as the youngest-ever player to appear in an FA Cup final when he faced the Gunners aged 17 years and 256 days, was out of contract and, after rejecting a new offer from West Ham, he chose a move to London rivals Tottenham Hotspur instead of Liverpool.

It was a double blow, because Lyall did not even manage to secure his £600,000-plus valuation of the player. With the 22-year-old Allen now a free agent, a tribunal decreed that all Spurs would have to pay for him was £400,000. An additional £50,000 would have been due to West Ham if Allen went on to make ten full England appearances but for all his prominence at under-21 level, he never made the step up to the senior national team.

Before the Allen deal finally went through, Lyall had abandoned the idea of signing Spanish-born midfielder Manuel Sanchez Torres, available for around £225,000 from Dutch First Division side FC Twente, after learning that government regulations would prevent him from obtaining the work permit he needed to play in Britain.

West Ham watched the 26 year old several times before turning their attention elsewhere in Holland.

The next (failed) target was £400,000-rated winger Rob de Wit, the 21-year-old Ajax star and full Dutch international. Lyall and his trusty chief scout Eddie Baily had made several flying visits to Holland in search of new blood but their efforts were rebuffed a third time when newly promoted NEC Nijmegen turned down Hammers' initial £100,000 bid for left-winger Danny Hoekman, who seemed keen to move to east London. Dutch Under-21 international Hoekman impressed over two days at Hammers' Chadwell Heath training ground but Nijmegen wanted more than double the figure Lyall was prepared to pay. After a lot of wrangling, Nijmegen eventually settled for £150,000 for their most promising youngster – but the deal collapsed in bizarre circumstances. Just as the transfer papers were en route to England for completion, Hoekman's mother invoked the rule that all Dutch Under-21s need the permission of their parent or guardian before they can move abroad – and Mrs Hoekman refused to sanction her son's switch to West Ham.

Lyall groaned: 'After working for over a month on the deal, this is a bitter blow, particularly as we considered it was all done but for minor details. Now we are back to square one with only five days left before the start of the season.'

On the home front, West Ham's squad had a depleted look about it. Long-serving left-back Frank Lampard had played the last of his 665 senior games for the club and was poised to join up with former teammate Bobby Moore, who was boss at Southend United, on a free transfer. Fringe players Paul Brush and Bobby Barnes were both seeking moves and more regular first-team action; veteran 38-year-old Billy Bonds, who had answered the call to help keep West Ham up at the end of the 1984–85 season, would be ruled out long-term by a badly broken small toe (in fact, Bonzo wouldn't make a first-team appearance all season); hard-working midfielder Geoff Pike faced a stomach operation that would keep him out for the first few months of the new campaign; and striker Dave Swindlehurst was sold to Sunderland for £25,000.

There were just two days left before the start of the new Canon League First Division season, and club photographer Steve Bacon had already taken the official team picture, when Lyall found the answer to his problems and made his second significant signing of that summer. Again, however, Hammers' long-suffering fans saw no reason to crack open the champagne, for, like Frank McAvennie,

Oldham Athletic's Mark Ward was a relative unknown who had never played in the top flight.

A diminutive, pacy winger, Ward was a 22-year-old former baker's boy who, having earlier been released by Everton as an apprentice, re-emerged from non-league circles with Northwich Victoria to become a star at Second Division Oldham, where he had recently signed a new three-year contract. The Latics' asking price of £250,000 (£25,000 of which became due after he had played 25 games) was met without hesitation.

Ward was effectively a replacement for Paul Allen on the right of midfield and Lyall spoke with prophetic accuracy when he enthused: 'Joe Royle, the Oldham manager, feels the boy could go right to the top and we have given Mark that chance. I have watched him many times and he was considered to be the best in the Second Division. You have to pay for quality.'

Martin, who was the first player to greet little 'Wardie' on his arrival at Chadwell Heath, says: 'You can never read too much into a pre-season campaign. We'd struggled the season before and with Frank and Wardie we were now going into the unexpected. We knew we weren't a very good side because we'd only just stayed up.'

A pocket dynamo at 5 ft 6 in, Ward was shocked to be told by Royle that Lyall would be driving up the next day to collect his new signing in person and would take him back to London.

'Imagine the manager of a Premier League club driving up to collect a new signing today,' says Ward. 'It was pandemonium in our house as my wife, Jane, and I told our families we were moving south.

'John drove along our little cobbled street in his immaculate Jaguar, but he immediately put us at ease by cracking a joke about paying a little scally a quid to look after it. I knew West Ham had watched me a lot of times the previous season and even during that pre-season. I think Eddie Baily was there against Runcorn when I happened to score twice, which was unheard of.

'When I got to the ground to sign my contract, Frank McAvennie was already there in the office. We were staying at the same hotel at Epping for a short while but there was a communication problem. He was very broad Glaswegian when he first came down and with me being a Scouser, we couldn't understand each other. It was a good idea to separate us, so Frank moved out to Brentwood way and I stayed in Epping for a few months. But we hit it off straight away.

'What struck me at first was the sheer vastness of London – I'd never been there before.'

BOYS OF '86

Ward wasted no time making his mark on his new teammates. Martin recalls: 'John Lyall rarely left training to his coaches. He was always out there doing the coaching himself but on this particular day he was nowhere to be seen. We knew something was going on, transfer-wise. He was always very secretive.

'Being the only other Scouser at the club, I got called in from the session and was asked to have a welcome chat with Mark and Jane. It lasted about half an hour but I hated it because I was missing training. We were having a really good game of "keep-ball" that day. I was quite pissed off about it.

'In the end, Wardie put on some kit and came out with me. At times he looked awkward and clumsy during that first session, although he was obviously hard. He went in for every tackle. Training sessions are meant to be competitive but they're not supposed to go over a certain line. Wardie didn't know where to draw that line and he was booting people and going in for every tackle as though his life depended on it. I was thinking, shit, he's going to hurt somebody or he's gonna get hurt himself. I didn't know what to expect from him during the season to come.'

Ward admits he had even started to doubt himself: 'I was mesmerised by the likes of Alan Devonshire. It was all one and two-touch football and I wondered whether I was good enough to be in this team. The pace and the quality I witnessed in that first session was unbelievable and that was the first time I'd ever doubted myself as a player. I'm glad there was just the one training session before my first game, otherwise the self-doubts might have increased, but all the lads made me feel so very welcome. They were such a great bunch, quality players and quality people as well.

'I always loved training. Joe Royle used to put on a heavy running session every Tuesday at Oldham and I'd always want to do so well that I would end up being physically sick. Joe would stand over me and say: "So what have you had for breakfast today, son?" I soon learned not to have breakfast on Tuesday mornings. But at West Ham I never struggled to keep up with the others. My fitness level was superior to most other players and I always prided myself on being fitter than the opponent I was going to be up against in the next game. I was very fit when I arrived at West Ham.'

But would Ward and McAvennie be equipped for the English First Division?

Tony Cottee, who had established himself as the club's main striker and their hottest property, surprisingly admits that he was filled with trepidation after a dismal pre-season for the team and personal doubts about the effect the Scot's arrival might have on his own future. Cottee, whose goal at Ipswich Town ensured Hammers' safety with just one game left of the previous season, says: 'I'd had a good season the year before even though we only just stayed up. I got 24 League and Cup goals so I just wanted to beat that target. I was apprehensive, though, because Paul Allen had gone to Tottenham and Frank had arrived. I'd been scoring goals but I didn't want to lose my place.

'I remember going to John Lyall's house at Toot Hill, near Abridge, to seek reassurance from him in the summer because I didn't know anything about Frank except that he was an attacking player. John was very good and convinced me that I was definitely a big part of his plans. He told me to get my head down and give everything in our pre-season games. He told me that he'd bought Frank to play behind Paul Goddard and myself up front. He described Frank as an attacking "in the hole" type of midfielder, which came as a relief to me.

'I wanted the club to progress and do well but when West Ham signed Frank and Mark Ward, to be honest, I didn't even know who they were. I wanted us to sign some big-name players so we could move on, but I also appreciated it was tough for John because we'd only just missed relegation by two points. How many big names would want to come to us?

'I was concerned about what the coming season would hold. We had some good players at the club, and Alan Devonshire was just coming back after being out for so long with a bad knee injury, but I just didn't know how good Frank and Wardie were going to be. I was really worried about relegation and being a supporter too, I just wanted the club to do well.

'The pre-season was a shambles. We were appalling, so I certainly didn't exactly go into the first League game at Birmingham filled with hope.'

BOYS OF '86

Chapter 2

INTO THE GROOVE – Madonna

Chart Position: Number 1, August 1985

It was symptomatic of the malaise surrounding the English game that Hammers' opening match of the season at Birmingham City on Saturday 17 August was ordered to start at the earlier kick-off time of 11.30 a.m. at the request of the home club and local police.

City's St Andrews ground had been the scene of frightening fan violence in each of the previous two seasons. In February 1983 the FA Cup fifth-round tie between Birmingham and West Ham was halted by pitch invasions as Hammers crashed to a 3–0 defeat. Worse was to follow in May 1985, when City's match against Leeds United was marred by the death of a teenager and injuries to 96 policemen after crowd trouble caused a wall to collapse. However, this tragedy was largely overshadowed by the fire at Bradford City's Valley Parade which claimed 56 lives on that same fateful afternoon.

On that warm summer's day in the Midlands, more attention seemed to be focused on David Gower's exploits for England in the Test at nearby Edgbaston than the start of the football season, as a crowd of only 11,164 turned up to see Ron Saunders' newly promoted City win a dull game 1–0. Despite the closure of Hammers' travel club, several hundred visiting fans made their own way to the Midlands and, after a minute's silence for the lad who had died at the ground the previous May, there were encouraging signs as Mark Ward looked worth every penny of his £250,000 fee and the returning Alan Devonshire impressed on the opposite flank.

There were less than five minutes left in the first half when an incident occurred which would soon change the course of West Ham's season. Paul Goddard, a stockily built striker with a neat touch and good eye for goal, was clattered to the ground by City's Ken Armstrong. Hammers' record signing from QPR had badly damaged his left shoulder and although he tried to shrug it off, he had to make way for substitute Alan Dickens in the 42nd minute. Dickens, a local youngster who was still looking to establish himself after scoring on his début as an 18 year old at Notts County in December 1982, was unlucky not to score when his shot struck keeper David Seaman's upright and rebounded clear within four minutes of the restart. But it was City who snatched all three points through Robert Hopkins' 65th-minute strike. The effect the injury to Goddard (nicknamed 'Sarge' because of his past links to the Boys' Brigade) would have on West Ham's season would soon become evident, as 'Dicko' moved into the attacking midfield role and Frank McAvennie pushed further forward to join Tony Cottee up front.

Cottee says: 'In the first game at Birmingham it wasn't happening. We were lightweight in midfield because we effectively had three attacking players. I remember it was a poor game. I had a couple of half-chances and perhaps should have scored but in the end even if we'd got a draw it would've been a good result for us. It was a disappointing start. There was nothing to suggest we were going to have our best-ever season, and to make matters worse Sarge dislocated his shoulder.'

Dickens, who was closest to Cottee after having played against him in schools football and come up through the youth ranks with him at West Ham, had suddenly been given an unexpected first-team chance he was determined to take.

He says: 'When Frank was signed to play just behind Tony and Paul, I still thought I'd have a good chance of being in the side. I didn't feel at all threatened by Frank's arrival, because I never used to think about too much that was going on around me. I just concentrated on my own game. But when Wardie came to play wide right, I knew then that I wouldn't be starting at Birmingham.

'You're always a bit hurt when someone is bought to take your place and if Paul hadn't got injured, I wouldn't have played for at least the first half a dozen games. Sarge was a quality player and any manager would have to stick with his new signings for a good while. I'd always been in and out of the side anyway and can't think of a time, at that stage in my career, when I played loads of games in succession.'

The first home game, against Queens Park Rangers three days later, heralded the arrival of McAvennie as the new hero of Upton

Park, although Dickens played a key supporting role as Hammers registered a stylish 3–1 victory under the lights. McAvennie opened his account after just ten minutes, turning in Cottee's cross. Ward fired a 40-yard effort just inches wide of Peter Hucker's goal before crossing for Dickens to score with a stooping header in the 24th minute. And although John Byrne pulled one back for QPR nine minutes after the interval, Hammers remained in control of an enterprising game and made it 3–1 when McAvennie chased Steve Walford's long through ball and brushed off the challenge of England defender Terry Fenwick to score his second in the 66th minute.

Frank enjoyed his home début but it was not simply his two goals that won him the acclaim of the small 15,530 crowd that night. His dyed blond hair ensured he stood out and he combined style, skill and pace with an incredible work rate. The theory goes that any new signing at West Ham who demonstrates his passion for the team by clattering an opponent into the Chicken Run wall as soon as possible after arriving, will guarantee himself instant hero status. Whether he was aware of this or not, McAvennie immediately won the hearts of the Hammers faithful by dispatching QPR defender Ian Dawes beyond the touchline and into the East Stand wall.

He recalls: 'It wouldn't have mattered if it had been Hackney Marshes or Upton Park, that boy was getting it whatever happened! It's something I've done on numerous occasions. It shows the fans how much you care for their team. That incident is memorable because I'd had some hassle with the fella and it was only a matter of time before he got it. And, of course, the fans loved it, so I started playing up to them and was knocking everyone around.

'Before a game I'd tell Alvin Martin and Tony Gale to put a ball up high towards the keeper so that I could go and clatter him in the first few minutes. Well, you very rarely get booked or sent off in the early minutes, so I'd try and make a point of charging the keeper in the hope that he'd think twice about coming out to catch the next cross. It did work a lot of the time but, occasionally, the biggest keepers would come out and batter me!'

After the unfortunate injury to Goddard, the Hammers' line-up for the QPR game would remain largely unchanged throughout a season luckily devoid of any other serious injuries.

The regular 4–4–2 formation lined up as follows: Goalkeeper – Phil Parkes; right-back – Ray Stewart; central defenders – Alvin Martin and Tony Gale; left-back – Steve Walford; right midfield/wing – Mark Ward; central midfielders – Neil Orr (defensive) and Alan Dickens (attacking); left-midfield/wing – Alan Devonshire; strikers – Frank McAvennie and Tony Cottee.

Phil Parkes, who cost £565,000 (a then world record for a keeper) from QPR in February 1979, had reclaimed the number one shirt from Scot Tom McAlister after missing all but the last ten League games the previous season due to an elbow infection. At just turned 35, he was by far the oldest in the team and despite his notorious 'dodgy knees', he remained one of the finest goalkeepers in the English game. But for the consistently brilliant performances of Peter Shilton and Ray Clemence, who shared the keeping duties for England over many years, Parkes would have added to the one full cap he received in Portugal in 1974.

Even if he was no longer as sprightly as he used to be, and enjoyed an occasional cigar and a brandy on the coach journeys back from away games, this tall colossus with the Midlands accent was still a very commanding figure, much respected, and his presence oozed confidence among the back four.

No one at West Ham knew Parkes better than Tony Gale. They, in common with Ealing-based Devonshire, lived to the west of London – Parkes at Wokingham in Berkshire, Gale at Walton-on-Thames, Surrey – and all three would meet up en route to the club's Essex training ground each day. Goddard, who also lived that side of the capital, would often join them on the journey to and from Chadwell Heath.

Parkes and Gale are both big, chirpy characters in their own right and Tony, who had just completed his first season with Hammers following his £200,000 move from Fulham, got to know Phil better on West Ham's '85 summer tour to Japan.

Gale says: 'We were flying to Japan to play a tournament; it was a long haul, and Phil and our physio, Rob Jenkins, were at the back of the plane enjoying plenty of drinks. There seemed no problem with that, because John Lyall had informed Phil earlier that he wouldn't be starting the first game against the weak Malaysia side – to be played the day after we landed – and that youth-team keeper John Vaughan would be playing instead.

'Anyway, while the rest of us slept, Parkesy and Rob continued to enjoy their bender and by the time we arrived Phil was fairly well gone. The problem came the next morning, when John told Phil he would be playing after all.

'The match was comfortably going our way. I think we were two up before half-time when one of the Malaysians scored with a hopeful 30-yard shot that went straight in the middle of our goal. It was a shot you'd expect a keeper of any quality to save comfortably. We all looked round at Parkesy in disbelief and as we came off the field at half-time, he said to me: "If John says anything, just say the shot took a deflection." I wasn't having that, because it was so obvious that the ball hadn't been deflected on its way into the net at all and that Phil, clearly much the worse for wear, had totally misjudged the flight of it.

'Anyway, we're sat there in the dressing-room and after saying all the usual things about keeping it neat and tidy, and pressing on for more goals, John turned to Phil and said: "So what happened with their goal then, Phil?"

'Parkesy looked sheepishly towards me, hoping I'd stick up for him and say the ball had been deflected in. But I turned the other way and there was only silence. After a few more seconds, sensing that he'd been rumbled by the manager, Phil replied: "Sorry, John, I saw three balls and thought I'd better dive for two of them!" We all fell about laughing and, in the end, even John saw the funny side.'

Parkes confirms the Japan story and admits: 'I felt really ill before the game and thought I was going to throw up. John knew I'd had a skinful on the plane coming over but he obviously thought I'd overdone it and he wasn't happy about it. That's why he changed his mind and told me I was playing in the first half against Malaysia – it was my punishment for drinking too much. He didn't look too pleased with me either when I joked at half-time about seeing all those balls but, thankfully, the laughter from the other lads defused the situation and John bit his tongue. He made me play the second half as well, though.'

Rob Jenkins succeeded his father, Bill, as Hammers' physio. A true East Ender and one of the old breed who administered the magic sponge for the best part of two decades before the club appointed John Green, a qualified chartered physiotherapist, in the early '90s. Rob, who still runs his clinic opposite the Boleyn Ground in Green Street, was a real character in the camp, well liked by staff and players.

Alvin Martin says: 'Rob was the vital ingredient that you used to have in any workplace. He would give you a rub down and a slap on the arse, laugh, and shout: "Now get out there and show 'em!" That was his little saying. He always had a one-liner and would muck in. Rather than just sitting on the coach coming back from away games, he'd be up and down the aisle helping our catering manager, Alan

Young, to serve the players' food. There would be a few beer cans floating about, while Parkesy would have a large brandy and a cigar. That was all right as long as we'd won. If we'd lost you wouldn't dream of it happening.

'If ever you had to go in for treatment from Rob on a Sunday morning, you had to give him a token of your gratitude for making him work – four cans of lager.'

Frank McAvennie rarely suffered injuries in his first stint at West Ham but he, too, recalls Rob's Sunday morning 'payments' plan: 'I remember once, before going out to play a pre-season friendly, I saw one of the lads sipping a drop of brandy he'd got from Rob. I didn't know then that this was something one or two of the lads liked to do and thought to myself, this is great, here – they give you a drink! I asked for a drop myself before the next game but instead of taking just a wee sip, I swigged back the miniature and as I went out for the kick-off I was positively glowing!

'Rob was a different class. I remember at half-time in one game, Alvin had some dirt in one of his eyes and as Rob went to treat him, he accidentally poked him in his other, good eye! Alvin was in a right state, cursing Rob, but I couldn't stop laughing.

'If you got injured on a Saturday, you were meant to turn up for treatment on the Sunday morning but if I'd been out on the booze on a Saturday night, sometimes I wouldn't bother to go in and see Rob. John would ask me on the Monday if I'd been in for treatment and Rob would confirm that I had – before demanding six cans of lager as payment.

'I remember at Stoke in 1989, when I broke my leg and my ankle and also tore my ligaments. Rob came running on and asked me if I could get up and run it off! Georgie Parris said: "He's fucking broken his leg!" I don't think Rob could see all that well, you know.

'Rob was a typical sponge and Deep Heat man. He'd rub Deep Heat into my hamstrings before the game – because I didn't warm up – and just before I got up off his bench, he'd grab me by the goolies with Deep Heat still on his hands. "That'll warm you up!" he'd laugh.'

Parkes explains how he occasionally came to share a bottle of the hard stuff with the popular physio: 'When I first arrived at the club, I think Rob had a little system going whereby a bottle of Scotch or brandy came down from the boardroom once a week, for medicinal purposes. But I don't think much of it was used medicinally, so I suggested to Rob that it was only fair that we should share whatever was going.'

BOYS OF '86

Apart from that isolated drinking binge on the flight to Japan, Parkes never incurred the wrath of the manager again. He made the point: 'John trusted me and was quite happy to let me have a couple of drinks the night before a game as long as I did the business on the field.

'It was Gordon Jago, my former manager at QPR, who introduced me and the other Rangers players to the idea of having a couple of drinks the night before a game, to help calm our nerves and settle the players down. He said there was no point in players sneaking out of the hotel for a few drinks behind his back, as they had been doing under previous managers. As long as we didn't take liberties, he was okay about us having a couple of halves of lager or glasses of wine. And when I was at West Ham, I would enjoy a couple of glasses of wine in my hotel room the night before a game, or with a meal at home, but I never went out to pubs or hung around hotel bars where people would get the wrong idea.'

Martin and Gale became regular room-mates on the away trips, even though Tony described them as 'opposites'. Alvin would invariably get to sleep first, while Tony liked to stay up watching TV until the dot appeared, as it did in those days. In the morning Alvin would usually rise first, while Tony slept in.

One morning Alvin was given a rude awakening. He complained to his room-mate that he had had difficulty getting a lather from his toothpaste . . . only to be informed by Tony that he'd used Galey's haemorrhoid cream in error! 'No wonder he was always talking out of his arse,' quipped Gale.

Galey's piles assumed legendary status behind the scenes at Upton Park. McAvennie says: 'Galey and Ronnie Boyce both had piles and they would sit at the back of the coach and compare notes. They'd be going on about their "Farmer Giles" and at first I didn't know what they meant.'

Although Gale was the biggest joker in the pack, his teammates did occasionally exact revenge. Ward describes one embarrassing experience that caused the centre-back to lose some of his renowned composure.

'One of the funniest sights I've seen was Tony's fat arse bent over the physio's table in the medical room, with the doctor's fingers stuck up it! Rob had tipped us off that the doc was coming in to examine Tony's piles, so Alvin and me waited until the examination was under way and then strolled into Rob's room, cool as you like, as if we didn't have a clue what was happening. Galey wasn't amused and started effing and blinding at Rob for allowing us in.'

Ward also witnessed at first hand one of Galey's cruellest moments while the players were having a meal after training: 'We were eating salad at Chadwell Heath one day and – this is how bad Galey's sense of humour is – he spotted Steve Walford about to open a large jar of beetroot. Steve sometimes had trouble with spots and boils on his face and neck, which hadn't escaped Galey's attention.

'While getting stuck into his own meal, Galey cast a sharp eye around the room, slaughtering people here and there, as usual. All of a sudden he clocked Wally out of the corner of one eye and waited and watched as Wally proceeded to unscrew the lid and then drop the jar onto the floor.

'There was beetroot everywhere and Galey, quick as a flash, turned to Steve, then looked down at the mess on the floor and said: "Fucking hell, Wally, there's no need to squeeze your spots here, can't you see we're all eating?" The room was in uproar. Poor Steve, he was a great bloke, and didn't have a bad bone in his body, but he really lost it with Galey that time.'

Although Alvin Martin was Tony Gale's regular room-mate on away trips, he also occasionally shared with Phil Parkes before the keeper roomed with Alan Devonshire.

'Phil and I were both really laid back,' says Gale. 'Ray Stewart and Alvin couldn't understand how we could be like that. Phil was the best keeper in the division that year. A gentle giant, he never used to shout and bawl.'

Gale claims his chauffeuring duties prolonged the career of his good mate Parkes.

'Parkesy hadn't played the season before and was thinking about jacking it in but because I picked him up at Waterloo every day he decided to carry on. It was before the M25 had been completed. I used to get up at 6 a.m. and drive to my mum's in Pimlico, where I'd go back to bed until 8.45 a.m. After a brief kip, I'd pick up Parkesy at Waterloo before collecting Dev [Alan Devonshire], who always got the tube to Barking station. When we got to Barking, Dev would be stuck into the *Racing Post* and eating a fry-up in the Wimpy. He used to be thin but now he's paying for it. He's got more chins than a Chinese telephone directory.'

Parkes did all his teammates a favour when he signed for West Ham. He was so concerned that the journey in from Wokingham to Chadwell Heath each day would take him so long, he spoke to John Lyall about it and the manager moved the start time back from 10.00 to 10.30 a.m.

Devonshire has never learned to drive. He says: 'It was just something I never bothered about. My wife, Chris, used to take me anywhere I needed to go, and I was also very friendly with two fellas, Carlo Delamura and Clive Palmer, who also drove me around. I don't know why I didn't take my test. I suppose it just didn't interest me. The British School of Motoring approached me and offered to give me free lessons and a car but I just said no. Even so, a Fiat dealer was still really keen to provide me with a car, so I must have been the only footballer with a sponsored motor who couldn't drive!'

By the start of the 1985–86 season, Londoner Gale had been at Upton Park a year and had firmly established himself as the dressing-room joker. No one could escape his wicked sense of humour. He was not a practical joker in the sense of a Martin Allen, Julian Dicks or John Moncur, who got their kicks from simple pranks, but his timing and delivery were invariably lethal.

His nickname 'Reggie' derived from the evil exploits of '60s East End gangster Reggie Kray, who was notoriously ruthless, cunning and cutting in his own murderous way. Tony Gale too had his own way of slaughtering his victims.

He explains: 'David Swindlehurst and Steve Whitton nicknamed me Reggie in my first season at the club. There wasn't a piss-taker in the camp when I arrived. People looked around as if to say, "It's the Academy, we don't do things like that here."'

But as Cottee points out: 'Even though Galey could be cruel – not nasty – we didn't have a vindictive dressing-room. There was just a lot of banter.'

Even the new Golden Boy, McAvennie, didn't escape Gale's humour. Like all good comedians who observe their audience very closely, Gale was among the first to expose the truth behind Frank's good looks. He reveals: 'Frank was like Captain Cosmetic – he had no teeth and ginger pubes. His gleaming white teeth were all capped and he always bleached his hair.'

McAvennie laughs when he hears Galey's stories and his ability for self-mockery is an endearing part of his nature. Pinpointing the moment when his ginger roots were finally exposed to his new teammates, he recalls: 'It got out when I started banging in the goals and TV were beginning to take an interest in me. I'll never forget, we were all sitting around the hotel before one game, watching Trevor Brooking going on about me, and they were showing old clips of goals I'd scored for St Mirren. I could see the expressions on the boys' faces change as each goal was shown and then Dev looked over at me and piped up: "So where were you then?" That was when they discovered I was really ginger. I got some absolute pelters from the lads, especially after Bob Wilson came on the telly at the end of the show and mentioned the fact that I'd changed my hairstyle and hair colour as well as my club.'

Frank admits that his decision to bleach his hair was a conscious effort to get himself noticed. He laughs again as he admits: 'I used to get my hair done at a place in Wanstead High Street. I didn't bother with toner, I just used bleach. My hair was yellow – like custard. I was determined to get myself noticed in London, although fortunately I soon got recognised for my goals rather than just the colour of my hair.'

If the 3–1 home win over QPR signalled the arrival of Frank McAvennie as Hammers' new crowd favourite, the team itself had flattered to deceive. The following Saturday, Mick Harford's 48th-minute penalty – after Ray Stewart had tripped Mark Stein in the box – gave Luton Town a 1–0 victory they had scarcely deserved. Even in the dying minutes, the home side were only denied the win by Hatters' keeper Andy Dibble who pulled off saves from Mark Ward and Greg Campbell (who subbed for Tony Cottee eight minutes from time) that John Lyall described as 'world class'.

Of equal concern to chairman Len Cearns and his fellow directors was the size of the Upton Park attendance – just 14,104 – more than 1,000 down on the first game, which had been won handsomely. Attendances around the country had dipped in the aftermath of the hooliganism of the previous seasons. But the gate for the Luton game was some 4,500 down on the 1984–85 average of almost 18,500, which in itself was 13 per cent down on the previous term. These were dark days for English football and there seemed no light at the end of West Ham's tunnel either.

After Luton, a midweek visit to Manchester United ended in a 2–0 defeat. West Ham had not played badly but the visitors' spirited start went unrewarded as little Gordon Strachan increasingly took control, setting up Mark Hughes for the 55th minute opener and then netting the second himself, 15 minutes from time, after latching onto Tony Gale's back-pass.

The month of August ended on a more promising note, with a 2–2 home draw against Liverpool, who were missing Kenny Dalglish through injury. A crowd of just under 20,000 saw the stylish Hammers twice take the lead thanks to the flying McAvennie. He was the new, big favourite and each goal he scored was greeted with the terrace chant of 'One Mac-A-Ven-eeeee, there's only one . . .'

Some of the football Hammers played against Liverpool, especially in the first half an hour, was of a very high quality. With Alan Dickens growing in confidence, linking up well with the front two, the home side threatened on numerous occasions and were unfortunate to see Cottee's 15th-minute 'goal' dubiously ruled out for offside.

McAvennie finally made the breakthrough after a 21st-minute mix-up between central defender Alan Hansen and keeper Bruce Grobbelaar, leaving Frank to roll the ball into the unguarded goal at the South Bank end. And after Craig Johnston headed home Steve Nicol's right-wing cross to equalise seven minutes after the break, McAvennie again caught out the eccentric Zimbabwean in the 71st minute with a lob from the edge of the box after running on to Ward's angled through ball. The Reds refused to buckle, however, and several neat triangular passing movements reaped dividends just seven minutes from time when Johnston crossed from the right for Ronnie Whelan's header to make it 2–2.

The two dropped points would prove costly at the end of the season but Liverpool had been given an early warning that West Ham were no pushovers, despite their poor start. They had showed too, that in McAvennie, they possessed a striker who could trouble any defence.

But there would be no prospect of a top-half finish, never mind a Championship challenge, unless the Scot could gel well with Cottee, who was seething after being denied what he claimed was a perfectly good goal in the early stages of the Liverpool game. Goals were like a drug to Cottee, a renowned poacher in the Jimmy Greaves mould who did all his best work in the opposition's penalty area, especially the six-yard box. A former Essex sprint champion, he was as quick as anybody in the country over 20 yards and his little legs boasted calves the size of tree trunks. After five goalless games, Cottee was badly in need of his next fix, but things would get worse for him before they got better.

Chapter 3

ONE VISION – Queen

Chart Position: Number 7, November 1985

If the first turning point of Hammers' season came with the unfortunate injury to Paul Goddard at Birmingham, the second, and more significant development followed early in September when the players held a no-holds-barred private meeting before training. There have been very few such gatherings, either before or since, but what was said that morning would ultimately prove the catalyst to the greatest-ever season in the club's League history.

The meeting was called by Alvin Martin and the main crux of the debate was the work rate of Tony Cottee – or rather the lack of it, in the opinion of some of his teammates. Martin, a natural leader who had taken over the captaincy from Billy Bonds at the start of the 1984–85 season, decided the time was right to get all the players together in one room to resolve the problems that were threatening to undermine the team as a whole.

This is how some of the players who played a key part in that crucial meeting saw it . . .

Alvin Martin recalls: 'John had done as much as he could. Then I heard a couple of lads making comments about Tony Cottee's work rate without actually saying it to his face. That's always dangerous. We had a good dressing-room but sometimes it can get too nice. This was the only time in 22 years when I felt that the situation was unhealthy. The worst thing that can happen is backbiting. It has to come out in the open. I thought the time was right to have a players' meeting and I cleared it with John, who was all for it. It was unique at a time when players' meetings were very rare. We held it at Chadwell Heath before training. I didn't know whether anybody was

going to get up and start speaking, so I began by saying that no grudges were to be held. All we wanted to do was get ourselves together and win.

'I said to Tony Cottee: "I see him [Frank McAvennie] working his bollocks off, yet you're not. You're a great athlete, you're a cross-county champion, and you can do a lot more."

'To be fair he took it really well and replied: "Yeah, okay, I'll go along with that. Maybe I can work harder and I will work harder." Already, we knew we'd got something out of the meeting. Neil Orr was told he was over-complicating things at times and a few others said that Galey and myself were defending too deeply. We had debates and everybody put his point across. From that moment on we all knew what we wanted from each other. I told John the meeting had gone well. It had been constructive and we just hoped it was going to translate into better results on the pitch. In the context of the season it was very important. It improved our team spirit and organisation a lot.'

Cottee admits he deserved much of the criticism aimed at him: 'I only vaguely remember the meeting. Frank was like Ian Rush, he was such a team player but that wasn't a natural thing for me. Later on, with Howard Kendall having a go at me at Everton and then with Leicester's style, it became easier for me to appreciate that side of the game. At the time I was 20 years old and I was pretty arrogant, which isn't a bad thing because it helps you to become a good player. I felt I was a goalscorer. I didn't think I had to contribute anything else. It was a case of the others around me playing to my strengths, giving me opportunities and letting me score goals. It was arrogant and self-confident but that was how I saw it.

'The other players were saying: "No, you should be contributing to the team. If you haven't got the ball, what are you doing?" Looking back now, they were absolutely right. I think Frank stuck up for me. You've got strikers and you've got defenders and they'll always stick together. Galey always used to call me "Harry" and I could never work out why. When I asked him later, he said I was like the old man who helped clean the training ground – a bloke named Harry who would do a little bit of work, then disappear behind the wall to have a fag. Galey wasn't one to beat around the bush, he was pretty up front. The point is, after that clear-the-air meeting, we didn't have another one all season. We had players-only meetings at Everton and Leicester but I can't remember too many at West Ham.'

Cottee matured as a player and came to realise that he had to combine his predatory goalscoring skills with a more industrious approach to the game.

'John Lyall would always say that there were other aspects to the game, apart from scoring goals, and he tried to make me aware of that,' Cottee continues. 'As I got older I realised what those people were getting at. At the time, though, a lot of training was designed for West Ham going forward and for Frank and myself to score goals. Anyway, by the end of the season no one was moaning any more, because I'd got 26 goals.'

With equal candour, McAvennie did, indeed, come to the defence of Cottee, although he also recognised the need for his strike-partner to work harder for the good of the team. He says: 'One or two of the lads were chatting about the problems on the coach coming back from Man United and it was agreed that something had to be done. I was bang on time for the meeting – never early, as always. One or two of the staff came in, Ronnie Boyce and maybe Tony Carr, but Alvin asked them to leave us to it. He said to us: "Whatever is said in this dressing-room, stays in this dressing-room. Nobody is having a go at anybody, but we've got a few new players and if we're gonna be a good team, we need to sort things out and find out what everybody wants." I think Alvin, with all his experience, and playing at the back, could see that we had the makings of a very good team.

'I had my say about Tony but he took it really well and in the way in which it was meant. I told him that I can't bust my arse with a 40-yard sprint to close somebody down for nothing, if he didn't shut off their keeper. At that stage, I didn't realise what a good finisher he was. I also explained to him about the need for us to talk to each other as well. I mean, if he wasn't perhaps in a position to close down their keeper after he had thrown the ball out, then he should shout to me to let me know, because then there would be no point in me making my 40-yard run. It was constructive criticism but it was never personal and as the season went on we built a great partnership. I knew what he wanted and he knew what I wanted, so we didn't need to have a lot of conversation out there on the park.

'It wasn't just Tony who was to blame and it was one of the few times when I really made sure the other lads fully understood me. Ray Stewart and Neil Orr understood what I was saying – they're Scottish – but when I was shouting and bawling my mouth off on the pitch during games, maybe the others couldn't understand me because of my accent.

'Even when we beat QPR in the first home game, things weren't

right. As a striker, I'm a great believer that I'm a defender when the other team have the ball. So if I'm busting my arse to get out wide to close down defenders, I wanted Tony to shut the goalkeeper off so that they couldn't pass back to him. But at the same time, I don't want the defender in possession – the one I'm closing down – to be able to pass the ball into midfield, so they had to shove up, too. Tony got abuse because defenders were able to pass the ball back to the keeper too easily, but we were all involved.

'I think it was Dev who made the point that it wasn't always possible for the midfielders to move up and prevent the "out" ball from the opposition's defenders, because our own defenders were usually positioned so deep, as they often liked to be. But if Alvin and Tony Gale were not going to move up, then the midfielders and forwards had to hold it and maybe step back.

'Neil [Orr] got told to keep it simple and concentrate on doing his own job. John used to remind him that he wasn't Michel Platini, so he should give the ball to people like Dev. It amazed me at first how John spoke to Neil in those terms. He'd say to him: "You can't play, so give it to the players who can. On the other hand, you can tackle and defend, but he (pointing to any one of a number of us) can't do that part of the game as well as you." The meeting lasted a good couple of hours and it had the right effect.'

Alan Devonshire adds: 'We had that meeting because we wanted to be successful, and if we wanted to say something, we would rather get it all out in the open than hide it between a few of us. The players made sure that no one ever took liberties. If someone wasn't working, the other players would say: "Why are they not doing it?" and we'd be on them like a shot.'

Scottish international Ray Stewart acknowledges the part Martin played in uniting the team at that time: 'He was a strong-willed guy who brought us all together. He was the kind of leader every good club needs.'

Gale explains it from the defenders' perspective and tells how the shape and tactics of the side evolved: 'We weren't happy with the way we were defending up front. The opposition's right-back always seemed to be giving us problems even though Wardie was getting up and down and Dev was holding midfield. We decided that as soon as their keeper got the ball Tony had to sprint wide and block off the ball to their right-back. That was his job, while Frank had to take care of their two centre-backs. Tony was a lazy sod but he took it on board and he needed a kick up the arse, which he got when he was dropped.

'Some may say that meeting was a turning point but for me it was more a case of Frank, Tony and Wardie getting to know each other better. Meanwhile Dev was getting fitter and fitter. That takes seven or eight games just to settle in and get going. Tony ended up having a great season. It did him good because he was the typical goalscorer – he shot with little backlift and he was really quick.

'Frank was one of the most hard-working forwards I've ever played with. He put up with Tony when he first came into the side but then I reckon he started thinking: "If I'm doing all the running, then he's gotta do some too". In the end they complemented each other very well, while at the back we had the ability to play from deep, which is the way I think the game should be played. Alvin and myself might not have left too much space behind us because we weren't quick enough to turn and chase back, but we were both comfortable on the ball. Sometimes the others felt we played too deeply but Alvin and myself knew we couldn't play up on the halfway line and it suited us to play like that. Whenever one of us went forward, Geoff Pike or Neil Orr sat in. As a back four we defended narrow and tight. We also knew we could chip balls behind their defence for Frank or Tony to sprint onto.'

Cottee suffered the indignation of being dropped for the midweek visit to Southampton on 3 September. His replacement was Greg Campbell, the son of former Chelsea manager Bobby Campbell, who had been scoring freely in Hammers' successful reserve team.

Campbell's career had suffered a massive setback in September 1984, when, in only his second first-team appearance, he broke his jaw in the home game against Watford. It knocked the stuffing out of him for a while but he battled back and showed glimpses of his potential when introduced as a sub for Cottee in the earlier games against Luton and at Old Trafford.

Campbell was desperate for another chance in the first team and admits: 'I used to sit on the bench and cheekily say to John things like "Tony's looking a bit tired", in the hope he'd bring me on. Instead, John would just tell me to shut up and keep my thoughts to myself. The trouble with Cottee and McAvennie was, they bloody well never got injured! The other players used to call me "The Judge" because I was always on the bench. Even when I finally got my chance at Southampton, I was up against one of the best young central defenders in England in Mark Wright.'

Campbell's one and only game in the starting line-up that season – indeed, his last-ever start for the first team – ended in the 69th

minute when he was replaced, almost inevitably, by Cottee. Cottee had been chomping at the bit, his head a whirlwind of emotion as he sat on the bench and watched Southampton take a lead when Alan Curtis diverted home Danny Wallace's deflected shot in the 52nd minute. As a young man who prided himself on his reputation as one of the most prolific marksmen in English football, Cottee – who still keeps scrapbooks of his career – didn't take kindly to being left out. However, he contributed to his own demotion.

'In the first five games I can remember having only two chances up at Birmingham and was getting concerned about my form,' he says. 'I hadn't started the season very well and chances were very few. It wasn't really happening for me. While I hadn't even had a decent shot, Frank had scored four goals in five games. In my younger days the main thing for me was scoring goals and if I wasn't getting them, then I was always concerned. I went to see John because I didn't feel happy in myself. He said: "Do you think it would be best if I gave you a rest?"

'"Maybe," I replied. He then put Greg Campbell in for the game at Southampton. I remember watching from the bench and thinking how well Frank was doing. It was like he was having a one-on-one duel with Peter Shilton. But I was also sitting there watching Greg and thinking, he's playing in *my* place. That's not right! Equally, I knew it was partly my fault because I hadn't started the season at all well. It fired me up and by the time I came on with 20 minutes to play, I felt I had a point to prove.

'In my first season John had rested me but this was the first time I'd been dropped. John did it in a nice way but it still hurt. I wasn't unhappy particularly because it was Greg replacing me – it could have been any player. In hindsight, though, John did the right thing, because I then went on a terrific scoring run.'

Not, though, before McAvennie made it five in five with a Hammers' equaliser nine minutes from time at The Dell. Devonshire sent over only the visitors' second corner of the match, Martin headed the ball down to Dickens, who set up Ward for a driven cross-shot that was flying past the far post until McAvennie stuck out a boot and diverted it past 'Shilts' for a fortunate equaliser.

Alan Dickens, a clean-living young lad, shy and unassuming, remembers celebrating more than usual on the way home after an unlikely point gained on the south coast. 'It was my 21st birthday that day and I was feeling good at the back of the coach . . . drinking lemonade. How sad is that?'

The major turning point for Cottee came in the next game, away to Sheffield Wednesday on 7 September. An injury to Devonshire paved the way for the inexperienced 21-year-old George Parris to make his first appearance of the season in midfield. The Ilford-based youngster, a local lad who starred for the Redbridge Schools district side, made an early impact by laying on the pass for McAvennie to open the scoring in the ninth minute.

Lee Chapman, whose limited ability on the ground brought him much derision from fans when he played for West Ham between 1993–95, showed his strength in the air by heading the Owls level on 18 minutes and this see-saw thriller tipped Wednesday's way when Garry Thompson fired them in front and Phil Parkes was forced to make three outstanding saves.

With Lawrie Madden also hitting the underside of the crossbar, Hammers rode their luck and an equaliser seemed improbable when McAvennie had to make way for sub Bobby Barnes – his only outing of the season – after 73 minutes due to a knee injury. It was an eventful afternoon for the Scot, who also had his name taken by referee Neil Midgley in the first half for failing to retreat ten yards at a free-kick.

But McAvennie had already done his bit, and now it was finally Cottee's turn to grab the headlines. The pint-sized striker never cared whether he scored with a spectacular 30-yard rocket or a tap-in from six yards. The way things had gone for him in the early weeks of the campaign, he was just relieved to score the 88th-minute equaliser.

Cottee says: 'The ball went through both the defender's and the keeper's legs. There was so much relief on my part – I really needed it. Once the first one went in I was off and running and scored in the next four games too. Frank had been doing his bit but I hadn't been doing mine. From then on, though, as a partnership, Frank and myself started to click.'

Chapter 4

HOLDING OUT FOR A HERO – Bonnie Tyler

Chart Position: Number 2, September 1985

Although Frank McAvennie and Mark Ward were the only two official signings at the start of the season, West Ham effectively had three. For after an agonising 19 months in the wilderness, Alan Devonshire had not only proved those who had written him off after a terrible knee injury wrong, the cultured midfielder had returned in fine style.

Leicester City were swept aside, 3–0, at Upton Park on 14 September. Although McAvennie and Tony Cottee were now sharing the goalscoring limelight (31 minutes and 70 minutes respectively), it was Dev's goal in the first minute of the second half that rightly captured the fans' imagination.

As Trevor Smith reported for the *Newham Recorder*: 'Dev took a return pass from McAvennie to put the skids under troubled Leicester with a superb second for Hammers. It was the highlight of the match and just what the doctor ordered for the fans who have been supporting and willing Dev back to his exciting former self. In fact, in the very next minute, Dev almost grabbed another with a powerful shot that exploded on the chest of City goalkeeper Ian Andrews, who clutched it safely.'

Only 12,125 turned up to see Hammers slice Leicester apart – the lowest Upton Park crowd of the season It was the worst attendance for a League game there since 11,721 hearty souls stood frozen on the virtually deserted snow-covered terraces for the Friday night visit of Cambridge United on 21 December 1979, when announcer Bill Remfry orchestrated a half-time knees-up to the sound of Mike Oldfield's hit, 'In Dulce Jubilo'. Those who stayed away from the Leicester game missed the reincarnation of a midfield messiah.

BOYS OF '86

Alan Devonshire was 29 years old in September 1985 and should have been in his prime but the serious knee injury he suffered in a collision during the home FA Cup third-round tie against Wigan Athletic in January 1984 had almost ended his career. There were genuine fears that the extent of the injury – three ruptured ligaments in his right knee – would finish the left-sided goal creator whose long, dark, flowing locks and trademark moustache would disappear into a blur as he tore past helpless full-backs – as he did to such devastating and high-profile effect in the semi-final and final of the triumphant 1980 FA Cup run.

At the time of his injury, Dev had been capped eight times at full international level and, along with Tottenham's Glenn Hoddle, was rated one of the most exciting, highly skilled midfielders in England.

When Dev was running at and tormenting opponents, there was no finer sight in the English game. Trevor Brooking, who starred alongside Alan on the left side of Hammers' midfield for the best part of seven years, rated him right up there with the best of his generation and, between them, they illuminated many a match with their deft touches, vision, passing ability and creativity, all of which mark them both down in Hammers' history as all-time greats.

Indeed, Brooking paid Devonshire the ultimate tribute when he decided to retire – somewhat prematurely according to many – because he didn't relish continuing without his injured midfield partner.

In the space of 19 months between the injury and the start of the 1985–86 season, Devonshire played just two first-team matches – the home and away FA Cup fifth-round clashes with Wimbledon in March '85 that proved to be an abortive comeback attempt. He fought a long and lonely personal fitness battle but it was a battle he was determined to win. As befits a former forklift-truck driver from a Middlesex Hoover factory (who came into the pro game late and almost anonymously in a £5,000 transfer from non-league Southall in 1976), Devonshire was not going to give up on his football life without a struggle.

He says: 'I loved my job. Football is the best job in the world and I can't believe it when players moan about training or playing too many games. I remember splitting up with my missus for five days a week during my spell out injured, as I had to live down at the rehabilitation centre in Leatherhead all week. I said to her: "If you stop me doing this, I will never forgive you, because I've got one chance of playing again and I've got to give it everything." My marriage suffered at that time but, thankfully, Chris understood.

'To be honest, though, when I came back, my general fitness was probably the best it had ever been, because I worked so hard on my rehabilitation. I had been busting a gut from 8.30 a.m. until 4.30 p.m. every day and that obviously helped me.'

Devonshire reveals, however, that the restricted movement of his right knee forced him to adapt his running style and, with typical honesty, and despite the brilliance he produced throughout the 1985–86 season, he admits now that he never managed to quite regain his pre-injury form. He explains: 'The strength in my leg was fine and I never worried about it giving way. I just didn't have a complete bend in it, which stopped me from sprinting properly. So I had to change my game. I just worked it out for myself and gradually realised what I could and couldn't do.

'As soon as I had the chance early on in the game, I used to like to run their right-back on the outside, just to test how quick he was. But I wasn't able to do that any more, so I'd tend to come inside, onto his weaker left side, and make the play from there. Looking back, I know I was only playing up to 80 per cent of my true potential after the injury. The '85–86 season should have been the peak of my career but it wasn't as good as it would have been if I hadn't done my knee. The team played well and I had a good season but I do regret the fact that I know it could have been even better for me personally.'

McAvennie and Cottee both thrived on the service they received from Devonshire, as well as from Dickens and Ward in particular.

Dev says: 'Frank was the best striker I ever played with. I think he had everything. He was good in the air, could hold it up, would dig a centre-half if he needed to, and he could finish. I think he should have achieved more than he did but he was the best I've played with, and that includes the England strikers in the early '80s.

'He was just magnificent that season. Players know who are good players, as much as the fans do, and I could tell that Frank was a top-class player by the way he handled himself on the pitch. And he was a team player too. I like to think that I was the same, in that I would work my bollocks off for the team when I didn't have the ball. The accolades I received from my teammates over the years mean more to me than anything else.'

McAvennie returns the compliment to the player who created so many chances and goals for him that season: 'He [Devonshire] used to have a simple philosophy on the game. "The ball's round," he would say, "so let's get it down on the grass and pass it." When I first arrived, he'd say to me: "Just show for me when I get the ball and lay it off. I'm not the sort of winger who can run by three or four players." I thought: "Oh yeah." But he was right. I said I didn't want to hold the ball up and get clattered from behind, so he just told me to lay it off, one touch, and then turn quickly. It worked a treat.

'Dev's right up there among the best players I've ever played with, along with Dalglish. They played in different positions, but they're both top quality. Dev was unbelievable, a breath of fresh air to me – but he's the worst finisher I've ever seen. He'd go past six players, beat the keeper and then knock it past the post. I'd look at him and shrug, and he'd just say: "I was fucked!" He's a great fella.'

Devonshire doesn't disagree: 'To be honest, finishing was my main weakness, but no one ever pulled me aside to work on improving it. I used to beat eight players in training and then miss an open goal. Looking back, it was something I should have worked on more seriously. I remember a game that season against Ipswich, one of the FA Cup replays in the snow, when I picked the ball up on the halfway line, jinked past several of their players, got into the box and then stroked the ball wide of the post from about 12 yards out. It would have been the goal of the season if it had gone in.'

The players described Devonshire as an insomniac and he admits: 'I can get by with only an hour's sleep. That's the way I am. I could never switch off. I used to go back over the game in my mind and think about the mistakes I'd made. If I gave the ball away four or five times, I knew I'd had a bad game and I'd think about what I should have done instead. That way, when I found myself in the same situation again, I'd know what to do differently.'

Explaining his link-up play with the two forwards, Dev adds: 'With the way my knee was, I couldn't run properly but I still had enough about me to help the forwards. Someone like TC [Cottee] never got injured, because he didn't have many touches of the ball. It would be one or two touches to control it, then a short lay-off and he'd sprint off into the box. He never took the sort of knocks that Frank did, because it wasn't his game. When TC went to Everton, I asked him: "Why are you going there?" I knew they were a long-ball team and wouldn't play to his strengths like we did.'

One of Devonshire's many strengths was his change of pace. He would suck in the full-back, show him the ball and then knock it to one side and leave him for dead. Even after he lost a yard or two of acceleration, he still had the intelligence on the ball to bewilder opponents.

He says: 'An American sports specialist came to the club once and he said to me: "I've been watching this game for about six months and you are the only player I know who has gears."

'I said to him: "You what?"'

'He said: "Well, you slow down and then quicken up again when you are running."'

'It was just something that I did naturally. I used to slow down to suck players in and then speed up as they approached.'

On his return from long-term injury, Devonshire reclaimed the coveted number six shirt that had been worn throughout the previous campaign by Gale. Numerous players have worn the six shirt made famous by Bobby Moore, since he left the club in 1974, but none with the style and distinction of the former World Cup winner, whose hero status at Upton Park will never be matched. Moore was a class act no one would wish to try and follow and, as Mick McGiven – the first man to pull on the shirt after Moore's departure – discovered, unfavourable comparisons were inevitable.

Alvin Martin tells the story of the time, before a game at Manchester City, when Gale was glancing through the matchday programme in the dressing-room and came across a reference to McGiven, who had long since quit playing to become one of the two first-team coaches, alongside Ronnie Boyce.

Martin smiles as he says: 'Galey is always slaughtering everyone in sight and on this occasion he turned his attention to Mick. It was all quiet and we were sitting around the dressing-room when Galey said with a snigger: "Mick, it says here that you were bought to replace Bobby Moore . . ." Mick thought about it for a second or two and came back at Galey, who I think was wearing the six shirt himself that day, with that immortal line: "Galey, they've never replaced Bobby Moore!" All the other players fell about laughing and, for once, Galey was speechless.'

Gale did his best to retain number six but the return of Devonshire meant he had to make do instead with the number four shirt, previously shared between Paul Allen, Steve Walford and Neil Orr.

Gale recounts his fruitless battle to keep the prestigious six on his back: 'Dev wouldn't let me wear six. I wore it at Fulham and also in my first season at West Ham, when Dev was out injured.

'He'd say: "I'm not being funny but I've always worn six."'

'I said: "You're having a laugh, only good-looking geezers wear six!"'

'He said he was really superstitious. I insisted: "I can't wear four, I'm supposed to be in control."'

'In the end, I gave up trying to argue with him. I didn't mind because at least the shirt was being worn by Dev, who was a pal of mine as well as a great footballer.

'I'd never played with Dev before his awful injury but as left-sided centre-back, I developed a great understanding with him. Dev would invite two players onto him and always release the ball just at the right time. He was a great one-touch player, too. Dev was my favourite player in that side.'

Devonshire gives an example of his special understanding with Gale: 'We had a throw-in idea that wasn't planned. If there was a throw around the halfway-line area, I used to shape to throw it long down the line, and Galey would quickly sprint over and I would turn and throw it to him instead. He used to just give it straight back to me, and I was away – simple as that. We never, ever spoke about it, it just happened, yet we got away with it for the whole season and it set up a countless number of attacks.'

Tactically, West Ham's swashbuckling football was starting to reap rich rewards. The enterprising 3–0 victory over Leicester City began a marvellous unbeaten run of 12 wins in 14 matches, stretching from 3 September to 14 December. The two draws were away to Manchester City (2–2) and at home to Arsenal (0–0).

Cottee's renaissance continued at wet-and-windy Maine Road on 28 September, when he received McAvennie's cross and sidestepped débutant keeper Eric Nixon before rolling the ball into the empty net in the seventh minute. But the lead lasted just three minutes, when Jim Melrose punished a mistake by Gale to set up Mark Lillis for the equaliser. Devonshire showed his speed of thought on the halfway line four minutes before the interval when he beat City's offside trap to slide an incisive through ball wide on the right to the overlapping Ray Stewart. His first-time cross was intended for Cottee but big central defender Mick McCarthy – now managing the Republic of Ireland – turned the ball into his own net. Hammers had to settle for their fourth draw in five games when Melrose headed City's second equaliser in the 49th minute, despite a valiant attempted goal-line clearance by McAvennie.

Three days later a crowd of just over 9,000 saw West Ham's Milk Cup bid begin with a comfortable 3–0 second-round, first-leg, home win over an experienced Swansea City. Swans' overworked keeper Jimmy Rimmer did well to keep the game goalless at the break but the now rampant Cottee hammered home Dickens' low cross on 49 minutes and then McAvennie – who else? – headed the second following a cross from Walford. The second leg was rendered a formality in the final minute when Devonshire was tripped in the box

and Ray Stewart stepped up to unleash his first penalty of the season into the North Bank netting.

This was the third consecutive match for which Paul Goddard was named as sub – only one was permitted then – but Lyall still resisted the opportunity to give his most experienced striker even a brief run out against lower-league opponents. One of the criticisms fans levelled at Harry Redknapp before his sacking as manager in May 2001 was his use (or rather lack of) of his three substitutes. Redknapp seemed to regard the men on the bench as mere replacements for injured players, rather than as tactical tools who could turn a game. The same criticism was aimed at Lyall from time to time, although with only one sub at his disposal this particular season, he had to exert a degree of caution. And besides, having waited for Cottee to slip into the scoring groove, he wasn't in any rush to break up his blossoming partnership with McAvennie. This was, however, of no consolation to the unlucky Goddard, who would be left kicking his heels for some time yet.

Before two more Stewart penalties and another Cottee strike (all three coming before half-time) completed an emphatic 6–2 aggregate success in Wales on 8 October, Hammers would cut down Nottingham Forest (4–2) at home and notch their first away win of the season at Newcastle United (2–1).

Brian Clough's Forest didn't know what had hit them and were 3–0 down inside 20 minutes, although, in mitigation, they conceded the first two after losing keeper Hans Segers with just 13 minutes gone and had to play midfielder Neil Webb between the sticks. The Dutch keeper hurt his knee in a collision with Alan Dickens in the move that led to Cottee's seventh-minute opener.

Cottee then turned provider to set up McAvennie for the second goal just six minutes later, and Frank made it 3–0 by scoring at the near post from Ward's cross. Wardie, enjoying his battle with left-back and future Hammer Stuart Pearce, also supplied the cross that Dickens steered home on the hour.

As Hammers eased off the gas, Johnny Metgod abandoned his defensive duties to try and salvage some pride for Forest, who pulled back two goals in the last half an hour through the balding Dutchman and the manager's son, Nigel. Clough senior, however, wasn't impressed to see his side suffer their first Upton Park defeat in seven matches, a sequence dating back to the 1971–72 season.

This convincing home win put Hammers in good spirit for the difficult trip to Newcastle United on 5 October. The Magpies were flying high in fourth place and had conceded just four goals in six matches at St James'. But West Ham were now oozing confidence and on a sunlit, windy day in the North-east, they attacked with purpose from the kick-off. Once again, it was the 'Cottee and McAvennie show' and the former was again unhappy to see an offside flag rule out his seventh-minute 'goal' following a pass from his strike partner.

Burnley referee David Scott did the visitors no favours, booking four (three for dissent), refusing two clear-cut penalties for fouls on Ward and Devonshire and missing entirely the off-the-ball incidents that left Stewart and Ward battered and bruised.

But there was no disputing West Ham's first goal, McAvennie running onto Ward's intelligent pass in the 12th minute to expose keeper Martin Thomas. After 25 minutes it was Cottee's turn to shine. He controlled Phil Parkes' long clearance and turned inside the future West Ham manager, Glenn Roeder, before slamming a right-foot shot into the net for his sixth goal in as many matches. Although Hammers had to weather some predictable second-half pressure, George Reilly's header two minutes from the end came too late for the Geordies.

It was a torrid afternoon for Roeder, the Cockney youngster who lived in Essex and grew up supporting West Ham but who had gone to the North-east after beginning his pro career with Leyton Orient. He missed a couple of good chances to score himself – but Newcastle got off lightly compared to what they were to suffer at the hands of the East Londoners later in the campaign.

Hopes of a third consecutive First Division win were dashed by Arsenal at home on 12 October. There were faint echoes of the trouble that had damaged the sport so badly in the previous year when referee Alan Robinson had to start the London derby five minutes late after a minor crowd disturbance. When the action began though, the fans got their money's worth in a game of high quality that produced everything but a goal. Hammers threatened to run riot in the early stages, despite losing Dickens with concussion after 35 minutes. Don Howe's Arsenal, with Charlie Nicholas prominent, recovered well from the early onslaught, but West Ham were inches away from snatching the winner when Cottee just failed to connect with Devonshire's low cross in the 63rd minute.

It was the first game in eight that neither Cottee nor McAvennie had scored – but it was no more than a temporary blip. The deadly duo were cheekily planning a spectacular goal feast at the expense of Aston Villa . . .

Chapter 5

TAKE ON ME – A-Ha

Chart Position: Number 2, October 1985

Once Tony Cottee clicked into the groove and was sharing the goalscoring duties with Frank McAvennie, their partnership flourished to the point where not only did they both go into every match fully expecting to find the net, they were also having side bets with each other on who would score the best goal.

Their harmless wagers were a sideshow to the 4–1 home win over Aston Villa on 19 October. Villa looked on course for a hat-trick of Upton Park wins in successive seasons when Simon Stainrod shot them in front after just six minutes, but it was one-way traffic thereafter as Hammers stretched their unbeaten run to 11 matches.

McAvennie equalised in the 23rd minute after a fine long ball from Alvin Martin and the big centre-back was also involved in the second, 11 minutes later, when his header rebounded off the bar and Cottee pounced to the net from close range.

Neither goal would win goal-of-the-season, however, and with the match now comfortably within Hammers' control, the twin strike force set about winning their personal private battle.

Cottee seemed to have one hand on the winnings when he burst through in the 57th minute and blasted a volley past Villa keeper Nigel Spink from 25 yards.

Cottee says: 'When I scored with that chip, Frank ran up to me laughing and said: "You little shit!" He knew it would be hard to top that.'

But there were ten minutes of a one-sided match remaining when McAvennie capitalised on a mistake by Brendan Ormsby. Knowing it would take something really special to beat Cottee's stunning long-

BOYS OF '86

range strike, the canny Scot ran with the ball and took it as close to Spink as he dared before executing the most audacious chip from just inside the penalty area.

McAvennie laughs out loud at the memory of his impudence: 'When Tony scored a cracker from about 25 yards, I thought, I'm never gonna top that. Then I was clean through onto goal with Spink, who's about 6 ft 4 in, in front of me. I just kept running towards him and he must have been wondering what the hell I was up to by not shooting earlier, but I dug the ball out of the ground like I was using a seven iron, and it went so high before dropping into the net. I couldn't believe it went in and Tony knew I'd beaten his great effort. It was arrogant stuff. And it was also good fun. I can't remember how much Tony and I had bet on it – it wasn't much – but I think John Lyall found out about it and docked the stake money from our wages anyway!'

Cottee scored the only goal of the game in a 1–0 win at Ipswich Town a week later, while McAvennie scored twice in the 2–1 home win against Everton on 2 November. The win at Portman Road was Hammers' fourth in succession in Suffolk. Mark Ward's overhead kick on 26 minutes caught Town's defence flat-footed and Cottee ran through to nod the ball over the advancing Paul Cooper, who was making his 500th appearance in goal.

Hammers were some way short of their best and this win owed more to defensive solidity, with Martin and Gale outstanding. George Parris replaced Ray Stewart (hamstring) at right-back, while 18-year-old reserve-team skipper Steve Potts made his one and only senior appearance of the season as cover for Alan Devonshire, who limped off in the 64th minute.

Three days later Hammers returned to Milk Cup action with a very tough visit to Old Trafford to face unbeaten league leaders Manchester United. These were the days when even the elite clubs viewed the League Cup as a worthwhile piece of silverware – and before top clubs like United began treating the competition with disdain by fielding largely reserve teams in order to rest their star players – and the two sides fought an enthralling battle in front of more than 32,000 fans.

Few teams have gone to Old Trafford and attacked the mighty Reds in the manner in which West Ham did on 29 October. Even after Norman Whiteside scored what turned out to be the winner in the 77th minute, the white-shirted Hammers surged forward and, but for a grave injustice, would have taken Ron Atkinson's men back to Upton Park for a hard-earned replay.

A storm of controversy surrounded the free-kick Hammers were awarded after McAvennie was fouled just minutes after United had gone ahead. The ball was placed some 30 yards from goal when Ward stepped forward and lashed a searing drive into the net, despite the valiant efforts of keeper Gary Bailey, who appeared to get fingertips to the ball as it flew past him and into the net. But the celebrations were cut short by Welsh referee Frank Roberts who, after consulting a linesman, disallowed the 'goal' because the kick was indirect and he had not seen Bailey touch it. Gale led the protests as irate Hammers players surrounded the official, but he wasn't going to change his mind.

After visiting the officials' room after the match, Lyall emerged with a typically diplomatic comment: 'I certainly thought Bailey touched the ball and all the lads who were close to goal were adamant he had.' The manager took some positives from the night, however, and oozed a growing sense of optimism when he added: 'The important thing is that we have shown that we can match the best teams both defensively and in attacking play. Our overall performance reflected great credit on the lads, and I think we have given United their hardest home game of the season so far. Not many sides will come here and dominate them as we did in the last stages.' West Ham would exact revenge on Manchester United when the teams were drawn out of the hat together again in the FA Cup later in the season but, for now, it was back to League business . . . and some pruning of the Upton Park wage bill.

Experienced left-back Paul Brush finally got his wish to move granted when, after two months on loan at Selhurst Park, he joined Second Division Crystal Palace in a £30,000 deal. Plaistow-born Brush was substitute for the '80 Cup final and made 188 League and Cup appearances for his local club in nine years. At the age of 27, he needed first-team football. More than that, the change of scenery was all the more welcome after he also suffered the heartbreak of losing his wife, Marion, who died of leukaemia shortly after she had given birth.

Diminutive 20-year-old midfielder Warren Donald had played only two first-team games for the Hammers before joining Northampton Town for £11,000. Fellow reserve Keith McPherson, a 21-year-old centre-back who made his only senior appearance in the final game of the previous season against Liverpool, initially went on loan to Cambridge United before moving on to Bournemouth and then Reading, and keeper John Vaughan, 21, had loan spells with Bristol Rovers and Wrexham.

Although the first team picked itself, Lyall had strength in depth. In addition to Goddard waiting in the wings, the reserves were also going strong in the Combination League. In the space of three matches, the table-topping Hammers thrashed London rivals Spurs 6–2, Chelsea 4–2 and crushed Swindon Town 9–3. George Parris and Greg Campbell were the two second-string players persistently knocking on the door of the first team but there were also others making their mark.

Tricky winger Bobby Barnes hit a hat-trick in the slaughter of Spurs. Steve Whitton, who returned after summer knee surgery, provided the experience, but there was plenty of promise, too, from younger players like Steve Potts, Paul Ince, Kevin Keen, Paul McMenemy (nephew of Sunderland boss Lawrie) and Stuart Slater, who had been catching the eye at youth level. The present was good and the future looked just as bright.

With talk of a proposed Super League still being mooted by the game's hierarchy, Lyall's belief after the Old Trafford cup tie that his team were very capable of taking on, and beating, the best was borne out on 2 November in the next game at Upton Park, where champions Everton were beaten 2–1.

The Toffees played their part in an absorbing, high-quality contest and looked to have all the points in the bag when Trevor Steven shot them into the lead on the hour. But McAvennie would upstage the visiting strike duo of Gary Lineker and Graeme Sharp with two match-winning goals in the space of eight minutes. Parris, substituting for Walford, put McAvennie away for the equaliser in the 74th minute and the new golden boy of east London sent the home crowd into raptures with a well-struck winner nine minutes from the end of a pulsating match. It seemed that everything McAvennie and Cottee touched turned to goals and Hammers had not celebrated a forward partnership this successful since Johnny Dick and Vic Keeble amassed 47 League goals between them (27 and 20 goals respectively) on West Ham's return to the First Division in 1958–59. On the field McAvennie and Cottee had developed an almost telepathic understanding, yet they were different personalities off the pitch.

Cottee, from the start of his pro career and with the benefit of financial advice from his father Clive, an insurance broker, had shrewdly invested a chunk of his earnings in a pension fund that would mature when he reached the age of 35 in the summer of 2001.

53

At the age of 20, he was about to leave his parents' place at Collier Row and buy his first home, a £42,000 flat off Upminster Road, Hornchurch, which he would later share with his girlfriend and future wife Lorraine Blackhall. The couple had known each other well since they both attended Warren Secondary School in Chadwell Heath, just a stone's throw from the club's Saville Road training ground.

Tony Cottee has always been a steady character. The worst thing he ever did in his schooldays was spray-paint his initials and the crossed Hammers symbol on the pavement outside his home. (He was immediately ordered to clean the pavement by his dad, or else pay the penalty – miss watching the next West Ham home game. Tony cleaned the pavement.) He didn't drink more than the occasional few beers at his local pubs in Essex, listened to soul music by the likes of Luther Vandross and enjoyed a game of snooker more than he did a night out on the town. His biggest luxury then was his pride and joy – a white Ford Escort Cabriolet with black go-faster stripes and alloy wheels.

In contrast, McAvennie, a much more happy-go-lucky character, drove a dark-green metallic 2.8i Ford Capri Ghia, the type of 'jam jar' Del Boy raved about in *Only Fools and Horses*. Being so far away from his family in Glasgow, he had the time and opportunity to indulge himself. He was, and is, great company, full of laughs and his infectious personality ensured he was never lonely after the initial settling-in period.

To this day, Cottee and McAvennie remain good friends and are full of admiration for each other. If anything, the 15 years that have elapsed since their famous season in tandem have only served to enhance their appreciation of each other's game. McAvennie says: 'I'd rate Tony at the top. I don't know whether he was the best partner I ever played with, because I played with Kenny Dalglish for Scotland. But Tony is without doubt the best finisher I've ever played with. I rate him a better finisher than Gary Lineker. Lineker was simply a goal poacher, and maybe Tony was that when he first came into the side, but he added much more to his game that season. The whole team made him a better all-round player. His awareness improved and he played more for the team. He understood that he needed to, whereas I'd played four seasons in midfield, so if I was getting starved of the ball up front, I'd come back and help out. But Tony has never played in midfield. He could score goals for fun but he also learned how to hold the ball up. We got on well, despite what some newspapers tried to claim. We never had a cross word on the pitch. If he did something I didn't like, I'd just have to look at him and he'd know he should have passed it. The only time we criticised each other was at the team meeting early on in the season.

'You could see from the videos of the games that we were so pleased for each other, no matter which one of us scored. We'd chase each other and be the first to congratulate each other. We were so full of confidence. It got to the stage when we knew we were both gonna score, and then it became a case of who could score the best goal.'

Cottee says: 'Even though I couldn't understand Frank at first, we were always talking on the pitch. We got on really well. Frank got more verbal abuse than me from opposing defenders, probably because of his blond hair, and he'd be more inclined to have a go back. I'd just keep my head down as usual. I never really got involved in the banter. Frank was full of it. He was brave and he unsettled defenders. Eventually they'd drop off and then we'd start receiving the ball to the feet. Once we became the regular two up front we'd work on improving things in training – crossover runs and extra shooting especially. We'd have competitions against Parkesy and Tom McAlister.

'Wardie, Frank and myself – the others called us "The Three Stooges" or "The Three Musketeers" – would also back ourselves to beat each other over 50-yard sprints. We were very competitive but it was a healthy rivalry. Frank and I wanted to do better than each other. I wanted to get more goals than him and he wanted to do the same. But it wasn't as though either of us would get the hump when the other one did well.

'Our philosophy was pretty basic. We wanted to play through the midfield and get the ball into the channels for Frank and myself. Little passing movements, third-man runs, everything John worked on in training. We had good players and it was enjoyable. Most teams played 4–4–2 and we tried to peel off behind the centre-backs. It was total football. There was no real secret to it.'

After he left West Ham to join Everton for a then British transfer record fee of £2.05m in the summer of 1988, Cottee often played alongside another Scottish international, Graeme Sharp – a tall, old-fashioned style centre-forward who liked the ball delivered to him in the air. Cottee had to feed off the scraps and knock-downs from the bigger man. Nine times out of ten, the ball never reached him and he was left feeling frustrated, wishing he could renew his dream partnership with McAvennie. As Cottee confirms: 'Those 46 League

BOYS OF '86

55

goals between us that season support the fact that it was the best partnership of my entire career.'

It was not until 1987 that rumours of a rift between West Ham's prolific strike pairing began to circulate, but both men adamantly deny such talk as rubbish.

Cottee made himself clear in his 1995 autobiography, *Claret & Blues*:

'The same day the report appeared in the paper claiming that we weren't getting on, we were playing golf together at Warley Park in Brentwood. Now if there was any hint of friction between us, or we disliked or felt jealous of each other in any shape or form, do you really think that we'd spend all afternoon together playing golf?'

Mark Ward compared the deadly duo: 'Frank worked his balls off for the team whereas, at first, Tony thought his job was done if he'd scored a goal. But having said that, you can't have everything and Tony would be in my all-time top 11 players for his ruthless finishing.'

Although Cottee and McAvennie did not often mix socially, as players they thrived on their healthy, though competitive, rivalry. Apart from betting on who could score the most spectacular goals, they would also wager a fiver in the gym before home games. McAvennie describes their unusual pre-match routines: 'I never used to like warming up before a game and preferred to read the papers instead, but John would make us go into the gym under the main stand. While a few of the boys were going through their exercises around us, Tony, Wardie and me would play this game of trying to chip a ball onto the light switch in the corner of the hall. We'd go in there before every home game and after a bit of jogging – and with Boycey having left the room – we'd play our usual game. Every time one of us hit the light switch, the room was plunged into darkness and the other players would be falling over themselves! We'd switch the light back on and try to hit it again. Well, it would have been a bit too arrogant to have tried to turn the light back *on* again with a chip!'

Cottee adds: 'It was a game of skill but, of course, nowadays players all have a proper warm-up before each game. We all had our own little routines, then, though. Dev, for instance, would take himself off into Rob's medical room and fall asleep for half an hour, then go out and be the best player on the pitch.'

Not that Cottee and McAvennie took their goalscoring responsibilities lightly. They would both regularly stay behind after training for extra shooting practice, firing shots from all angles and distances at keepers Phil Parkes and Tom McAlister, with 64-year-old goalkeeping coach Ernie Gregory (who celebrated a record 50 years with the club during that season) barking advice and encouragement from the sidelines. Ernie didn't need to throw himself around to demonstrate the art of goalkeeping and Parkes had the greatest respect for one of the club's most loyal employees.

Parkes says: 'Some of the training we did as keepers was quite innovative at the time and you couldn't help but respect old Ernie. What he didn't know about goalkeeping wasn't worth knowing and he was a big help to both Tom and myself.'

Parkes also speaks highly of the Scottish understudy, who had taken over the number one jersey from him for most of the previous season.

Parkes continues: 'Tom was a great lad, we got on really well. He was so unlucky with injuries throughout the early part of his career and, to be honest, I wasn't even sure of getting my place back at the start of the '85–86 season. I knew I had to keep on my toes once I did get back in.'

The players invariably enjoyed Lyall's training methods which were obviously geared to getting the best from the Cottee/McAvennie partnership. Players did not have big egos then and weren't shy of seeking advice from their peers, or from the coaching staff. They wanted to improve and believed in the age-old maxim that you are never too old to learn.

Ray Stewart says: 'The attitude was so good that players still came in on their day off to work on certain aspects of their game. And if anyone messed about, which was rare, the other players would pull them into line. I used to work mostly on improving my control and passing, the things that would sometimes let me down in games. But after working on it, I think that accurate passing over long distances became a strength of mine. We worked hard on organising the back four and it's a sign of how hard the boys worked at it that you could almost do it with your eyes shut. There was a togetherness. We often played it into midfield and we always had players in front of us who would take a pass.'

Devonshire says: 'I always talked to Boycey. He was a midfield player, so we thought along the same lines. I was the type of person who liked to talk about the game and ways of improving myself, and Boycey was like that too, so we got on well. My first real football memory was of him scoring the winner in the 1964 FA Cup final, so I had a lot of respect for him.'

BOYS OF '86

Alvin Martin adds: 'Boycey was the popular link between the players and the manager. You could always trust Ron. If he came up to you and said "well done", it meant a lot to you. He simplified everything about the game – just how he'd played it – and wouldn't ever over-complicate things. I'd been brought up in the youth team and Ron played a big part in my career. We both knew that he'd done his bit in everything I was achieving. He'd been there for me from the very first day I'd arrived at the club. He was a lovely man, a real West Ham person alongside the likes of Ernie Gregory, Billy Bonds, Eddie Gillam and, of course, John Lyall. They're synonymous with what the club used to be all about. It was a unique club, and Ron was the nicest, most genuine man you could ever meet.'

McAvennie saw other, less obvious qualities in Boyce, a true East Ender who shared Lyall's smoking habit. He says: 'I used to steal his fags. Well, I couldn't very well nick them off John! If I fancied a fag on the way home from an away game, I used to entice Boycey to the back of the coach. If he ever refused me, I'd torment him by saying that if he didn't give me a ciggy, I'd tell John that he'd been supplying me with them all season! Wally Walford and me were the only regular smokers in the team at that time, although if we had a night out and the boys got a few drinks inside them, they all suddenly became smokers – and they'd nick them from me! I was only a light smoker – I smoked Silk Cut – so I never really considered it real smoking. I never smoked more than ten a day at that time.

'Wardie was a pest to room with, though, and used to complain about my smoking. He'd even offer to buy me my own hotel room. In fact, if there was an odd number of players on the trip, John would let me have a room to myself. He was good like that.'

Mick McGiven, a Geordie signed from Sunderland to succeed the irreplaceable Bobby Moore in 1973, was a more demonstrative man than Boyce and adopted a more disciplined approach that perhaps didn't always endear him to the players, although those who know him best will testify to his dry humour and likeable qualities.

Alvin Martin says: 'Mick was a good right-hand man. He was more of a dour personality and a bit more abrasive than Boycey but you can't have all really nice people at a football club. Mick would always get the job done. If John needed to rattle a few cages, Mick would be the one to do it. He had an important role to play.'

The influence Alan Devonshire had on the free-scoring duo has already been illustrated but fellow midfielder Alan Dickens had a pivotal role that was certainly not underestimated by the players, even if the supporters did not always fully appreciate his value. With Neil Orr playing the holding role in centre midfield, it enabled the 21-year-old Dickens to get forward and link up play with the two strikers, as well as to spray accurate passes to Devonshire and Ward on the flanks. 'Dicko' was the forward-running midfielder in the third-man runs mentioned by Cottee but the tactic had already become second nature to him.

Dickens explains: 'We'd done those sort of things since the age of 15, in the grids at Chadwell Heath. I just played the same way for the first team as I did as a youth player. In fact, I played the same way for my schoolboy Sunday side, Ascot, before I went to West Ham. It was all one and two-touch, playing balls into the forwards or into the space behind them.

'When I got the ball, I knew that Tony and Frank would want it played in behind the centre-halves. You couldn't lay the ball behind the full-backs for Dev and Wardie, because they always liked it to their feet. When I had possession, there were always a lot of options. We used only 18 players all season and we all knew each other's game.'

Dickens had all the ingredients to become the complete midfielder. Tall and elegant, he stroked the ball around effortlessly in midfield and could score goals with both feet or his head. And although aggression was a quality that didn't come naturally to him, he was more fired up this season than at any other time in his career. He remembers few details from the games and, being so young and inexperienced at the time, was simply very happy to be part of the team's success. He was carried along on the crest of a wave.

If Dickens lacked anything it was self-confidence. A quietly spoken man and completely unassuming, Dicko would be worth £15m in today's Premiership market but after a big-money move to Chelsea in 1989 he lost his way in the game, became disillusioned under a succession of managers at lower and non-league level and drifted out of football by the age of 30.

After passing the 'Knowledge' in 1997, he now gets up at 5.30 a.m., sometimes six days a week, to drive his black taxi cab from his Barking home to earn a crust in and around central London. While agreeing that he lacked self-belief, Dickens suggests he could have benefited more from stronger words of encouragement from the manager and coaches, too.

He reflects ruefully on the season when he arrived as a First Division star: 'Sometimes I would get too nervous. It's good to be on

edge and wanting to do well, but to be too nervous is not a good thing. I don't think anybody helped me in that way. John never used to say anything to me. He never told me I'd done well or played badly. Nothing. Even when I was in the youth team, I don't remember the manager, Tony Carr, boosting my confidence with a few words of encouragement.

'I know it doesn't do any good to build up some kids, because praise can easily go to their heads. But where I was quieter than most, it would have brought me out of my shell more and made me feel much more confident of my own ability. It would definitely have helped me. If John had said to me, "You're doing a great job, son, keep it up", I would have run through brick walls for him. If someone is nice to me, I'll do anything for them.

'My little boy, Luke, is like me in that he needs a regular confidence-booster. He can be a bit of a worrier but I recognise that in him and will always encourage him in whatever he wants to do. John was a good coach but I don't think he gave me the guidance and help I needed to get the best out of me. Having said that, he's still the best manager I ever played for.'

The inferiority complex that hampered Dickens' football career is perhaps evident in a story he tells about the first car he owned. This time he had cause to question his dad, Alan senior: 'I was 18 when my dad advised me to buy a Triumph 2000 for four hundred pounds. Honestly, it was embarrassing. The exhaust was blowing and it was a right state. I'd just broken into the first team but instead of driving into the players' car park, I used to park around the corner from the stadium, in a side street, and walk to the ground. I didn't want anyone to see me because the car was a disgrace. One Christmas, after training, the players were travelling in convoy up to The Bell at Epping, where we'd meet up and stay before playing the next day. But my car was so bad, so slow, that I couldn't keep up with the others and I'd be left behind. I remember getting lost the first time that happened!

'Mind you, George Parris had a car worse than mine. His first car was a white Morris Marina, a really bad-looking car, and he always sat so low in the seat, you could hardly see his head over the top of the dashboard. George wasn't the best of drivers either. One of the things I find so amazing about football today is the fact that young players, who have never even played in the first team, are driving around in thirty-thousand-pound cars.'

Dickens should by rights be driving an expensive car himself today, and his teammates from the 1985–86 season are still in no doubt about his worth to West Ham's most successful League campaign. And despite what Alan says about a lack of verbal encouragement from the management and coaches at the club, his teammates claim they did their bit to bring out the best in a great talent.

Alvin Martin says: 'Dicko had an exceptional one-off year. He was as talented as any player we'd ever had. He made a good start, believed in both himself and his game and kept going. We were lucky that we got the best out of him. We kept telling him how good he was because he was exceptionally talented. He was one of the nicest men ever to walk into Upton Park but you just felt that sometimes he had to be that little bit nastier. The likes of Mark Ward and Frank McAvennie had that streak in them.'

Despite what Dickens himself believes, Devonshire claims he recognised Dickens' weakness at the time and says: 'Dicko always needed an arm round him. I knew he wasn't a confident boy and I tried to look after him, the way Trevor Brooking and Billy Bonds had looked after me. When I first came into the game, they kept an eye out for me and helped me settle into things, on and off the pitch. I was grateful for that and I never forgot it. And I was like that myself years later, when young lads like Kevin Keen, Paul Ince and Steve Potts came in. I always had time for them, because they were the future of the club. I knew when Dicko went to Chelsea that there would be no one there to put an arm around him or look after him. To see him go out of the game at such an early age was terrible. A real waste of genuine talent.'

Cottee, who roomed with Dickens on away trips, says: 'As the left-sided forward I was lucky because I lined up with Dev and Alan Dickens. Dicko never got the credit he deserved in that team. He linked everything up and had a great season. He was my best mate because we'd come through the youth team together. We'd grown up together and played against each other from the age of ten. He was head and shoulders above everybody at that time.

'When we got to youth level he was a bit ahead of me and he made his first team début at Notts County just before I made mine against Spurs. We went through everything together and he was great for my game. He knew my runs and I knew where his passes were going. We had a great understanding. He made everything happen for us but he wasn't fully appreciated. Today, he would definitely be in the England squad. He ran games. He did sliding tackles, could head the ball and made runs. Dicko had everything except perhaps, at times, confidence. He was pretty quietish.

BOYS OF '86

'When things went right for him – as they did all that season – his confidence was high and he looked a fantastic player. Confidence is the biggest thing in football. Without doubt he was the type of player who needed an arm around him and in the latter stages of his West Ham career some people were having a go at him and that didn't get the response you wanted from him. In the end he went to Chelsea but no one should underestimate his contribution to the West Ham team of '85–86. He was one of the players who made it happen. To be fair to the fans, they didn't get on his back during that season but during the following one they seemed to pick him out now and again. I could never understand why and in the end it destroyed his confidence. He was never quite the same player again. He shouldn't be driving a black cab.'

Dickens was never money-motivated, however, looking back, he now wishes he had pushed himself more. But he was by no means the only West Ham player who felt intimidated by John Lyall when money and new contracts were on the agenda.

Chapter 6

I'M YOUR MAN – Wham!

Chart Position: Number 1, November 1985

Whenever people talked about West Ham United being a family club with a long-held tradition for playing entertaining, attacking football, they were really talking about John Lyall and all the good beliefs he inherited from his mentor, Ron Greenwood, who he succeeded as team manager in August 1974. When they talked about the caring side of football, the honesty, dignity, high morals and intelligence, they echoed the same qualities embodied by Lyall, that Ilford-born son of a former policeman. And when they grumbled about West Ham's careful handling of the purse strings and a refusal to pay not a penny more than a player's true worth, they were also thinking about John Lyall. For in Lyall, the east London club had much more than a team manager who looked after affairs at the training ground and on matchdays. He was also the best bank manager the board of directors could have wished for.

Of course, he knew the value of a player and the facts confirm his willingness to spend big if he felt the deal was right; Phil Parkes, Paul Goddard and Ray Stewart were very expensive purchases at the time they joined the Hammers. But Lyall ran West Ham United from top to bottom, as if it was his own club. In many ways it was.

We can only guess at the true reasons why the man who led West Ham to two FA Cup successes (1975 and 1980), the Second Division Championship and League Cup final (both 1981) *and* the highest-ever League placing (1986) no longer wishes to publicly associate himself with the football club with whom he spent 34 years of his life.

He was undoubtedly shocked and bitterly hurt to be sacked after West Ham were relegated to Division Two in 1989, having given so

much to them over such a long period – especially so since the Hammers' Board had effectively prevented him accepting a lucrative offer from QPR supremo Jim Gregory to succeed Barcelona-bound Terry Venables at Loftus Road in 1984. As Lyall lamented in his autobiography *Just Like My Dreams*, he would have joined Forest's Brian Clough and Manchester United's Ron Atkinson among the mega-earners in Football League management, almost doubling his West Ham salary over the period of the mouth-watering five-year contract Rangers had offered him. But the West Ham Board demanded £150,000 compensation from QPR before sanctioning Lyall's release, so the deal collapsed at the eleventh hour. Lyall, true to his principles, bit the bullet and got on with the job of managing the Hammers to the best of his ability. Indeed, in May 1985 he signed a new four-year contract. Little did he imagine then that when it expired in June 1989, he would be discarded so shabbily.

Although he claims not to bear any grudges against the club he transformed into a family institution, Lyall is no longer prepared to discuss in public any aspect of his time at West Ham. One has to respect his reasons but there remains the feeling that, deep down, one of the aspects of his sacking he finds most galling is that he spent – and saved – the club's money with such care and diligence that he thought he deserved as much loyalty from the directors as he had given them.

Managers are usually dismissed after irresponsibly squandering their employer's money in the transfer market, or lavishing fat contracts on players who don't produce the goods. Like even the very best bosses, Lyall made his mistakes in the transfer market, most notably in the two years that preceded his downfall (the names of David Kelly and Allen McKnight should have long since been erased from his Christmas card list). But he still largely managed West Ham's football budget as if it was his own. He wouldn't gamble the family silver on a whim.

Not surprisingly, the two biggest stars, Frank McAvennie and Tony Cottee, were the most frequent visitors to the manager's office in search of the financial rewards they felt they were worth as the goals continued to pile up. West Ham climbed towards the top of the First Division table and attendances increased accordingly.

McAvennie reveals: 'I got four wage rises in the first six months. But John was crafty because every time he gave you more money, he made you sign an extra year on your contract. I started on a three-year contract and I think I finished up signing for something like

The official 1985–86 squad picture (minus Mark Ward, who had not yet been signed from Oldham Athletic). *Back, left to right*: Swindlehurst, Martin, Bonds, Gale, Walford, Parkes, Vaughan, McAlister, Campbell, Devonshire, Hilton, Dickens, Whitton, Goddard. *Front, left to right*: Orr, Stewart, McPherson, Pike, Barnes, McAvennie, Cottee, Donald, Potts, Keen, Parris, Brush.

(© Steve Bacon)

Frank McAvennie scores with a looping header against Birmingham City.
(Courtesy of Frank McAvennie)

Ray Stewart shows his power in the tackle against Watford.
(Courtesy of Ray Stewart)

Looking the part, Frank McAvennie poses with his
Ford Capri Ghia after training at Chadwell Heath.
(Author's Collection)

BELOW: Alvin Martin leads the protests after referee Tyson's
hotly disputed penalty award at Anfield.
(© Steve Bacon)

Alvin Martin celebrates his match-winning volley against Southampton.
(© Steve Bacon)

Tony Cottee turns away after scoring against
Nottingham Forest, while Alan Dickens (number nine)
checks the condition of injured keeper Hans Segers.
(© Steve Bacon)

Mark Ward arrived as an
unknown but proved
an inspired signing.
(Courtesy of Mark Ward)

Tony Gale – a classy centre-back
who was always comfortable
on the ball.
(Courtesy of Tony Gale)

WEST HAM UNITED

1 **PHIL PARKES**
Played his 650th Football League game in our home match with Birmingham City.

2 **GEORGE PARRIS**
Has been playing in midfield for the injured Neil Orr but reverts to fullback to cover for the suspended Ray Stewart this afternoon.

3 **STEVE WALFORD**
Makes his 100th League appearance for the Hammers today. Joined us from Norwich City in the summer of 1983.

4 **TONY GALE**
Tony will make his 340th League appearance this afternoon. Made his debut with Fulham v Charlton Athletic in August 1977.

5 **ALVIN MARTIN (capt.)**
Surely the best central defender in the country at the moment. A Liverpool lad he made his 270th League appearance at Anfield a fortnight ago.

6 **ALAN DEVONSHIRE**
Will make his 297th League appearance this afternoon. Signed from Southall for £5,000 in September 1976.

7 **MARK WARD**
This is only Mark's third season of League football. Joined us from Oldham Athletic last summer.

8 **FRANK McAVENNIE**
Has shot to stardom as a prolific scorer in this his first season in the League. Aged 25, he was signed from St. Mirren last June.

9 **ALAN DICKENS**
Still only 21 but already a firmly established midfield player. Set to play his 75th League game today.

10 **TONY COTTEE**
It was New Year's Day 1983 that he made a scoring League debut v Spurs. Has now scored 48 goals in 113 League games. Age. 20.

11 **NEIL ORR**
Had made 186 Scottish League appearances for Morton before arriving at Upton Park in January 1982. Made his 110th League appearance at Spurs on Boxing Day.

12

MANCHESTER UNITED

1 **GARY BAILEY**
Lost his place for a couple of games last month but is now back between the posts. Has made 24 League appearances this season.

2 **JOHN GIDMAN**
Experienced defender with nearly 100 League games for United to his credit; 197 for Aston Villa and 64 for Everton.

3 **ARTHUR ALBISTON**
Had made 309 League appearances before the commencement of this season, and had scored five goals.

4 **NORMAN WHITESIDE**
Still only 20, yet has scored 31 goals in 130 League games for United.

5 **KEVIN MORAN**
Very competitive defender who has suffered more than his fair share of injuries. Has been at Old Trafford since January 1978.

6 **PAUL McGRATH**
Back after injury. Made his League debut v Spurs in November 1982 but did not establish himself in the side until last season.

7 **JESPER OLSEN**
Scored 5 goals in 36 First Division games last season and has already netted five in the League this season.

8 **GORDON STRACHAN**
Recovered from a dislocated shoulder. Missed only one League game last season, his first in English football.

9 **MARK HUGHES**
Has scored 12 goals in the First Division this season to bring his tally to 32 in games.

10 **FRANK STAPLETON**
Six goals this season boosts Frank's total to 52 in the League for Manchester United.

11 **COLIN GIBSON**
A newish face in the United ranks. Signed from Aston Villa last November, he has come into midfield and contributed 3 goals in 8 League matches.

12

Match Referee

REFEREE:
JOHN BALL
(Kirby Muxloe, Leics.)
Police Inspector. Married with two boys. Commenced refereeing in 1968 progressing via Leicestershire Senior and Southern Leagues. Interested in all sports, active in cricket, badminton, golf, swimming/lifesaving. In leisure moments when not working around the home, enjoys reading. Qualified F.A. coach and coaching secretary for Leicestershire. In 1983 lined a U.E.F.A. Cup match and in 1984 refereed Southern League Challenge Cup Final.

Linesmen:
M. H. BROWN
(Buckingham) Red Flag

P. DON
(Hanworth Park, Middx.) Yellow Flag

Matchball Sponsor

TODAY'S MATCHBALL SPONSOR

Stellana
AN SKF TRADEMARK

MILTON KEYNES (0908) 565154

SUPPLIERS OF
WHEELS, CASTORS & ROLLERS

Match Mascot

This afternoon we welcome Guy Underwood, aged 10½. Guy lives at Beresford Gardens, Cliftonville, Kent. He attends Chartfield School, Westgate, Kent and his hobbies are all types of sport, swimming and tap dancing. At present he plays football for his school team, in a midfield position. Guy's special team is of course West Ham United and his favourite player is Phil Parkes . . . We take this opportunity of wishing Guy and his family a very enjoyable afternoon with us at Upton Park.

WEST HAM PLAY
adidas

How the back cover of the matchday programme looked when Manchester United visited for the live TV game on Sunday, 2 February 1986.
(© Manchester United)

ABOVE: Golden Boy Frank McAvennie runs towards the South Bank terrace to signal yet another goal – this time against Watford.
(© Colorsport)

INSET: John Lyall, Hammers' much respected manager.
(© Steve Bacon)

Frank McAvennie and Tony Cottee netted 46 League goals between them – Hammers' most formidable strike partnership since the Dick/Keeble pairing of 1958–59 and one that has not been emulated in the past 15 years.
(© Colorsport)

fifteen years! I thought I was the top-paid player but Tony, Wardie and me were playing cards one day and it came out – I don't know how – about what we were earning. Tony said what he was on and me and Wardie looked at each other in amazement. Typically, Wardie started giggling because he knew what I was thinking. We used to share a room, so we already knew what we were both earning. I was straight in to see John the next Monday morning. When I asked him about what he'd said earlier about me being the top-paid player at the club, he said: "Well, you were at the time!"

'I said: "Cheers!" and sorted out a new deal.'

Cottee confirms this story of Lyall's stipulation that new contracts were only sanctioned if the player agreed to tie himself to a longer deal. After seeing Paul Allen end up out of contract and defect to rivals Tottenham for the relatively low tribunal fee of only £400,000 in the summer, the Hammers' boss was determined not to lose any more of his star players. In *Claret & Blues* Cottee described how he successfully renegotiated his contract in November 1985:

'I explained that I was ready to buy my first property and he told me that as I'd done well, he'd talk to the Board to see if they could do something for me. He came back and said what he always said in those situations: "The Board have done brilliantly for you." John never took the personal credit for giving you a pay rise, it was always "we" or "the club has done this". That was his way.

'John's only condition was that I had to sign for the next five and a half years. I didn't receive a signing-on fee but the slight increase in my basic pay was topped up by appearance money for each first-team game I played. It wasn't as much as £1,000 per game but it was a hefty sum.

'I had nothing written into my new contract about any additional bonus for scoring a certain number of goals, as more and more strikers insist on including in their deals today. In 1985 it didn't occur to me to ask for such a clause to be inserted in my contract and I'm sure the club would have said no to it anyway.'

Cottee also recalled a meeting, some 15 months earlier, when, as an 18 year old, he had been 'scared' by Lyall's forceful and off-hand manner when he didn't immediately accept the contract offer John had put before him. 'Although I thought highly of him as a person and a football manager, and he did very well for me in my career, I always found it hard to approach John and had difficulty communicating my true feelings to him. He was like a headmaster-type figure in his office.'

Money was not on Mark Ward's mind as he left Oldham Athletic for his big chance in the top flight. But he soon had first-hand experience of Lyall's persuasive powers. He says: 'I accepted whatever was offered. I can't remember how much I actually signed for but it was buttons. I don't think I got a signing-on fee and my wages were just a little bit more than I was on at Oldham. I'd been at West Ham two months and hadn't missed a game but Jane was really homesick. Our daughter, Melissa, was only a baby at the time and they were both back in Liverpool visiting family a lot of the time. It didn't affect my game because I was still focused on trying to be the best, but John actually came round to our house one evening to put things right.

'His first words to Jane were: "Don't think about going home. I've bought him for a quarter of a million pounds. I couldn't replace him and you're staying where you are." He sounded like a school headmaster. John was a clever sod – and do you know what he did next? I wasn't on that much money and had just moved into our new house at Loughton, which cost £73,000. Compare that to the one we had in Liverpool which cost £16,000. It was a massive jump. So John said to us, "Right, I'll give you an extra £100 a week." It was a sweetener but, looking back, if I'd had an agent, as all players do today, who knows what I could have got, considering the level I was playing at? I don't think John expected me to do as well as I did. John was a bit of a bandit when it came to money, but he was doing a good job for the club. But money wasn't an issue then anyway, it was all about enjoying the football.'

Earning big money was not an issue for young Alan Dickens either. He'd been living with his parents, Alan and Wendy, at Mortlake Road, Custom House, just a few minutes' drive from the Boleyn Ground, before moving into a flat at Goodmayes. Although he roomed with Cottee, Dickens expressed shock when he finally read a copy of Cottee's autobiography 15 years on and discovered, for the first time, how Cottee had instigated talks with Lyall for improved contracts. As Cottee says: 'As a player and a person, you owe it to yourself and your family to get what you believe you are worth.'

No one in that West Ham side doubted Dickens' worth, except perhaps Dicko himself. Talking about what players were earning then, he can't disguise his own inner feelings of regret when he opens his heart and confesses: 'When it came to money I was so naïve, it was quite embarrassing. I had never, ever thought about money until

I had to start driving a cab to provide for my family. Money had never come into it for me while I was a footballer.

'My first contract as a pro was worth about £160 a week and I think by the '85–86 season I was on £300 a week. I used to share a room with Tony for away games but it was not until I recently read his book that I was so shocked to find that he would knock on the manager's door to ask for a better deal if he thought he deserved it. I never did that in all my time at West Ham and didn't think it was necessary. I just thought you signed your contract and that was what you got until it ran out. The way I thought it worked was that if the manager thought you deserved better, he would call you into his office and offer you better terms.

'On the few occasions that I did see John to sign a new contract, I felt quite intimidated. He made you feel that whatever the club was paying you at the time, it was all you deserved. It never once occurred to me to ask for more money and I never received a signing-on fee from the club. I remember that Greg Campbell used to earn more money than me and he hardly ever used to play. He had a nice new car and he was obviously well advised by his dad, who was steeped in football. But my mum and dad didn't know anything about football in the financial sense.

'I'm not money-orientated but, looking back, I felt a bit hurt that John never called me in, told me I was doing well and offered me a little bit more. But I think he would try and give the kids, who didn't cause any fuss, the least possible, whereas the ones who knocked on his door got better deals. That's the wrong way to do it and if I were a manager, I'd look after the good kids. It would give them a big lift to know that their manager thought so highly of them. But at that time, all I worried about was whether I had played well and the team had won. Money didn't come into my thoughts. I wouldn't have felt bitter towards Greg, Tony or anybody else – good luck to them.'

Ironically, if Lyall had not been dismissed on 5 July 1989, Dickens might not have left in a big £600,000 deal to Chelsea just weeks later.

'I had a couple of meetings with the new manager, Lou Macari, and I think I would have got more money if I'd stayed at West Ham – my next contract would have taken me up to my testimonial – so leaving for Chelsea had nothing whatsoever to do with the fact that we had just been relegated, or money. I left for football reasons, but wish now that I hadn't. I wish instead that I had sought advice from experienced people like Bonzo, Alvin Martin or Boycey. I wasn't quite sure what I was doing and when I heard stories about the way

BOYS OF '86

Lou was going to change the style of play, introducing a longer-ball game, I felt it wouldn't suit me.

'Bobby Campbell, the Chelsea manager, rang me a couple of times and I just got the feeling that I was wanted more by Chelsea than I was by West Ham. I think Macari wanted me to stay but he didn't really know me. But if Billy Bonds had maybe been manager at the time, I'd have stayed. I needed someone to say I was still needed and wanted at West Ham. I received a signing-on fee from Chelsea, but I negotiated my own terms and I messed up there really. If I'd done the deal properly, I would probably have paid off my mortgage by now. But, again, money wasn't on my mind at that stage. All I thought about was playing football until the age of 35, or as long as I could.

'People moan about agents in the game now but people like me need an agent. Me and money don't get on well. As I say, I'm not bitter, but I wish I'd done better for myself for the sake of my wife, Annika, and my two sons, Luke [7] and Sam [5].'

Tactically, Lyall had the full respect of his players and was rightly regarded then as one of the best tracksuit managers in the game. It was a measure of the esteem in which he was held by his players – as both a man and a football manager – that when he left the club so suddenly, they rallied round him to offer words of support in a string of phone calls.

Alvin Martin, Lyall's trusted leader on the field, summed up the general view:

'John was excellent at the technical side of the game. Everything was geared towards touch and control. He was a great organiser and the best manager throughout my time at West Ham. Although he paid a lot of money for Phil Parkes, Paul Goddard and Ray Stewart, he built something solid and reliable without spending millions. John ran the club's finances as if it was his own money. He was always trying to balance ambition with the budget. It was his club and he wasn't going to bankrupt it.

'At the end of the 1985–86 season you could have said to John, go out and buy the best three players you can – say, Dalglish, Souness, Hansen – and he wouldn't have done it. John would've said, "I don't think we can afford it and what if it goes wrong? We'll suffer." He had a wonderful attitude towards the club. Even when you tried to negotiate a new contract with him it was as if it was his own money you were talking about. That was the way he did the job.

'He was great and the most disappointing thing is that he's no longer at the club. He should be on the Board now. I don't think there was one player who didn't get on with him. Even the difficult ones, like the teenage Paul Inces of this world, had great respect for him. He never got the credit he deserved and people don't understand how good he was. John Lyall had everything. If you'd put John in charge of Liverpool, for instance, it would have been unbelievable what he could have achieved. Put him in charge of the Sounesses and Dalglishes and he could have gone out and bought the top players.

'All the way through the '85–86 season, he never, ever showed any signs of pressure. If we hadn't played well we knew we were in for a hard day's training on Monday morning. John was tough but he wasn't the sort of bloke who would walk through the club and see somebody injured and then treat them in the wrong way. That's why he was so popular. He was a father figure whom you knew you could always turn to.'

Tony Gale is typically forthright: 'The club has never recovered from John Lyall's departure but the Board probably thought he was too powerful. I was on a golf course when I heard the news he'd been sacked and I just couldn't believe it. West Ham has always been a great club – always will be – but it has never been the same. It hasn't got that family feel any more. That was down to John. He used to go to see the players in hospital if ever we were badly injured. He made a point of knowing all the wives' first names and would arrange for flowers to be sent to them if they were ill. And he'd always ask how your kids were doing.'

Alan Devonshire valued the manager's insight into the game. He says: 'I was a player who needed straight talking and I used to go in to John's office every Monday to chat about Saturday's game for ten minutes. What had I done wrong? What should I work on? That sort of thing. You can always learn something new in football and I always kept that on board. I had a great relationship with John and he knew what made me tick. Every now and then he would pull me in and say: "What's the matter? You haven't looked too sharp lately."

'I might say to him: "Yeah, I've felt a bit heavy-legged."

'Then he'd just as likely say: "Have Monday and Tuesday off – just tell the other boys you've got a bit of a thigh strain and need to rest it."

'It always seemed to work for me. He knew just how to deal with individual players and I had so much respect for him because of that.'

Mark Ward agrees: 'I learned so much from him. As a manager and a coach, he brought things out in my game that I never thought I had. In the first few weeks after joining the club, me and Boycey would be back out in the afternoons working with a couple of youth team kids.

BOYS OF '86

They'd give me the ball out wide and I'd have to beat a full-back before whipping in a cross. Frank and Tony weren't the biggest lads up front, so it was important that I could whip the ball into the near-post area at pace, instead of just pushing the ball to one side and lofting it towards a big guy like, say, Niall Quinn, who I played with at Man City. John was very much hands-on, he was superb.'

Lyall's team-talks were generally well received, if an occasional source of amusement to one or two players. The West Ham manager would often use real-life situations to help explain his point, or the values he treasured most or as a way of cultivating good team spirit.

McAvennie, who has a knack of finding humour in even the worst tragedies, says: 'John had a great way of getting his point across, using fictional characters he'd made up, which sometimes made you laugh at the same time.

'At half-time he might say something like: "If Billy the Burglar walked by your back door and saw it open, he may walk past once, he may well walk by twice, but he'll nae walk by three times – he'll go inside and nick all your furniture!" Whenever he told that one you knew he was having a pop at our defenders.'

Ray Stewart adds: 'John would be talking about the value of team spirit and saying things like: "If our ship was sinking and there was only one life raft available, you boys would look after yourselves, but I'd make sure all 11 of you got on it and found safety." That was his way of saying that one or two players were playing for themselves and not the good of the team.

'Then he'd talk about the tie salesman. I'd occasionally try selling ties to the lads, so John would say to the others: "Some of the ties he's selling are disgraceful, horrible colours, but you'd end up buying one from him just to get rid of him." The point he was making was that I had the right attitude because I was persistent and wouldn't give in until I got what I wanted.

'He was always trying to make you think and be realistic in life, put things into perspective. The bottom line was that you could call him "John", which meant you could have a friendship with him, too. If you had a problem, he'd be the first to try and help. Sometimes players would go to him to advise him that one or two of the other lads needed a helping hand. It was all about maintaining a good team spirit.'

Alvin Martin illustrates Lyall's attention to detail before signing a player: 'We all believed in John's judgement. He had ultimate respect in the dressing-room. Nobody ever questioned him. He was a strong character and a great coach but he took a big risk on Wardie. Nobody knew whether he could step up to the top division. John was meticulous in his groundwork and intelligence before he signed a player. He wouldn't touch anyone with a bad reputation but he'd reached the stage where he desperately needed somebody up front. He knew he had to take a chance with Frank McAvennie. It was a last roll of the dice but history says he made the right decision. Those two signings were as good as any John ever made.'

Neil Orr reveals: 'Yes, John spoke to me about Frank before signing him. Having played against Frank early on in his career in Scotland, I was one of the few who knew about him up there, so John sought my opinion on him. But he always did his homework well. There was no doubt as far as I could see that John had already made up his mind to sign Frank, but he just wanted to make sure that there were no problems with him that he wasn't aware of. He just wanted to make sure that Frank was a decent guy as well as a good footballer.'

While Lyall's analogical team-talks brought a smile to the face of the fun-loving McAvennie, he adopts a more serious tone when he adds: 'John's man-management and coaching methods were of a different class. He was very hands-on that season.'

Mark Ward had cause to appreciate the caring side of Lyall's nature and the consideration he had for his players, especially new signings: 'I always felt at home at West Ham. John took me and Jane around for two weeks after I signed to visit all the estate agents in the area. I'd wait around for John for an hour or so after training each day and then he'd drive us, pointing out the best places to live and areas to avoid. He really went out of his way to make us feel welcome and help us settle down.'

Perhaps John Lyall's loyalty to West Ham was summed up best when McAvennie left Hammers the first time to join his boyhood heroes Celtic for £750,000 in October 1987. McAvennie had asked for yet another pay increase and although the manager agreed to it, he insisted on the usual contract extension which, in theory, tied the player to the club for a much longer period.

But, Frank says, 'I told him I wasn't signing for any more years, so I asked for a signing-on fee instead and John refused. When the deal with Celtic was just about to be completed, I told John that if he gave me a £50,000 signing-on fee, I'd stay at West Ham. He gave me a cuddle, and was genuinely pleased for me when he heard what Celtic had agreed to pay me, but he wouldn't give me the fifty grand. He said it was club policy and he wasn't going to break those principles.'

BOYS OF '86

Chapter 7

WEST END GIRLS – Pet Shop Boys

Chart Position: Number 1, December 1985

In accordance with his contract, Frank McAvennie received another pay rise at West Ham after playing for Scotland against Australia in the World Cup qualifier in Glasgow in November that clinched the Scots' place in the following summer's 1986 finals in Mexico.

It was not John Lyall's policy to refuse permission for any of his players to represent their countries in full international matches, so Frank was given the all-clear to spend ten days with Alex Ferguson's squad for the second leg Down Under, before resuming his incredible First Division scoring spree that, following the home win over Everton, yielded another four goals in the next six matches.

He did not make it onto the score sheet, however, at Oxford United on 9 November, when Hammers came under early pressure and Phil Parkes and Alvin Martin had to be at their best to deny the U's, who were inspired by former Hammers midfielder Ray Houghton. After John Aldridge headed the home side in front on 21 minutes, Mark Ward led the fight-back, crossing for Tony Cottee to equalise in the 38th minute. And as the visitors continued to gain control in the second half, it was the little winger who came up trumps again in the 68th minute. Ward had been cruelly denied a goal from that free-kick in the Milk Cup tie at Old Trafford but this time his 35-yard strike flew into the net past Steve Hardwick. It was a spectacular way to open his West Ham account and a delighted Lyall enthused: 'You could not have asked for a better winner.'

Ward, who always insists he was a midfielder who worked tirelessly up and down the right flank, rather than an out-and-out winger, should really have scored more goals in his career for someone possessing such a ferocious shot with his size-five right foot.

He invariably stayed wide on the right touchline to help maintain the overall balance of the side but, as a player who later played many games in a more central midfield position, one wonders how many more goals he would have scored if he had drifted inside or got into the penalty box more often. He would not take any nonsense from full-backs and tackled every bit as hard as they did – sometimes too hard. Although small in stature, Wardie had terrific courage and the heart of a lion.

In his four years at Upton Park, the tenacious Scouser never scored more League goals in a season than the three he netted in 1985–86 and a final tally of nine in four and a half years does no justice to his ability and shooting power. He scored for the second consecutive Saturday, however, as Hammers beat Watford 2–1 at home on 16 November.

Former manager Ron Greenwood, the only European trophy winner in Hammers' history, was back in the stands to see the men in claret and blue produce a brilliant display for the first hour in which incisive, fast, flowing football threatened to completely overwhelm Graham Taylor's side. Alan Dickens and Neil Orr both got forward at every opportunity to good effect and it was from the hard-working Scot's cross that Cottee flicked on for McAvennie to score with a diving header at the South Bank end in the 27th minute.

West Ham should have had the game sewn up by the time Ward netted from a trademark free-kick in the 56th minute, his rocket shot squirming through the hands of crestfallen keeper Tony Coton. But the Hornets were stung into life and dominated the last half an hour in which they scored a 66th-minute deflected goal through Worrell Sterling, missed two sitters and were denied by the superb Parkes.

Lyall directed most of his praise at his defenders: 'The little fellows up front have rightly been getting all the headlines, which is nice for them and us. But today it was Phil, with his late world-class saves from John Barnes, and the rest of the defence which really made sure we took our unbeaten run to 14 games.'

But the headline writers still had their eyes firmly fixed on the sensational form of McAvennie. His reward for the amazing early-season form was a call-up to the Scotland squad for his first full cap against Australia in the vital World Cup qualifying play-off at Glasgow's Hampden Park on 20 November.

The new caretaker boss Alex Ferguson's decision to play the blond bombshell from the start was fully justified when the West Ham

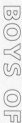

number eight scored the vital second goal on the hour mark in a 2–0 victory that virtually secured Scotland's place in the World Cup finals. After Davie Cooper had netted from a free-kick three minutes earlier, it was a typical piece of improvised skill by the Hammers hero, who cleverly chipped the ball over the advancing Aussie keeper Terry Greedy.

Said a proud McAvennie: 'I knew when Kenny [Dalglish] had the ball that he would give me the right kind of pass. I waited for it and it was like a dream come true. It was the perfect ball and when it went in, it meant something very special to me.'

Ferguson, who had taken charge following the sudden death of Jock Stein during an international in Wales, had earned respect way beyond Scotland for guiding Aberdeen to victory in the European Cup Winners' cup in 1983, and he was among those John Lyall consulted before completing the signing of McAvennie. Indeed, Lyall made the trip to Hampden to see his man grab international glory.

McAvennie wouldn't remain a big favourite of the future manager of Manchester United for much longer, but as the Scots were preparing to book their ticket for Mexico, Fergie was unreserved in his praise of the new cap: 'It was a goal of sheer brilliance. The goal showed how special Frank can be. He did everything we wanted,' said Alex.

Ex-Manchester United boss and fellow Scot Tommy Docherty joined Fergie on the McAvennie bandwagon, saying: 'That took me back 20 years. I thought for one minute that it was Denis Law. World class.'

It was a memorable week for McAvennie, who followed his magnificent début goal for Scotland with his 26th birthday on 22 November and then, the next day, netted the 55th-minute winner for Hammers in their 1–0 win at Coventry City – their fourth consecutive away win in the First Division and the fourth in successive visits to Highfield Road. City's Scottish manager Don Mackay revealed afterwards that he had tried to sign McAvennie three times while he was boss at Dundee, and Ferguson had also failed in a bid to lure Frank from St Mirren to Aberdeen, shortly before Lyall swooped after having watched Frank three times in the previous two seasons. Their loss was certainly Lyall's gain.

Ward, Dickens and Cottee all played a part in the goal at Coventry, an opportunist effort from McAvennie who arrived unmarked at the far post to net his 16th in the League with a diving header. But the Scottish scoring machine might have had a hat-trick and, similarly to the Watford game, Hammers' defensive players earned most of the plaudits, especially the outstanding Neil Orr who cleared a Terry Gibson effort off the goal-line.

Orr, so often the unsung hero, was seen more in advanced positions than in his usual covering midfield role when bottom-of-the-table West Bromwich Albion – the team whose navy-and-white striped shirts bore the 'No Smoking' sign as their sponsor's logo – were well and truly extinguished at Upton Park on 30 November. The former Morton star scored from an easy tap-in in the 66th minute to complete a 4–0 rout that left Albion's caretaker manager, former World Cup winner Nobby Stiles, fuming.

The big talking point before the game was how Hammers would perform without McAvennie, who had left with the Scottish squad for a ten-day visit to Australia for the second leg of their World Cup play-off. Paul Goddard, who had not appeared in the first team since dislocating his shoulder just 42 minutes into the season on the opening day at Birmingham, was champing at the bit for another chance but he was again dealt a cruel blow. Although he recovered from that knock to play in several Combination League and specially arranged friendly matches, Sarge suffered an ankle injury in training that robbed him of the chance to deputise for McAvennie against West Brom.

Instead, Lyall pushed Dickens into a more attacking role alongside Cottee (who had been named the Fiat Uno Young Player of the Month for October), with George Parris coming into midfield. With football still absent from TV screens because of the ongoing dispute between the Football League and television companies, the club finally introduced its own video coverage from this game. Commentator Colin Benson was perched on the gantry beneath the East Stand roof, his howls of delight audible at the other end of Green Street as he heralded young 'Smokey's' first senior goal.

After firing the low shot that rebounded for the livewire Cottee to open the scoring in the 13th minute, Parris struck another low drive that went in off Ally Robertson on 31 minutes. Alan Devonshire made it 3–0 at the end of a typical jinking run, two minutes into the second half, before Orr sealed Hammers' biggest win to date.

Even allowing for the obvious deficiencies of woeful West Brom, Hammers had climbed into third place – three points behind Liverpool and another two adrift of leaders Manchester United – as December dawned. The national press were starting to take notice of Lyall's team, as one Sunday newspaper declared:

'Vibrant Hammers – unbeaten in 15 League games – are gliding up the treacherous slope to the top of the First Division like a refurbished Rolls-Royce. The power is there. The smoothness is there. The winning touch is there. Now West Ham are ready to step up a gear to mount a serious title challenge.'

Almost as if he had given his less celebrated teammates a rare chance for personal glory before returning to reclaim the limelight, McAvennie dominated the headlines once again as Hammers prepared for the daunting trip across London to face Queens Park Rangers on their infamous plastic pitch. Having played in Scotland's dour goalless draw in Melbourne, which clinched their World Cup finals place, the previous Wednesday, 'Supermac', as the headline writers soon dubbed him, flew back into London just 24 hours before the Loftus Road clash . . . but insisted on playing.

McAvennie must have been physically shattered after the 12,000-mile flight but still found the energy to rifle home the only goal of a scrappy game in the 77th minute, after Alvin Martin – who was outstanding throughout – outjumped Steve Wicks to nod down Ray Stewart's first-time cross into his path.

McAvennie typically played down his heroics: 'Was I tired? Nah, I'm used to it . . . anyway, I'd had three hours sleep a couple of days before that! Everything was going so well and I was just busting to play.'

Clubs are now very reluctant to release their players for international friendlies but this was not Lyall's attitude. As well as releasing McAvennie for Scotland's trip to Australia for ten days, missing one Hammers game in the process, he also allowed Phil Parkes to go to Marbella, Spain, to compete in a charity golf event only 48 hours before the match. Lyall reasoned that Phil was contributing to a worthy cause and that, in any event, he would be back in good time for the visit to his former club.

As well as completing West Ham's first League double of the season, the victory at QPR also earned Lyall the Bell's Whisky Manager of the Month award for November – his 11th such success in eight years. But, typically self-effacing, he explained why he had signed a new contract to stay at the only club he had ever known.

He told journalist Joe Melling:

'My chairman asked me to stay and the players said one or two things to me. I have people around me who have been tremendously loyal. I owed them. I could not have done the job at West Ham alone. All of the staff have worked hard to try to make me a successful manager.

'Obviously it's hard to topple the giants of football with their vast resources. But that doesn't mean to say it cannot be done. It's going well for us at the moment.'

On McAvennie's unbelievable baptism in English football, Lyall added: 'If he'd only got 10 goals in 20 matches I would have been saying he looks a fair buy.'

As it happened, Frank had only to wait until the 37th minute of the next match, at home to Birmingham City on 14 December, to notch his 18th League goal. The tone of the game was set after just 36 seconds when ref Lester Shapter booked Brian Roberts for chopping down Alan Devonshire. Inexplicably, no more cautions followed but Mark Ward and Nicky Platnaeur were both lectured after a touch-line fracas and Steve Walford had to leave the field to have four stitches in a head wound just before half-time.

But City's hopes of ending a poor run of ten games without a win ended with two goals in the space of three minutes near the end of the first half. Cottee set up McAvennie, whose arcing shot beat the despairing dive of David Seaman, while the future England number one had no chance of stopping Ray Stewart's penalty, awarded after Jim Hagan scythed down Alan Dickens. Birmingham showed more ambition in the second half but Parkes was equal to their best effort – a low-driven shot from a young Julian Dicks.

On the last Saturday before Christmas, Hammers created a slice of club history when a 0–0 draw at Luton equalled an all-time club record of 18 successive League games without defeat – but they had no cause for celebration. Ward and Devonshire both collected heavy knocks, the latter departing Kenilworth Road in club director Jack Petchey's 'Roller' for a hospital check, while a fifth booking of the season for Orr left the Scot one short of a first-ever suspension. At least the defence held firm to prevent a Town side including Les Sealey and Tim Breacker from completing a League double on their new and much-maligned artificial plastic surface.

It was a former Hammer, Paul Allen, who played a part in the Boxing Day defeat at Tottenham which ended Hammers' unbeaten run. A 70th-minute sub for Ossie Ardiles, 'Ollie' was involved in the move that resulted in Steve Perryman's rare winner just five minutes from the end of a full-blooded derby played in driving rain.

'We were certainly too cautious in our approach,' bemoaned Lyall after his side failed to force Spurs keeper Ray Clemence into making even one save of note.

The final home match of 1985, against Southampton on 28 December, was postponed just 90 minutes before the scheduled kick-off after an overnight frost left the pitch unplayable. However, the disappointment of those closing days of December could not dampen the atmosphere at the club and, in particular, the mood of McAvennie. The charismatic Scot, with his bright, bleached-blond hair, gleaming smile and smart clothes, had transcended football stardom and became an overnight celebrity. After a terrible period when hooliganism scarred the people's game, football was slowly becoming fashionable again and the big-name players were rivalling pop stars and TV celebrities for media attention. Leslie Grantham, one of the main characters in the BBC's new hit soap *Eastenders*, was genuinely thrilled to meet McAvennie for the first time, and 'Dirty Den' Watts became a regular face in the Upton Park crowd and the sponsors' lounges that season, while fellow Eastenders Nick Berry and Ross Davidson often kept him company.

McAvennie was a magnet for the girls and his fondness for glamorous, leggy blondes was evident when he brought his Scottish fiancée, the erotic-sounding model Anita Blue, with him to London. Their relationship soon came under heavy pressure, however, as he became the man-of-the-moment on the capital's celebrity scene, enjoying the delights of the West End nightlife with increasing frequency.

Frank can easily pinpoint the moment which changed his life off the field – his appearance, just before Christmas '85, on *Wogan*, the Beeb's big thrice weekly chat show hosted by the genial Irishman and watched by a massive 15 million viewers.

McAvennie says: 'John gave me permission to appear on the Terry Wogan show on the Friday and I went on with Denis Law, who's a great hero of mine. As I left the training ground for the studio, Galey told me to talk slowly, so that everyone would be able to understand me. Denis had a hole in the sole of one of his shoes and he asked me beforehand to give him a nudge to remind him if he forgot and crossed his legs, revealing his holey shoe to the cameras and the millions watching at home! I remember that Denis seemed more nervous than me and, for some reason, he kept slapping me, which I found a bit annoying.

'Whenever I look at the tape of the show again, the sight of myself in that grey Gucci jacket with black trousers gives me nightmares! My new Cartier shoes could have cost me a fortune – the bloke who sold them to me wanted sixty quid but I only gave him £30! – but my colour coordination wasn't the best.

'Appearing on *Wogan* was the turning point of my life. Suddenly, all the women who didn't read the back pages knew me. The show was on the Friday and after playing on Saturday, I went to Heathrow the next day to meet my mum, who was flying to Australia. As I walked into the departure lounge, people were coming up to me for my autograph. I loved it but it was a shock to the system.'

Despite the well-publicised drug problems that would later tarnish his name and effectively cut short his playing career in the early '90s, McAvennie was at pains to point out that he had never touched cocaine or any other such substances at this stage in his turbulent Hammers career. He insists that it was not until after he badly broke his leg at the start of the 1989–90 season – a few months after Lyall's departure – that he really embarked upon the downward spiral that would lead to his arrest for drug possession, bankruptcy and, finally, a crown-court appearance for possessing drugs with alleged intent to supply. If convicted, Frank would face a lengthy jail sentence. But he maintained his innocence throughout the trial and won the biggest victory of his life when he was acquitted of all charges.

'I couldn't have played as well as I did at the time, and scored all the goals that I did, if I'd been out living that kind of lifestyle,' says Frank. 'I had too much respect for John to do that anyway,' he says.

McAvennie's teammates certainly never thought of him as unprofessional or unfit for action. Alvin Martin says: 'I wasn't worried about his lifestyle, I was just concerned that he was still chasing every ball. And he was. Sometimes in training he'd be a lazy sod but put him in a game and he'd chase and run more than anybody else. He was one of the fittest players I've ever seen.

'Frank would be a nightmare to play against. He'd leave a foot in and wouldn't let defenders settle. We'd have been happy with him being lazy as long as he scored a few goals. Instead he was scoring lots and chasing and giving us other options.

'As a defender it was great. We could hit any half-decent ball into space and he'd use his pace and get after it, leaving everyone saying what a great ball we'd played out from the back! Frank was remarkable.'

Tony Cotttee acknowledges his and McAvennie's contrasting personalities and lifestyles but, again, insists he had no problem with Frank's enjoyment of a night on the town.

Cottee says: 'I can't say we ever went out socialising together. I

BOYS OF '86

liked a few beers but I didn't go to Stringfellows every Saturday. The one time when I did go there, it was three o'clock in the morning . . . and yes, I bumped into Frank! He was a great trainer. He never turned up pissed for training or anything and if he had had a few beers or glasses of champagne the night before, he always came in and worked his cobblers off anyway.'

Mark Ward remembered a chance meeting with his old room-mate in Glasgow, long after they had both stopped playing top-flight football in England.

He says: 'I was training at Motherwell for a week in pre-season five or six years ago. I didn't sign in the end but one night during that week I got tickets for Celtic v Hamburg and was sitting in this bar near the ground when, all of a sudden, I saw Frank, dressed in shorts, walking down the road. I was with an agent, Willie Mackay, and I said to him: "Don't say anything to Frank when he walks in, pretend I'm not here." So Frank walked into the bar and said to Willie: "Have you got eighty quid? I've been done for parking and must get my car back from the compound." As I turned round Frank was so shocked to see me. He lifted me up out of my chair, laughed out loud and said: "How ya doin', wee man?"

'Having arranged to meet up again after the game, we went on the piss. Well, it's the most frightening thing I've ever done! I've been to some rough places in my time, but that night was something else. I left Frank to it in the end – I couldn't keep up with him. Frank was great, we got on really well. I used to room with him and could tell you some stories!

'Frank and Maurice Johnston were very much the same. Despite the bleach, they were both really ginger. They both loved a bird, loved a pint – like proper men do – and they were both great footballers. If I was having a Last Supper and could invite ten people I'd met in my life, Frank would definitely be there. I'd put him and Mo next to each other and then I know I'd die happy!'

McAvennie developed his own social circle in London's West End but he was also a popular and regular guest at one of east London's most trendy night spots at the time, the Greek-style Phoenix Apollo restaurant on Stratford Broadway, owned by the Panayiotou brothers, known to their friends as Gil and Panay. Alan Devonshire, Tony Gale, Phil Parkes and Ray Stewart would also often be seen there and it became the popular haunt for sports and TV stars.

McAvennie explains: 'The players liked it at the Phoenix because it was quite private for us and their parties were ticket-only. I became quite friendly with other stars who went there regularly, like boxers Nigel Benn and Frank Bruno, *Eastenders* star Nick Berry and Glen Murphy from *London's Burning*, and there were always *Sun* and *Star* page-three models around. It was a happening place.

'I always felt very safe and comfortable there, in the heart of the East End. For some reason the East Enders took to me straight away and I have always liked their company. The people of east London are very similar in many ways to the people of the East End of Glasgow. They're very humble and although they're not the richest around, they're not the poorest either. They get on with their lives and try to keep laughing.'

The West Ham players held their annual Christmas parties at the Phoenix, a tradition that continued for a number of years, but one occasion lacked the usual festive spirit. As usual Frank was the centre of attention, as he explains:

'We held parties there three times a year – I think they had them before I joined the club – and someone thought it would be a good idea to invite the wives and girlfriends along just for a change. We all got a bit drunk and were having a laugh and a joke. There was a bit of banter flying about and women don't take things the way footballers do. Anyway, one of the girls poured a pint of beer over me, then one of the other players' wives stormed off and left him there. It was a great night! One version of the story is that one of the players' wives fancied me and it kicked off because of that, but it wasn't like that at all. Things were said and it got out of hand, that's all. I went back to the Phoenix earlier this year to film part of the Channel 4 documentary they did on me – and me, Gilly and Panay were sipping champagne again – only this time Channel 4 paid the bill!'

Tony Gale says it was a mistake that year for the players to break with tradition and invite their wives and girlfriends.

'There were 16 girls and 16 blokes and I remember Frank having a pint thrown over him by one of the wives, and another player got a slap from his missus for insinuating that she was chatting up Frank. She went home with the hump. The blokes were fine, it was a few of the women who turned it into a nightmare. We never invited them again.'

Devonshire enjoyed the atmosphere of the Phoenix Apollo as much as anybody. He says: 'I was a regular there for a few years before it became "The Place", and we all used to have a great time. I am a very good friend of Gilly's and we can phone each other every

BOYS OF '86

six months or so and talk as if we only saw each other yesterday. Their parties used to be unbelievable. I remember going there one night and Gilly cooked us all breakfast at 5.30 a.m. I went all the way home to west London at about 7.00 a.m., had half an hour's kip and then got on the train to come back east for training. Well, I always promised the wife I'd be home!'

It was around this time that high-profile footballers began to appear on the front as well as the back pages of the tabloids for their boozing exploits. Most notably, at Manchester United where, ten years after George Best, a drinking culture had developed under Ron Atkinson that brought problems for international stars like Paul McGrath, Norman Whiteside and the England captain Bryan Robson. Footballers have always drunk, of course, but in 1985–86 newspaper editors decided that, as celebrities, their excesses were fit for public consumption. The tabloids, caught up in a circulation war, used big names to sell their papers and footballers were prime targets for the paparazzi. McAvennie, with his new-found stardom on the field, eye-catching looks, bird-pulling ability and West End lifestyle, was a dream come true for Fleet Street.

Alvin Martin refutes any notion, however, that West Ham was a drinking club. He says: 'Frank was our Champagne Charlie but we weren't a big social side. The players lived in different parts of London, so we didn't get together as a group socially very often. We had a good squad but we didn't live in each other's pockets. I would never have a drink before a game. On a Wednesday before a Saturday game, I might have had a couple of bottles of beer but I certainly didn't get drunk. Maggie and I used to have dinner once a week with Mark and Jane Ward. Ray Stewart and Neil Orr were good mates while Dev, Galey, Parkesy and Paul Goddard all lived out to the west.

'John Lyall was firm in his discipline and he didn't want people drinking. We used to keep our Christmas party quiet but he'd always know where and when it was – and the following morning he'd give us a session and run our bollocks off.'

Gale adds: 'Players didn't go out after Wednesday and we drank sensibly, but when we went out we were largely all good friends and had a good time.'

Ray Stewart was another responsible player. He says: 'The other lads might call me a liar but I never drank until I was 28. I was dedicated to my game and stuck to Coca-Cola. You can enjoy yourself without getting bevvied. It wasn't until after my bad knee injury, when I spent so long out of the game that I thought it was all over, that I started drinking beer.'

Devonshire underlines the spirit among the players of that era: 'We were like a family and everyone genuinely cared about each other. You have to face reality and admit that West Ham has never been what you would call a "big club". Because of that, the team spirit has to be strong if you want to be up there with the best.'

Chapter 8

THE SUN ALWAYS SHINES ON TV – A-Ha

Chart Position: Number 1, January 1986

The freezing winter weather around the turn of the year caused widespread disruption to the Football League programme and no one was more badly hit in the top flight than the Hammers. Five days after the postponement of the home game against Southampton, West Ham secretary Eddie Chapman had the frustrating task of announcing the news that the derby clash against Chelsea on New Year's Day had also been frozen off as London temperatures continued to fall. The Upton Park pitch was still bone-hard on 14 January, and the Southampton game had to be cancelled for a second time.

There was some good news at the start of 1986, however. Hammers' entertaining brand of attacking football was about to reach a much wider audience after the long-running TV dispute ended with a £1.3 million compromise deal. The BBC scheduled West Ham's FA Cup third-round tie with Charlton Athletic for their first live Sunday transmission of the season at Selhurst Park, which the homeless south Londoners were sharing with landlords Crystal Palace. The Beeb's gamble on Frank McAvennie and Tony Cottee showing their continued incredible form looked to have backfired on them as the Second Division promotion contenders held the deadly duo at bay until two minutes from time.

When they got down to play, Cottee challenged for Mark Ward's forward pass and after Charlton defender John Humphreys sliced his clearance into open space, McAvennie burst through onto the ball. His chip cleared keeper Nicky Johns and bounced just short of the line before Cottee made sure by tapping home the winner and then leaping up to grab the crossbar in celebration of his 13th goal.

BOYS OF '86

It was harsh on Lennie Lawrence's Addicks – including former Hammer Alan Curbishley in midfield – who deserved the replay that looked certain until Cottee and McAvennie showed the watching millions that glimpse of what they had been missing.

An ankle injury, sustained in the defeat at Tottenham, kept Neil Orr out of both the Cup tie and the next League game, at Leicester City on 11 January, but McAvennie played at Filbert Street after recovering from the knee and ankle knocks he suffered against Charlton. Just as well, too, because the irrepressible Scot again decided the game. Alan Dickens set Ward free on the right wing in the 54th minute and Wardie's cross was met with a looping header from McAvennie that sailed over keeper Ian Andrews and into the net via the underside of the bar.

At the other end, Alvin Martin and Tony Gale made a fine job of shackling 16-goal Alan Smith and Mark Bright (who was jeered off in the 65th minute) while two minutes later, after Steve Walford had fouled the tricky Steve Lynex, Phil Parkes saved Gary McAllister's penalty kick with his leg.

Hammers could have no complaints about the penalty award at Leicester but it was a much different story at Anfield a week later. In a match that would ultimately have such a big impact on the outcome of the Championship race, the all-white visitors approached the game with a self-belief rarely seen among sides visiting Liverpool. It was a measure of the confidence running through the side at the time that they did not go there simply to try and contain the mighty Reds and accept yet another honourable defeat at a ground where West Ham still haven't won since 1964. Instead, Lyall's men went to attack whenever possible.

Martin and Gale were again resolute, restricting Liverpool to just a couple of first-half chances, from one of which Ian Rush hit the post. Dickens and George Parris – still covering for Neil Orr – worked tirelessly in midfield and Ward was typically forceful and busy on his return to Merseyside. For almost an hour of an enthralling match there was nothing between these two sides in pursuit of league leaders Everton, but the whole game hinged on a highly controversial penalty award by referee George Tyson.

The ball looked to be rolling over the byline as Alvin Martin made only the slightest contact in the back of Paul Walsh but, to Hammers' utter disgust, the Wearside official pointed to the spot in front of the Kop. To be fair to Londoner Walsh, he had not dived or attempted to make a meal out of what was a harmless challenge by the West Ham skipper. Martin was duly booked for his heated protest before Jan Molby scored from the spot but it soon turned from bad to worse for Hammers. Linesman Little called over Tyson, who then sent off Ray Stewart for something he had apparently said.

Not surprisingly, West Ham lost their shape and concentration in the remaining half an hour, which produced further goals from Rush and Walsh inside the space of three minutes. Cottee set up Dickens for a consolation goal eight minutes from time but it didn't matter by then, and the east Londoners went home in angry mood.

Martin couldn't hide his disappointment, and says: 'Throughout my career I'd never been to Liverpool and won but I really felt we had a chance that day. To be fair, we played exceptionally well but didn't take our chances to go in front. We still deserved at least a draw, though. I didn't think it was a penalty, and after the game Kenny Dalglish agreed. When you look back on how the season finished, it proved a crucial decision.'

But the performance acted as a spur for the long, hard schedule ahead.

Martin continues: 'After leaving Anfield, we looked back down the Liverpool teamsheet and thought to ourselves, if we can reproduce that kind of performance in our next few games, we'll have a good chance of winning them and continuing our challenge.'

Stewart, who, like Martin, always played with his heart on his sleeve, felt that he had particularly let down John Lyall at Anfield. The Scottish international explains: 'I had been sent off twice before during my time at West Ham – once at Villa Park and then after a flare-up with England's Mark Hateley while playing for Scotland Under-21s. I promised him then that I'd never be sent off again, but it happened once more at Liverpool.'

Just as Cottee and McAvennie had developed a marvellous understanding as strikers, so too, the back four became a solid, reliable unit with everyone on the same wavelength. They trusted and respected each other and no one earned greater respect than the captain.

Martin says: 'We had a right good goalkeeper behind us and we could soak up pressure. Galey and myself knew each other really well. Ray Stewart was dependable alongside George Parris or Steve Walford. With Dev, Dicko, Wardie and Neil Orr or Geoff Pike, we also had a team working very hard in front of the back four. Up front Tony Cottee and Frank McAvennie were working hard, too.

BOYS OF '86

'Before Galey arrived the season before, I'd played alongside Billy Bonds and we were both aggressive. Bill always wanted to chase everyone all over the place, otherwise he felt he hadn't used up all his energy. Galey and I used to mark the "wrong side" – in other words, we'd stand on the outside of the strikers we were marking, which would effectively deter their midfield from playing the ball into the channels, where we'd be quicker to the ball. We just started doing it and it suited us both. We could also both break down attacks and play balls into areas for Cottee and McAvennie to run onto.

'We never had too many disagreements, although in a game you will all have your moments where you have a pop. It's inevitable. I don't care what team you're in, you might have to have a row now and again just to get a reaction.'

Gale, who was in only his second season at Upton Park, says: 'I found working alongside Alvin hard at first. I'd been the main man at Fulham alongside go-and-head-it centre-halves like Roger Brown and Jeff Hopkins. Alvin normally took the big man and I took the smaller one. Obviously when I joined up with Alvin I wanted to play it all the way from Parkesy's roll-outs but Alvin thought I took too many risks. We had a couple of barneys along the way. He called me a cocky Londoner and I called him a few things! We were opposites really but we were room-mates and good friends off the pitch, too, and overall we worked well together. I never felt inferior to Alvin, though. West Ham encouraged us to play, so we weren't defenders like, say, Tottenham's Chris Perry, Sol Campbell and Ben Thatcher, who can defend well but are embarrassed whenever they get the ball.

'In training, John would split us up. The midfield would go and work on crossing, while we'd do one-on-ones and heading. Our back four were experienced so John would often leave us to our own devices. We'd sort things out among ourselves. Steve Walford was laid back, too, whereas George came in and would tear-arse around. It's true what Alvin says about us marking the wrong side but John wasn't too bothered. He was more interested in seeing us getting the ball down and playing.'

If either of the centre-backs were sidelined, Lyall had ready-made cover in Ray Stewart, who was equally effective in that more central position alongside Billy Bonds in the 1980 FA Cup semi-final replay against Everton at Elland Road, and on numerous other occasions. 'Tonka' was, of course, best known for his astonishing penalty record – 76 conversions in 86 attempts – but the ten-times capped Scottish international also scored his share of spectacular long-range strikes from open play. He invariably struck the ball with venom, whether he was shooting directly at goal from distance, or aiming a long-range pass to a teammate – hence his nickname. Ray wasn't one for subtleties, although his all-round game did develop over the years. Defensively, he was very difficult to beat, either on the ground or in the air. If his temperament was sometimes suspect, you could not question his commitment to the cause.

Martin agrees: 'Ray was solid and reliable. He could play a good long ball but we didn't always want him to hit it long because then it becomes predictable. Ray often played that one ball when he first came to the club but he adapted well and could also comfortably give it to Wardie or Dicko, or square to Galey or myself. In a game where you were under the cosh, you knew Ray would never let you down.'

Martin took over the captaincy from Bonds, who had succeeded Bobby Moore in 1974. By 1985–86 he had developed into a strong, influential leader although if ever he was injured or suspended, the club had another natural-born leader in Stewart.

On the captaincy issue, Martin modestly plays down his influence with the armband, saying: 'I grew into the role. I was only 27 years old. John offered it to me when there was another outstanding candidate in Ray. Tonka wanted it more than me and I never placed that much importance on it at first. John and I spoke about it and I agreed that I'd take it during the pre-season to see how it went. I was wary of being captain at first because I didn't want the extra responsibility I was taking on to affect my performances. With my sort of character it might not have agreed with me. But in two or three of those games Ray and I had a couple of rows and that made my mind up to take it. I thought, Ray wants this but, no, I'm having it. Anyway, Dave Swindlehurst told me in pre-season that a few of the lads wanted me to take the captaincy, so that decided it for me.

'I took over from Bonzo – the ultimate player. He was a role model and although I tried to live up to him, it was an impossible job. As captain it had been getting more of a strain in the 1984–85 season. I was worrying about results, thinking it was my fault, and I had a discussion with John about it. When I took over we definitely weren't a good side but in a strange turn of events, we became West Ham's best-ever side.'

Stewart offers a slightly different view of events: 'I didn't know that I was in for the job and, okay, I was maybe a wee bit upset at not being offered the captaincy, but Alvin probably earned it more than me. He wanted it more than I did and, besides, he'd been there longer than me and I couldn't have any objections.'

Not that Tonka lacks any respect for the big Scouser. He continues: 'I've got a lot of time for Alvin. We had our differences on the park – I'm Scottish and he's English – and long periods went by when we'd hardly talk to each other. But, deep down, I've got so much respect for the guy. At times I wished he was Scottish so that I could have played with him in our national team, and I think he thought the same about me at times.

'I like to think we were all leaders out on the park. Okay, Alvin was the captain but I didn't hesitate to make a decision for myself and I'd like to think the other players felt the same way. We all knew Alvin was the man and we respected him, and I'm not sure a lot of captains today get that same sort of respect from their teammates.'

Stewart has plenty of praise, too, for the role played by Gale, who could have been equally effective as a sweeper, or in midfield, because of his composure on the ball and his passing ability.

Says Stewart: 'Galey was one of the best defenders I've ever seen in one-on-one situations. People talk about what Alan Hansen could do but Galey was excellent and not many players beat him. You could leave him one-on-one because you knew he was good at dealing with it. Galey was decent in the air for his size and good on the ground. Alvin was different class in the air and also very comfortable on the ground. Galey knew the game, spoke well to people and although he's now doing very well for himself on the radio, I could also see him being a success in football management in the future, if he gets the chance to prove himself.'

Stewart and Martin led by example on and off the field and were more closely associated than the other players with the businessmen who frequented the sponsors' lounges at Upton Park. If commercial manager Brian Blower needed a player or two to perform the after-match niceties, win, lose or draw, he could usually count on those two experienced defenders to keep the Executive Club members entertained. They were both happy to perform the role of ambassadors. As Stewart says: 'We understood that it was the businessmen who were putting in money and providing our sponsored cars and other perks, so we were happy to mingle with them in the lounges after matches and also away from the club. We saw it as part of our job, but I don't think it goes on so much at any Premier League club today because the game has changed so much and players' earnings have gone through the roof.'

BOYS OF '86

Hardly a week went by without Stewart being pictured in the local press appearing at one charity function or another, helping to raise thousands for sick children and other needy causes. And while he benefited personally from the publicity (he even managed to secure a second sponsored car from Honda dealer Eddy Grimstead for his wife, Carolyn!) Ray always did West Ham United proud, too. He was a fine, hard-working representative of the club, somebody who put himself out for others and his attitude reflected well on West Ham.

Indeed, Stewart once speculated – probably only half-jokingly – that after his playing days were over, he might return to Upton Park one day in the capacity of commercial manager. He certainly knew everyone worth knowing and how to make a bob or two.

'Aye, I knew them all around that time,' confirms Stewart. 'Alan Mitchell at the Dovercourt VW Golf dealership in Plaistow was West Ham through and through. I had about six or seven cars from him. There were a lot of guys who mixed well with the players. Great characters like Terry Creasey, who'd take care of the tickets; the boys at the Phoenix Apollo; Ian Digby of Salian Building Supplies; Neil Davey of South Eastern Electrical; and John Simmons, of Weller Financial Management, who arranged all the players' mortgages, endowments and trusts. You never got near our club without John Lyall's permission but John Simmons was a friend to the players and we all trusted him to do what was best for us. Colin Wines, who ran a luxury car showroom in Gants Hill as well as a pub in Billericay, was another good friend of the players. Tragically, he later committed suicide.

'I became very aware of the commercial side of football. Trevor Brooking was a great example to me. He advised me about shop openings and things like that, and I loved that side of it. As players, we always realised that we had to mix with these supporters and sponsors. We were hand in hand with them and knew that we got the benefit of their support. But you wouldn't get players going out of their way now, which is sad.'

Billy Bonds could have provided experienced cover in defence, having played so heroically in the last 19 games of the previous season to ensure Hammers beat the drop, but the former skipper and Upton Park legend was ruled out for the entire 1985–86 season by a badly broken toe. The little toe on his left foot required two operations and at one stage there was talk of it having to be amputated after it became infected.

As one of the fittest, most dedicated trainers at the club, the 39-year-old Bonzo faced the growing prospect of having to hang up his boots after a record 746 League and Cup matches but, with typical grit and determination, he came through it and went on to play another 24 games in each of the next two seasons to take his appearance tally to an unbeatable 793. As today's players change clubs as routinely as Tiger Woods, it is safe to assume that Bonzo's astonishing appearance tally will never be surpassed at West Ham, or elsewhere in the top flight.

After his departure from the squad, Bonzo remained a constant source of inspiration to the players who will always hold him in the highest esteem. Gale, who now shares radio commentating duties with him for Capital Gold Sport, says: 'I remember Bonzo working his way back from injury and he came into the gym for a kickabout. We were playing two-touch football and the ball was pinging around here, there and everywhere. When he came out Bill said to John: "You've got a good team here. This is the best one and two-touch football I've ever seen. It's so quick, I can't get near anyone!" Bill wasn't a watcher but he even said he enjoyed seeing us play. When I first started he said to me: "If you ever get any problems here come and see me." That was very nice of him considering that I'd been bought to take his place because he was nearing the end of his career.'

Martin says of Bonds: 'Bill was struggling with his toe injury but he was still around. It was the only season of his career when he didn't play a single game. He was always in the dressing-room afterwards, though.

'Now and again we'd have the odd conversation and, because it was Bonzo, if he gave you a tap on the shoulder and said, "Well done on Saturday", that meant a lot because you had so much respect for what he'd achieved and all that he stood for.'

The only significant change to the defence, apart from a few minor injuries, was the emergence of George Parris, who took over the left-back spot from Steve Walford after Lyall abandoned his pursuit of Scottish Under-21 left-back Tosh McKinlay of Dundee. Parris, 21, started every match from the visit to Leicester on 11 January until the end of the season and no one was more surprised by his impact than the youngster himself, who had almost joined Southend United in the close season and only remained at Upton Park on a week-to-week contract.

Parris, whose various nicknames throughout his long Hammers career included 'Chicken George' (after one of the main characters in the hit TV series *Roots*), told the *Newham Recorder* at the time: 'At the end of last season I thought my future at West Ham was pretty limited. There were a lot of players ahead of me and when the manager told me he planned to make a couple of big midfield signings it seemed I would be even further out of the reckoning. I appeared in all of the games in the end-of-season trip to Japan but when we returned I thought it was time to start looking for another club. There seemed a good chance I might go to Southend but in the end I went for a week's holiday without settling anything definite. When I came back and found that nobody else had been in for me I decided I would stay at West Ham on a weekly contract and see how things went from there.'

Parris preferred to play in midfield but was just delighted to be chosen to appear anywhere in the side. In the end, he settled into the left-back slot, even though he was right-footed.

Reflecting on events some 15 years later, he recalls: 'I was quite lucky to come in when the team was already flying. With so many good players around me it was easy for me to fit in. To play in that quality side at such a young age – it set up my career. I just went out and played and didn't really appreciate at the time just how good the side was. I only realised that a few years later.' Parris, like Gale and Martin, would subsequently experience two relegation and promotion campaigns during his helter-skelter Upton Park career.

Of all the players around him, Parris not surprisingly singled out Alan Devonshire, who played just in front of him on the left flank, for special praise. He continues: 'No disrespect, but anybody could have played at left-back behind a great player like Dev. I just used to get the ball and give it straight to him. Even if he had two or three players marking him tightly, he always showed for the ball and would always want it from me. Sometimes I'd be frightened to pass to him in case we lost possession, but we never did. It was an education for me.'

Parris was not the most cultured player in the team but what he lacked in skill and subtlety, he more than made up for in a tireless work-rate and a steely determination to win the ball. It was these qualities which also earned him the nickname of 'Bruno', after the British boxing hero, when, following the arrival of Julian Dicks, he moved into central midfield.

Parris worked hard to improve on his left foot and admits: 'When I first came to the club as a schoolboy at the age of 14, I couldn't even kick with my left foot – full stop. I had to work hard at it and spent a lot of time in the afternoons on the training ground with Mick McGiven trying to improve myself.'

Parris would play a key role in the eventual FA Cup fourth-round defeat of Ipswich Town – but not until extra time in the second replay of a marathon tie. Upton Park reopened its gates to 25,000-plus fans – the largest of the season to date – on 25 January after a gap of six weeks since the home game against Birmingham City. Groundsman Stan Botham and his staff laid straw overnight on parts of the pitch to help thaw the frosty surface, which was still rock-hard at the South Bank end. There was little to warm the crowd, though, as Hammers failed to make the most of 11 first-half corners.

Paul Goddard had to wait until ten minutes from time to make his long-awaited reappearance, subbing for Walford. Ipswich were on top by then and the First Division strugglers were unfortunate not to win in east London.

Not that West Ham went to Portman Road with an inferiority complex, having won there on their previous four visits. The following Tuesday's replay became yet another casualty of the cold climate, so Hammers put their cup hopes on hold for another week and focused instead on the next home League fixture, against leaders Manchester United on Sunday, 2 February. The game was shown live by ITV, kicking off at the strange time of 2.35 p.m., and it said something about the apathy of some fans then that the previous matchday programme carried an appeal urging supporters to 'be here and savour the true excitement'. The Boleyn Ground capacity at that time was around 35,000, yet only 20,000-odd skipped Sunday roast to see a thrilling game that, as West Ham were already aware, would be a dress rehearsal for a fifth-round FA Cup showdown with the Reds provided they won the replay at Ipswich.

Hammers also wanted revenge for their controversial Milk Cup exit at Old Trafford back in October, so both teams were fired up for a pulsating clash. None more so than Mark Ward – cruelly denied his 'goal' in Manchester – who underlined his passion for the fight by ruthlessly despatching the much bigger Kevin Moran into the Chicken Run wall. He was booked and Leicester referee John Ball also took the name of top-scorer McAvennie after he followed through on keeper Gary Bailey, while Alvin Martin later became the third Hammer to be cautioned. West Ham and United contested a full-blooded match that had the crowd enthralled and the TV bosses drooling.

Either side could have taken the lead but it was United who did so,

Bryan Robson lobbing over Phil Parkes in the 25th minute. Robbo was in typically robust mood and accidentally inflicted a head injury on Geoff Pike, who returned to midfield for the first time this season after finally recovering from a stomach-muscle tear. 'Pikey' replaced the suspended Stewart whose right-back spot went to the versatile Parris.

The second half became even more frantic than the first but after 62 minutes Ward showed United that he was not just an uncompromising competitor. He could strike a ball, too. Dickens found Devonshire on the right, in front of the West Stand, and Dev cut the ball inside for Wardie to unleash a blistering shot that bounced just in front of Bailey before nestling in the far corner of the net.

With Parkes busy making excellent saves from Jesper Olsen, Norman Whiteside and Colin Gibson, it looked as though Hammers would be content with a point. But things soon turned their way. Robson, whose career was blighted by injuries – most of which seemed to occur at Upton Park – came off worse in a midfield challenge with Hammers 'hard man' Cottee, and had to hobble off midway through the high-tempo second half nursing an ankle knock. Cottee, one of the smallest players in the game whose tackles were as rare as trophies in the Upton Park boardroom, was about to inflict much more damage as West Ham surged forward in search of the winner.

First, Dickens and McAvennie created a great chance for Cottee to score at the far post, only for the normally clinical goal poacher to rap the upright with his shot. But Tony made full amends 13 minutes from time when, after pressure from McAvennie, Whiteside misjudged his back-pass and Cottee, with lightning reactions, beat Bailey to the ball before tucking it low into the net.

The worst winter freeze since 1963 meant Hammers were unable to play another home game throughout the rest of a snowbound February, which claimed the League matches against Ipswich Town (18th) and Manchester City (22nd), while the scheduled visit to Aston Villa (8th) had also had to be rearranged. The home clash with Southampton, already rescheduled once, for 5 February, had to be revised again because the Saints were still involved in the FA Cup. So, too, of course, were West Ham, who would play four more Cup ties before their next League fixture in mid-March.

The fourth-round replay at Ipswich looked to be heading Town's way when Jason Dozzell put them one up at the start of extra time.

Hammers had shown their character and resilience against Manchester United, however, and again fought back admirably. Neil Orr, making his first appearance since Boxing Day, came on for flu-ridden Walford at the start of extra time and there was a new tenacity about the visitors. With central defenders Martin and Gale both pushed well forward, the latter took control on the right and set free the overlapping Parris, who raced to the byline before cutting the ball back for Cottee to squeeze home the 107th-minute equaliser.

The visiting fans who had driven up the A12 almost forgot the biting cold as Devonshire went on a sizzling 40-yard run, leaving three Ipswich defenders trailing helplessly in his wake. But as he slid his low shot past Cooper, he turned away in despair as the ball rolled inches wide of the far post.

Whether it was the cost of watching another game in such rapid succession or just because the fans were still defrosting after the 1–1 draw, the gate for the second replay at Ipswich just 48 hours later was down by more than 10,000. What they missed was the Tony Cottee Show (or, more appropriately, 'Snow'). The Portman Road pitch was covered in the white stuff as the sides remained deadlocked at 0–0 after another 90 minutes.

Cue Cottee, who popped up in the 21st minute of extra time to pounce on a mishit back-pass from Mark Brennan, round Cooper and guide the orange ball home. Incredibly, Cottee had scored on five successive visits to the Suffolk ground, finally ending a fourth-round tie that lasted five and a half hours.

With his low centre of gravity and uncanny balance, Cottee was perhaps always destined for the Snow King headlines that were splashed across the back pages. And maybe it had something to do with the improvised training sessions going on at Chadwell Heath around that time.

Cottee explains: 'We were going outdoors for training and doing diving headers in the snow. We even played rugby in the gym. Frank, Wardie and myself were always the back three and whenever any of us got the ball we'd throw it straight to one of the others, who would then just get crunched. We played five-a-side in the gym with a rugby ball, too. Mick McGiven reckoned that, due to the bad conditions outside at the time, the ball was likely to bounce awkwardly in a proper match, played on a hard, unpredictable surface. He reasoned that the unpredictable bounce produced by an oval-shaped rugby ball would prepare us better for any football games that did manage to beat the weather.'

BOYS OF '86

Whether McGiven's dry humour had got the better of him on this occasion or not, the devilish Ward was not too impressed with the rugby theory. He was the only kid in his school to be put forward for a trial with rugby league giants St Helens but that was years earlier. At Chadwell Heath he deemed there was no value in playing rugby, even for fun, so he simply ended the bizarre training session by catching the ball and then booting it high into one of the gardens that backed onto the training ground.

John Lyall was not amused.

Chapter 9

MONEY FOR NOTHING – Dire Straits

Chart Position: Number 4, August 1985

Card schools are part and parcel of professional football, and have been since a group of workers who earned their money banging steel hammers decided to call their part-time football team Thames Ironworks. There was even a media outcry following England's dismal Euro 2000 campaign when there were claims that Kevin Keegan's players were distracted by betting – and losing – too much money playing cards on their way to and from training sessions and matches.

On that basis, given the wretched quality of their performances, the England players must have been playing cards and gambling at their horse-race nights 24 hours a day. In reality, their early exit from the tournament owed everything to the inadequate ability of the coach and his players rather than their spare-time antics.

But games of three-card Brag were commonplace on the West Ham team coach used for away match travel in 1985–86, killing the notion that footballers who lose at cards invariably lose on the football field too.

Alvin Martin says: 'We had some good card schools that year. We'd always have the third table back on the coach, away from John Lyall. If he got up to walk down the aisle towards us, we'd quickly whip our money off the table.'

Alvin was joined in the regular card school by Tony Gale, Frank McAvennie, Tony Cottee, George Parris and Mark Ward, but they were by no means card players of equal calibre. Frank was always a popular player at the table, as Martin explains: 'We used to encourage Frank to go to the bank before getting on the coach. He was a great

BOYS OF '86

goalscorer but a crap card player – it was another reason why he was so popular with the lads!'

'Reggie' Gale agrees and says: 'Frank once went "blind, blind, blind, blind – stack!" He's the only player I've ever known to stack a blind hand! We all took hits and we all won a few bob. It never affected our game. It helped us pass a lot of time away and we also enjoyed it.'

Indeed, McAvennie still laughs at the thought of Galey having to cough up his dosh. 'Galey used to pay in instalments – I called him the man from the Provident. In fact, I'm still convinced he owes me! Galey used to throw his cards down in disgust because he knew that Wardie, Tony and me would just keep going, no matter what cards we were holding. I used to hate Brag, but loved Blackjack. Liam Brady, who joined us later the following season, was the best Poker player I ever seen. Brady taught us all how to play and even brought along his own chips to use on the bus. He was a nightmare.'

Cottee describes the routine: 'We had a great three-card Brag school and even that was highly competitive. Brag's about bluff and you had to keep your nerve. People were winning on ten high when players holding pairs were stacking. There was a good atmosphere on the coach. It was cards all the time. On the way to the hotel, Friday night, Saturday morning, on the way to the game and then all the way home, too. Sometimes you lost hundreds of pounds, which in the mid-'80s was a lot of money. I don't remember it having an adverse effect on anyone's game but sometimes the losses got a bit out of hand. One of the lads lost a couple of grand in one session. It was never nice to lose but it was all part of the team spirit.'

When he became a manager himself, Ward understood, however, that players could be psychologically affected by these heavy losses. He says: 'When I was player-manager at Altrincham last year, I banned the playing of cards from the team bus. Some of the players were losing too much and I didn't want it to get out of hand.'

Although the continuing arctic conditions played havoc with the English and Scottish fixtures, Alvin Martin was delighted to enjoy much warmer temperatures as he headed for Tel Aviv to earn his 14th full England cap in the friendly against Israel, some 12 months after Bobby Robson had awarded him his last cap against Northern Ireland in Belfast. The recall was his reward for an outstanding season and the courage he had shown for months in ignoring a troublesome knee injury that was obviously in need of surgery.

BOYS OF '86

Martin's partnership with Ipswich Town's Terry Butcher (they were reunited at the expense of Mark Wright and Terry Fenwick) had been remarkable. In their seven previous internationals together, England were undefeated and conceded just one goal. That became two in Israel as winger Eli Ohana put the home country ahead, but Glenn Hoddle and Bryan Robson inspired the fightback that resulted in a 2-1 away win.

The joy of Robbo's two goals in Tel Aviv contrasted starkly to his mood at Upton Park where the FA Cup fifth-round tie against Manchester United – postponed four times – finally went ahead on 5 March in front of the biggest Boleyn crowd of the season to date. Only two minutes had gone when the combative Robson tangled awkwardly with Cottee, fell heavily and dislocated his right shoulder again. It was the England captain's fifth injury of the season – and his second bad knock inflicted by 'Tiny Terror' Cottee in a month – but this one cast doubts over his fitness for the upcoming World Cup finals.

United's problems increased in the 25th minute. Receiving a quickly taken free-kick, Devonshire found Cottee who scuttled to the byline before crossing for McAvennie to squeeze the ball in from a tight angle at the near post. The flying Scot had registered his first FA Cup goal, his 21st of the season, and was a thorn in United's side all night.

But the Cup holders, who had just seen Everton overhaul them at the top of the First Division, kept their grip on the silverware for a little while longer after the diving Frank Stapleton headed home Mike Duxbury's cross in the 73rd minute. Under normal circumstances, the prospect of visiting Old Trafford would fill Hammers (and most teams) with fear but Lyall's men were made of sterner stuff and the self-belief kept flowing through the players as the season gathered momentum.

Just four days after the Upton Park humdinger, Old Trafford was almost only half full – the crowd down by more than 20,000 on the attendance for the League game between the teams in August – but millions more watched at home on ITV as West Ham produced one of the biggest shocks of the season. No – make that in Hammers' history.

The Reds' early raids came to nothing before one of the visitors' only two corners in the match produced a stunning first goal, and from one of the least likely sources. Mark Ward admits he miscued his 18th-minute flag kick that sailed perfectly to the edge of the box

where little Geoff Pike sprung to send a bullet header over Arthur Albiston, who was guarding the near post, and into the top corner of the net at the Stretford End.

Elation turned to ecstasy after 54 minutes when Hammers were awarded a hotly disputed penalty. As he ran into the box to meet Ray Stewart's high free-kick, Martin stumbled and went to ground. He argued that he had been shoved in the back by his marker, Stapleton, while the Irishman protested his innocence, claiming he had stood his ground and the Hammers' number five had simply run into him.

An indirect free-kick for possible obstruction was an option many referees would have taken, so full credit to Gloucester referee Brian Stevens for bravely ignoring the fury of 30,000-plus rabid Reds by awarding a rare penalty against the home side. United had conceded only six times in the league all season, but they went 2–0 down as Tonka stepped up and thumped the ball past Chris Turner before celebrating in front of the travelling Irons' fans at the Scoreboard End.

The more cynical among West Ham supporters and neutrals watching at home were no doubt expecting Mr Stevens to try and balance things up by awarding a spot kick to United at the first opportunity. They would be shocked again, then, as he waved away hostile United protests as Stapleton went flying under a strong challenge from Stewart just minutes after the Scot had netted at the other end. Hammers defended like Trojans, restricting Barcelona target Mark Hughes to just two shots at goal, both superbly saved by Parkes.

It was a smug Tony Gale who walked off at the end of Hammers' first-ever FA Cup victory at the so-called Theatre of Dreams. He says: 'We'd murdered 'em in the first game at home but on the way down the Upton Park tunnel Ron Atkinson said: "You won't like it when you come up to Old Trafford." I had a few quid on us that day because I thought we'd win up there.'

For Pike, by now holding down the anchor role in midfield at the expense of Neil Orr, the Old Trafford Cup epic remains his most memorable moment in a Hammers career that spanned 367 matches and 12 seasons. He scored 41 goals in that period, some of them better than the header that floored Manchester United, but none that stir the memory quite like that one.

Pike still has the video of that game in his collection at home near Romford and he says: 'People asked afterwards if it was something we'd practised on the training field, but there was no way in a million years that we ever did. Wardie miscued the corner and I just happened to be there. I was fortunate that Arthur Albiston, one of the smallest players in the League at the time, was on the goal-line because the ball went in over his head, although there was a fair bit of pace on it.

'It was a tremendous feeling when it happened and it's amazing how, even now, people come up to me and the first thing they talk about is my goal at Manchester United. You would not believe the amount of times it happens. In terms of where it was, and the fact that it was an FA Cup tie, yes, it was a big highlight for me, but I wouldn't call it the best goal I've ever scored. For instance, we were playing at Sunderland in the League Cup and while Paul Allen was lying on the pitch injured, I picked the ball up and smashed it in from 30 yards. I scored against Norwich in the late '70s, when we were struggling against relegation, and that flew in from the edge of the penalty area. And I scored a goal against Tottenham where the build-up play was magnificent. So I can recall scoring better goals than the one I got at Old Trafford. The thing is, too, that I found scoring at Upton Park, in front of our own fans, gave me a better feeling than scoring elsewhere.

'One of the biggest personal highlights for me was playing in the 1981 League Cup final against Liverpool, one of the top teams in Europe at the time, in front of 100,000 people at Wembley and then being named man of the match in many of the following morning's papers. That meant more to me than scoring at Old Trafford.'

Pike, an FA Cup medal winner in 1980, was the longest-serving Hammer at Old Trafford that day, having made his League début ten years earlier. He had fought hard to overcome injuries in the past year and it was only right that somebody who had given so much for his local club over such a long period should be part of its success.

He says: 'I'd already had a hernia at the end of the season before, and then the stomach muscle injury kept me out for another 12 weeks at the start of '85–86. It was the result of wear and tear but we couldn't find out what the problem was for a while, so in the end I had to have an exploratory operation, when they discovered a hole in my stomach muscle about the size of a fifty-pence piece.'

Pikey seriously doubted if, once fully fit, he would be able to reclaim his customary midfield anchor role, and admits: 'Neil Orr did extremely well in my position and I wondered if I could get back in the side. Neil and I are very good friends, both our families get on well, and they only lived four doors along from us in Netherpark

BOYS OF '86

Drive, Gidea Park. My wife, Pauline, and Neil's wife, Julie, were very close and spent a lot of time together, while all the kids played with each other. So it was a very friendly rivalry but it was very frustrating seeing someone playing in my position and playing well. Neil's fairly quiet and unassuming and, as a player, possibly didn't fulfil his potential. He came to us as a centre-half but ended up playing in midfield.'

Once he had reclaimed the number 11 shirt, Pike enjoyed playing alongside the young Alan Dickens, who was enjoying his best-ever season at the club.

Pike continues: 'It was different playing with him on a regular basis compared to what I'd been used to, playing with Trevor Brooking for so long. Alan did things that Trevor wouldn't do, like run back with players and make tackles. Trevor did it sometimes but not as often as Alan, because he knew it would take away his best qualities, like being in a space to receive the ball. So I had to adapt my game a bit playing with Alan and didn't have to rush around as much. I knew that if I ever joined in with the front players, Alan would be there to cover for me. But you just did what you were asked to do and I was pleased to be playing in any role. My main job was to fill in holes, pick up loose pieces and keep the attacks going. If they did break down, I had to make sure I was in and around to help out defensively. I enjoyed every minute of it.

'When I went to West Ham as a kid I was a centre-forward and after I left to join Notts County I scored 15 goals in my first season as an attacking central midfield player. So I liked the chance to get forward and, in fact, I enjoyed it even when Trevor wasn't playing because it meant I could get forward more, knowing someone like Paul Allen would be covering for me.'

Pike identifies the problem that many felt hampered the progress of the immensely talented Dickens when he adds: 'I thought he was put under a lot of undue pressure because he had been portrayed as the next Trevor Brooking. With all due respect to Alan, I don't think he had the mental strength to be able to cope with something like that, but he had terrific vision, great passing ability and he always gave 110 per cent.'

Gale appreciated the more industrious qualities of both Pike and Orr, saying: 'They were much better players than people sometimes thought but because they were playing in a very talented team, they didn't get the recognition they deserved. If Neil hadn't have been such a hypochondriac he would've been an even better player! Pikey was there for the experience and alongside Dicko, Dev and Wardie it was a great balance. We could change from 4–4–2 to 4–3–3, or whatever, depending on how the game was going.'

After the euphoria of their 2–0 triumph at Old Trafford, West Ham were perhaps too drained, physically and mentally, to play three FA Cup ties in the space of just seven days, but those were the kind of pressures created by the catalogue of postponements and the fact that, unlike today, cup replays were arranged at the drop of a hat, long before local police demanded the introduction of the current ten-days' notice rule.

So it was a weary West Ham, London's last FA Cup survivors, who journeyed to Sheffield only three nights after their 'Super Sunday' in Manchester to face Howard Wilkinson's Wednesday, whose sharpness was evident from the kick-off.

After 13 minutes, Devonshire cleared Mark Smith's header off the goal-line, only for Nigel Worthington to drive the ball through a crowded area and into the net. The Owls pressed hard and in the 35th minute the in-form Carl Shutt outpaced Parris to score his sixth goal in three matches. Hammers' first shot did not materialise until the 48th minute. Dickens found McAvennie with a pass out towards the left flank and the Scot cut inside to pick out Cottee who fired his 17th goal at the ill-fated Leppings Lane end.

Cottee later directed a looping header onto the roof of the net but Wednesday had already done enough to book their passage to the semi-finals and a meeting with League leaders Everton, who beat Luton Town in the quarter-finals and were already eyeing the Double. Hammers' hearts sank because, for all their fine work in the League, the FA Cup had still realistically been their best hope of winning honours.

Lyall said after the Hillsborough frustration: 'The first half was a disappointment because we didn't play much football. We tried to battle with them and, in doing that, we didn't really play to our own strengths.'

Martin tried to refocus attention on the tough battle for First Division points when he added: 'It's important that we bounce straight back from that Cup defeat. There is still a lot to play for this season.'

With 16 games remaining and just seven weeks of the season to go, West Ham were in sixth place with games in hand on all the clubs above them.

BOYS OF '86

Chapter 10

WHEN THE GOING GETS TOUGH THE TOUGH GET GOING – Billy Ocean

Chart Position: Number 1, February 1986

Hammers' hopes of an immediate return to winning ways after their FA Cup exit were dealt a savage double blow in the space of four days in mid-March with defeats at Highbury and Villa Park.

After a gap of almost six weeks since beating Manchester United at home, West Ham renewed their First Division Championship challenge against Arsenal on 15 March. The tone for an ill-tempered game was set in the first minute when Gunners' abrasive midfielder Steve Williams was booked by referee Jim Borrett for a foul on Tony Cottee, followed soon by Graham Rix for kicking the heels of Mark Ward.

Cottee and Frank McAvennie saw plenty of the ball in a first half dominated by the visitors but, for once, neither could make the breakthrough. Frank missed three good chances in the space of the first 14 minutes and Hammers would pay for it.

Arsenal came out fighting in the second half – literally as it turned out – and after managing their first shot in the 55th minute, Tony Woodcock struck the only goal of the game in the 76th minute. He momentarily lost control of the ball in the box under pressure from Alan Devonshire and it appeared to strike his hand before he drove it into the net.

Hammers were furious and protested all the way back to the centre circle. Afterwards Woodcock admitted: 'The ball did hit my hand but it was unintentional.'

Even so, no one in a white shirt was more furious at the injustice than Alvin Martin who, with socks rolled down his ankles, moved into attack in search of the equaliser West Ham deserved. His anger and frustration simmered as he clashed several times with opposing centre-back David O'Leary in a torrid last five minutes and their feud boiled over with just ten seconds of the match to play.

Martin, who had just been booked following a clash with David Rocastle, won a free-kick at O'Leary's expense but with the ball some 40 yards away, angry words were exchanged and Martin floored O'Leary with an elbow to his face. It was quite out of character for the Scouser but the big Irishman was hell bent on retribution as he chased after Alvin and punched him in the back of his head. After the 'ugly brawl' subsided, the Norfolk official consulted a linesman before sending off the West Ham skipper, who could have no complaints. Inexplicably, however, the lucky Irishman escaped unpunished.

Arsenal's third win in consecutive games pushed them four points ahead of West Ham, who dropped to seventh place, albeit with games still in hand on those above them. Everton stayed top, two points clear of Liverpool, who had played two games more, and the Merseyside clubs threatened to pull away.

Both managers did their best to defuse the incident, which inevitably dominated the back-page headlines. Joe Lovejoy of the *Sunday People* quoted John Lyall as follows:

'Alvin got involved and he knows he was wrong. He will be suspended, and that's a big blow to him and his team.

'I think it was down to frustration because we felt we'd done enough to get something from the game, and my players thought Tony Woodcock handled the ball before scoring the winner.'

Gunners' boss Don Howe seemed as surprised as anyone that his player emerged from the fracas blameless in the eyes of the officials. He added: 'There's no way you can condone any player punching another. I'll be having a good look at our video of the match before seeing David about it.'

Howe, who came to know Martin well through their England connection, felt both centre-halves had acted completely out of character. 'They're two smashing lads. I can only think the competitive nature of the game got to them.'

O'Leary and Martin shook hands afterwards and the Republic of Ireland international said: 'Alvin lost his head and I can't explain it, unless he was upset at being a goal down. But there is no excuse for going around swinging elbows. It surprised me because he's a great player, and not at all like that.'

Although the players and their club were prepared to leave it at that, the media grasped the opportunity to condemn all concerned.

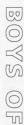

BOYS OF '86

Under the headline 'Howe and Lyall's Blinkered Excuse', *The Independent*'s Patrick Barclay penned a particularly patronising piece in which he felt the game had been 'dragged into the gutter'. Barclay went on:

'Martin will now be suspended from the Easter matches against Chelsea and Tottenham, as they chase the most realistic target left to them: fifth place in the League, which would be their highest ever.

'The irony is that their skipper had spent most of the afternoon underlining what a fine player he is. He may not be the best central defender in England, but he is the most skilful English footballer in that position and will surely be on the plane to Mexico.

'Between now and then, however, he must learn to control his temper. The World Cup finals will be full of outrageous fortune, unjust decisions and threats to one's pride. If Martin can't cope with them then – "smashing lad" or not – he will be a liability to his country.'

When the dust had settled on the Highbury incident, Martin told the *Daily Mirror*'s Tony Stenson:

'If we had played badly and got beaten at Arsenal I might not have got carried away so much. But there was no excuse and I was totally wrong.

'There's a lot of tension when you're near the top. We haven't experienced it here for a few years and it does get to you.'

More than 15 years on, Martin still accepts full responsibility for one of the rare blemishes on his long and distinguished career. When interviewed for this book, he said of the incident involving the successful Leeds United manager of today: 'We'd played particularly well that day at Highbury. We'd outplayed them and they scored against the run of play. It was a frustrating time and I'd already got the needle.

'I thought: "We've pissed all over this lot, we should be three or four goals up and they've ended up nicking a win." In those situations, John used to throw me up front to try and retrieve something from the game. It was my fault really. I was going for every ball and throwing my arms around. I was causing chaos.

'I did catch David O'Leary – I meant to – and he reacted and I got sent off. It was silly of me. A week or so later, David sent me a letter apologising. He was always the ambassador and I think he just felt that way inclined. He recognised he'd played a part in what happened but we both knew I was the instigator. It was my fault.'

There was no disgrace in losing by the odd goal at Highbury, but a 2–1 defeat at Aston Villa on 19 March – Hammers' third loss in a week – was certainly not in the script. Villa were languishing in the bottom three, along with fellow West Midlanders Birmingham City and West Bromwich Albion. Their troubles increased as early as the second minute, when West Ham were gifted an own-goal by Steve Hunt, who chested the ball between keeper Nigel Spink's legs. There were other opportunities to increase their lead but, just as they had against Arsenal, the visitors failed to take them and ended up counting the cost. The game, watched by a mere 11,579, swung Villa's way on 38 minutes. Andy Gray nodded the ball down for Steve Hodge to score the equaliser and, with 12 minutes remaining, the newly capped England midfielder thrust forward again to volley in Andy Blair's cross.

The cure for West Ham's recent travel sickness came in the form of a welcome 1–0 victory over their Cup conquerors Sheffield Wednesday at Upton Park on 22 March. After two games without scoring, Hammers took a sixth-minute lead through Frank McAvennie, who seized on a crazy back-pass by Chris Morris – later to become a teammate of Frank's at Celtic – before sidestepping keeper Martin Hodge and scoring from a tight angle.

The post prevented McAvennie from adding a second, while captain Hodge, their best player on the day, had to be at his best to make saves from Cottee, Geoff Pike (twice) and Neil Orr, who stayed in the side after replacing Alan Devonshire (who had injured his ankle) at Villa Park.

Owls' boss Howard Wilkinson said: 'West Ham played very well and I don't rule them out in what's going to be a tight finish to the Championship.'

It was Wednesday's 17th successive defeat in the capital in three years but the Yorkshire side still retained sixth place, one above the Hammers who shared the same points (54) with Luton Town. The Hatters had given the chasing pack hope that day by scoring two goals in the last nine minutes to beat Everton 2–1 at Kenilworth Road. It was a devastating blow from which Howard Kendall and his players never recovered. Ominously, Liverpool moved level with Everton at the top on 66 points after a 6–0 thrashing of Oxford United at Anfield.

West Ham were set to welcome back Devonshire for the vital Easter derbys against Chelsea, away, and Tottenham Hotspur, at home. The influential midfielder would play a key role in one of the most brilliant performances ever produced by the Hammers on their travels.

Chapter 11

CHERISH – Kool and the Gang

Chart Position: Number 4, July 1985

Every now and again, one is privileged to witness a match that encapsulates all the best things about football and the qualities normally associated with West Ham United: skill, invention, fast, flowing moves and spectacular goals.

At Chelsea's Stamford Bridge ground on Easter Saturday, 29 March 1986, the Hammers mesmerised 29,555 fans with a display of such brilliance that, in the words of Alan Devonshire, 'was breathtaking'.

Yet there was nothing to suggest, pre-match, that the visiting fans would be singing 'Bubbles' well after the final whistle. A thunderstorm had left the pitch in a puddled state, which raised some doubts about the game even going ahead. It did, but conditions were hardly conducive to neat football played mainly on the deck. It was probably suited more to the Blues' battling strengths.

More importantly, Hammers' line-up saw one significant change in the absence of Alvin Martin, the skipper serving the first match of a two-game suspension following that Highbury bust-up with O'Leary. It was a frustrating time for Martin, whose Highbury indiscretion had also denied him any involvement in England's 1–0 midweek friendly win against Russia in Tbilisi. Although he did travel to Georgia as part of the squad, the Hammers skipper was sensationally banned from playing for his country by Football Association chairman Bert Millichip – the first player to become an example of the FA's tough new World Cup disciplinary code. Alvin was not even allowed to sit on the bench and it was only at the insistence of manager Robson that he was allowed to join up with the squad.

Millichip said: 'I don't want to be thought of as a dictator, but it is vitally important we set the right standards for behaviour in Mexico.' English football was still under the microscope from UEFA after Heysel, so Martin became a scapegoat. Southampton's Mark Wright did too, after the FA also dropped him from the England squad following his bath-time punch-up with his club manager Lawrie McMenemy.

The governing body's crackdown was all very honourable but – hold on a minute – didn't Manchester United skipper Bryan Robson get sent off for kicking out at an opponent at Sunderland . . . and did he not still play for England in their next game, against Israel? Surely not double standards at FA HQ?

Alvin's short-term replacement at West Ham was reserve-team regular Paul Hilton, a tall, lanky 26-year-old centre-back who had made his mark in the lower divisions with Bury but had very limited experience in the top flight at Upton Park due to the commanding presence of Alvin Martin and Tony Gale. Not that the skipper was missed at Chelsea. For Devonshire, who had recovered just in time from an ankle injury, was invariably at the heart of all Hammers' best work and despite Blues' early possession, it was Dev who made the breakthrough after 25 minutes. Receiving a short free-kick from Gale, he accelerated inside and drove a crisp, right-foot shot from 25 yards that soared past stand-in keeper Steve Francis and into the top corner of the net.

If Dev's goal was a superb solo effort, West Ham's second, after 55 minutes, owed everything to team play of the highest order. After a headed clearance from the outstanding Gale, George Parris began the counter-attack deep in his own half. He played a short pass to Tony Cottee who turned it inside to Alan Dickens. Hammers' well-practised third-man run routine worked to perfection as Parris collected Dickens' exquisite pass from the halfway line and ran flat-out down the touch-line. And all those hours spent on the training ground trying to improve his weaker left foot paid off as he hit a cross low towards the near post, where the predatory Cottee – ending a third-man run all of his own – arrived to steer the ball inside the far post.

Muddied West Ham were ripping Chelsea to shreds and the third goal, on 64 minutes, said everything about the respect and harmony between Tony Cottee and Frank McAvennie. After Mark Ward left big Doug Rougvie for dead to find McAvennie, Frank passed up the chance to grab some personal glory by rolling a pass across the

penalty box for Cottee to score probably his easiest goal of the season from no more than six yards.

As Cottee points out: 'If, as some people had falsely claimed, there was any jealousy or ill-feeling between Frank and myself, there's no way he would have put that goal on a plate for me.'

Cottee repaid the compliment four minutes later, albeit unintentionally. In trying to complete his hat-trick, his sliced shot dropped nicely into the path of the unmarked McAvennie who finished with an imperious volley into the Shed-end net. He jokes: 'It was the best pass I ever got from Tony!'

Devonshire trotted off 14 minutes from the end, to be replaced by Orr, but Hammers kept going forward and should have won by more. Pike admits he should have made it 5–0 but shot past the far post from a great position.

Chelsea, who had surprisingly left out the pacy Kerry Dixon in favour of David Lee, didn't seriously trouble Phil Parkes until the big man was forced to tip over David Speedie's 25-yard effort ten minutes from time.

John Lyall, a man not given to exaggeration, could not conceal his pleasure after such a thrilling spectacle. 'That was as well as we have played away from home all season. We won in spectacular fashion and everything went right. It was a very special performance. You get days like that, days when everything you try comes off. If I'm not happy now, I never will be.'

Chelsea could have no excuses and, to be fair to them, they lavished praise on their rivals from the opposite side of the capital. The Blues still held on to fourth spot with 62 points, but sixth-placed Hammers' biggest-ever win at Stamford Bridge had closed the gap to five points. Chelsea manager John Hollins even popped his head around the door of the visiting team coach before it departed West London to offer his sincere congratulations, saying: 'Well done, lads, great stuff.'

And with a comment unheard of from an opposing skipper, either before or since in top-flight terms, Blues' Colin Pates added: 'If West Ham play like that for the rest of the season they will win the Championship. No one will live with them. They were brilliant – the best team to come here for a very long time.'

The TV cameras captured the magical Hammers in their prime but Lyall tried to play down the significance of the result, if not the performance, when he said: 'We'll just keep playing and maybe begin to talk about that possibility the longer the season goes on.'

This performance, above all others that season, reinforced Lyall's qualities as a coach of redoubtable quality – and the ability and intelligence of his players to carry out his strategy in the heat of battle.

Lyall continued: 'We knew it was important to keep together and play as a unit as this is not the easiest of places to come and win. We set out to make things as technical as possible.'

Lyall's philosophy was underlined by Gale, who said:

'We were aware that Chelsea like a battle. So the aim was to keep the ball on the move and make it impossible for them to get at us. After all, you can't be tackled if you are not in possession.'

Devonshire still maintains that the Hammers have probably never played better than they did at Chelsea that afternoon. He says: 'We were both fairly level pegging on the fringe of the title race and it was a big game. Even though the pitch was a mudbath, some of the football we played that day was breathtaking.

'By then, we had such a strong understanding going and the team had a pattern of play that was perfect for us. It all fell into place that day and there is no better feeling than when things come together like that.'

McAvennie paid tribute to Devonshire's brilliance: 'What was so good about it was that the pitch was knee-deep in mud and yet he was playing in moulded studs. And when he came off near the end, his all-white kit still didn't have a mark on it!'

Cottee also singles out the emphatic win at the Bridge as the pinnacle of West Ham's season, saying: 'If ever one game stood out above all the rest, this was it. We absolutely pulverised them. This was the result that made people sit up and take notice of West Ham. Not only that, but our players started to believe that perhaps we could go on and challenge for the title.'

Matches against Chelsea in the mid-'80s were traditionally bruising encounters where personal duels abounded. One such battle to emerge this time around was the David and Goliath encounter between Mark Ward and Blues' big, rugged Scottish defender Doug Rougvie.

Frank McAvennie knew of Rougvie's hard-man reputation from their Scottish League days and, before the two meetings between the teams in 17 days, the Hammers hot-shot had warned Wardie of what lay in store.

Still smiling at the memory of his old mucker Ward ripping into the Scottish man-mountain, Frank says: 'It was the funniest thing I ever saw on a football field and I'll never forget it until the day I die. Wardie, who is not much more than four-foot-three, was playing right wing, up against their left-back, Rougvie, who is about six-three. I knew Doug from his days at Aberdeen. I was winding Wardie up about how the big man was gonna do him and when he stood next to him in the tunnel Wardie must have feared the worst.

'Anyway, we're playing in all-white at Stamford Bridge that day and it's thick mud. Tony touched the kick-off to me and I put it straight out to the right, where Doug's gone – BANG! – straight into Wardie. Mark had dirt all down the side of his face and I said to him: "Told you, wee man!"

'Every time Wardie got the ball, Doug was going through him. At half-time we were all muddy – apart from Dev who came off still looking immaculate – but at the start of the second half Wardie had clearly had enough. This time, he knocked the ball through Rougvie's legs and as Doug's gone to turn and run, Wardie tripped him up. As Doug was falling, Wardie fell on top of him and head-butted him! Doug looked over at me. It was such a funny sight, the tears were rolling down my face. Wardie loved a scrap.'

Fleet Street – where the presses were still rolling before the Wapping revolution – had definitely taken a shine to the Hammers. Reporting on the Chelsea match, Brian Madley wrote: 'There was a time when everyone knew West Ham would blow any sort of title chance when the winter rains arrived. A fair-weather team. But they floated around in the mud as happy as pigs in fertiliser and, with three home matches in hand on the leaders, must still be in with a Championship shout.'

Ben Bacon wrote: 'It was football of the highest order and poor Chelsea could do nothing about it. They were swamped by a tidal wave of attacking play from their title rivals. When they tried to get their heads above water, West Ham pushed them under again. And again. And again.'

Patrick Collins added: 'Chelsea were simply overwhelmed by a team which offered pace, control, invention and all the other virtues one normally associates with the champions of the Football League.

'West Ham have added rigorous efficiency to their traditional charm and the sheer quality of their football rippled through the side, from the defensive composure of Tony Gale to the predatory speed of Tony Cottee.

'It was an exhilarating exhibition, orchestrated in its important phases by Alan Devonshire with a bright intelligence which Chelsea could not comprehend, far less contain.'

As for Paul Hilton, who had been linked with a possible loan move to Blackpool at the start of the season, he could hardly have dreamed of playing a part in one of the club's finest matches of all time. Ironically, some 18 months earlier, before his transfer to West Ham, Paul had played for the Bury team battered to a 10–0 defeat as Hammers established a new record League Cup score.

'Hilts' recalled being interviewed by the *Newham Recorder*'s Trevor Smith on the team bus after the game: 'I told him that I was just pleased and, at the same time, relieved that I came in and didn't let anyone down, and that Alvin being out hadn't upset the applecart. I remember how vocal our fans were at the open end of the ground. It was a great game to play in.

'The team was playing with such confidence at the time, it made it a lot easier for me to come in and play,' continues Hilton, whose early powerful header, from Ward's corner in the 17th minute, looked as if it had crossed the goal-line, only for Speedie to clear acrobatically with the back of his foot.

'Even though Alvin was missing, Galey and Tonka were both such good talkers that my job became that much easier. I felt more nervous before we beat Chelsea 4–1 at home in May 1988 – to win a vital relegation battle in which I managed to score – than I did at Stamford Bridge in '86.

'The thing about Galey is that no matter what, he never looked under pressure. Having said that, he didn't like getting his hair dirty . . . and that's probably why I lost all mine!'

But with a typical 'Reggie'-like retort, Gale says: 'With all due respect to Hilts, I told him before the game at Chelsea to just do what Alvin does. I said, "Get after the ball and attack it. I'll clear up all your shit. Don't try and do anything too clever. The last time you tried that you lost to us 10–0!" As it happened, Hilts did okay and he was pleased that we kept up our winning run after he came into the side.'

The tough, wholehearted Lancastrian, who had started just a dozen first-team games before his recall at Chelsea, did not need the more cultured Gale to point out his limitations. Looking back on a Hammers playing career that spanned 65 games in little over five years, before a knee injury cruelly forced him to quit, Hilts never got ideas above his station.

With complete candour, he now admits: 'I never had a problem being kept out of the side by Alvin and Galey. John Lyall made it very clear to me when I signed that if it hadn't been for all the injuries they had at the time, I would never have been at West Ham, and I fully accepted that.'

Before the Easter derby double, Cottee received the honour of being named as the PFA's Young Player of the Year. England manager Bobby Robson gave him special permission to leave the Under-21 squad that drew 1–1 with Denmark in a European Championship qualifier at Maine Road (Dickens was on the bench) to attend the PFA dinner at the Grosvenor House Hotel and receive his award from legendary Irish goalkeeper Pat Jennings.

Lyall commented: 'It is a tribute to all the hard work the lad has put into his game this year. Tony has been playing First Division football for three seasons now and has managed to maintain his scoring rate over this period. But this season he has added a tremendous amount more to his game and has developed into a better player.'

Cottee would become the club's biggest sale when he left to join Everton for a then British record of £2.05 million in the summer of 1988 and the value of that fee could perhaps be measured by the fact that, following their AGM around Easter, the club announced it had made a profit of over £400,000 in the year ending 31 July 1985. The days of British clubs paying more than £20 million for one player, with even average players earning £20,000 a week thanks largely to Sky TV's satellite television deal with the FA Premier League, were still light years away.

Just how much Cottee had improved his all-round game was again evident at Upton Park on Easter Monday, 31 March, when the eagerly anticipated visit of Spurs attracted a 27,565 holiday crowd to see West Ham complete an Easter weekend double that, in view of results elsewhere, threw the Championship chase wide open.

Cottee netted his 20th goal of the season after 17 minutes, having sprinted clear of Paul Allen to receive a slide-rule through ball from Dickens, after a deft McAvennie back-heel.

Only the goalkeeping excellence of Ray Clemence prevented Hammers from racking up the kind of score they had posted at Chelsea two days before, although the home side were stunned five minutes after Cottee's opener as Ossie Ardiles nodded Spurs' equaliser following Mark Falco's back-headed near-post flick on from Chris Waddle's corner. West Ham soon regrouped, however, playing delightful one-touch football that frustrated the visitors. Gary Mabbutt and Ardiles were booked for lunges on McAvennie and Ward respectively, while former Hammer Allen – who was mercilessly jeered throughout – entered referee Ray Lewis' notebook for dissent. In the second half Mitchell Thomas and Tony Galvin took the visitors' bookings tally to five – both for using strong-arm tactics on the irrepressible Ward, who got himself booked for an over-zealous, yet fearless, challenge on Graham Roberts, one of the game's true 'hard men'.

Despite all Tottenham's efforts to harass and contain, the Cottee-McAvennie spearhead again did the business two minutes before half-time. Ward's corner found Cottee at the far post and though Clemence did well to block the shot, the ball rebounded kindly to McAvennie, who lashed it home, left-footed, from six yards. McAvennie was denied his 25th goal of the season from much longer range midway through the second half when he outfoxed the England keeper with a delicate lob that bounced back off the crossbar.

Clive Allen, on for Ardiles, also hit the woodwork late in the game but the 2–1 victory flattered Tottenham, whose manager Peter Shreeves said: 'Cottee, McAvennie and Ward were just too quick for us at times.'

Shreeves visited the home dressing-room afterwards to say sorry for Galvin's wild challenge on Ward, who left the field clutching his damaged left shoulder that required hospital treatment. X-rays revealed no serious damage, and the Spurs manager said: 'There was one particularly nasty foul involving Galvin on Mark Ward and I apologised to John Lyall.'

Gary Tobyn, one of the youngsters who Wardie befriended at the training ground, and who, along with his father Mick and brother Danny, remains very good friends of Mark's, remembers the reaction to the Galvin incident from fans on the East Stand terrace. Wardie was perfectly equipped to fight his own battles but Gary says: 'The blokes in the Chicken Run could certainly dish out stick to opposing players and after Galvin fouled Mark, he suddenly became drenched in spit from the crowd. I can still see Galvin now, looking disgusted as he tried to wipe it off the back of his shirt.'

No one in a white Spurs jersey that day received more abuse from the Upton Park faithful than their number two, Paul Allen, who had still not been forgiven for defecting to White Hart Lane the previous summer, just days after winning the fans' vote for Hammer of the

BOYS OF '86

Year. 'Ollie' had no complaints, however, and was full of praise for his former teammates when he said: 'I was very impressed with the lads. There was not a weakness anywhere in the side. I can't see why West Ham should not go all the way to the title.'

While the first-team players at Upton Park maintained their belief that the Championship race was still on, it was a case of what might have been for several of the former fringe players who moved on.

Bobby Barnes followed a loan period at Scunthorpe United with a £15,000 transfer to Fourth Division Aldershot and quickly repaid their faith by scoring a hat-trick in ten minutes in a 6–1 win over Stockport County. Paul McMenemy netted 29 goals in his first season of reserve team football for the table-topping Football Combination side before joining Barnes at Aldershot on loan. And young centre-back Keith McPherson's loan spell at Northampton Town became permanent after a £10,000 deal.

Easter is traditionally regarded as the benchmark for confirming the eventual champions, and after taking a maximum six points against London rivals (Chelsea were also crushed by QPR, 6–0, on Easter Monday) West Ham had put themselves right up there in contention on 60 points. Lyall's men occupied fifth place, two points behind Chelsea, with Manchester United a further three points above them in third spot. United and Everton had cancelled each other out at Old Trafford, which meant Liverpool, who beat Manchester City at Anfield, went top for the first time with 70 points. However, the Reds had played a game more than their Merseyside neighbours.

One of Hammers' games in hand was used up at the City Ground, Nottingham on 2 April, their third match in five days. Devonshire, who made way for Orr late in the game against Spurs, his 300th league appearance, was still out, but Martin, now free of suspension, naturally returned at the expense of Hilton.

Forest, playing their best football of the season, took the lead in the 39th minute with Dutchman Johnny Metgod's free-kick thunderbolt that rocketed high into the net after scorching the paint off the underside of the crossbar. Phil Parkes took responsibility afterwards when he told the *Evening Standard*'s Bill Pierce: 'It was some shot from Metgod but nine times out of ten I would have expected to save it. The ball flew upwards at the last moment and I couldn't get my hands up in time. Metgod hit another one almost as good in the second half and again I didn't see it until very late. Thankfully, I just managed to dive across and keep it out.'

In the 69th minute West Ham scored a goal that almost rivalled the former Real Madrid star's wonder strike when Cottee received Ray Stewart's clever pass on the edge of the penalty area, swivelled to outwit both the Dutchman and Des Walker, and scored with a rare, curling left-footer.

A point would have been more than handy from a game in which Forest had done enough to take all three. Although Steve Sutton had to be sharp to deny late strikes from Cottee and McAvennie, the night turned sour for Hammers just two minutes from time when Brian Rice silenced the home boo-boys with his close-range winner after Stewart failed to clear Franz Carr's cross.

Parkes added: 'I was more disappointed with the second goal and not only because it came so late. We should have got the ball away and I know Ray just couldn't believe it.'

A 2–1 defeat proved a big setback and, perhaps for the first time, revealed clear signs that the heavy fixture backlog was beginning to take its toll on mind and body.

Cottee says: 'Towards the end of the season I definitely felt drained. It had also become harder for Frank and I to keep scoring the amount of goals we were getting earlier in the season. Teams had done their homework and, particularly at Upton Park, were tending to man-mark us both and/or play with a sweeper. We had found it hard to beat Sheffield Wednesday at home and it was the same against Southampton.'

West Ham were relieved to have the next Saturday after the Forest defeat off, as their title rivals Liverpool and Everton contested different semi-finals of the FA Cup, against Southampton and Sheffield Wednesday respectively. The mood at Chadwell Heath remained upbeat although tinged with realism. Whatever they may have been thinking, no one was openly talking of winning the Championship simply because Hammers were always trying to play catch-up with the fixtures. For West Ham to triumph against all odds, both of the Merseyside giants would have to falter at the final hurdle.

Lyall said after the defeat in Nottingham and before playing Southampton at Upton Park on 8 April: 'We have got four of the next five at home and so that could change everything again. We will now simply try to win all our remaining matches and see what happens. We certainly haven't given up.'

With seven of their last ten matches at home, where only Luton Town had managed to win, West Ham were genuine outside title contenders. They had the toughest possible schedule, however,

BOYS OF '86

having to cram those ten crucial games into just 27 days.

Southampton must have felt pretty weary themselves three days after losing their semi-final, 2–0, to Liverpool at White Hart Lane, especially as centre-back Mark Wright was among their injury victims. Even so, the Saints still managed to keep the Cottee/McAvennie goal machine at bay – perhaps more by luck than judgement, rather than simply thanks to the presence of sweeper David Armstrong – and for the first time since the goalless draw with Arsenal way back in mid-October, neither of the front two got on the scoresheet at Upton Park.

Instead, Hammers' winner came from an unlikely source in Alvin Martin, who cleanly volleyed home his first of the season, and the only goal of a one-sided match in the 26th minute. Neither striker was involved in the build-up as Stewart's piledriver produced a fine save from Peter Shilton. The resulting corner by Ward was then headed on at the near post by Gale for Martin to thump past 'Shils'.

Cottee and McAvennie made and missed a cluster of good chances, while Saints' Andy Townsend was unlucky to hit a post before seeing a vicious volley acrobatically turned away by Parkes.

Southampton boss Chris Nicholl said: 'Two years ago West Ham would have got a goal and then given it away. They don't do that now. Instead they get in and battle to guard it, and that is the big difference.'

After scoring his first goal since November 1984, Martin said: 'We believe the next two weeks will decide it. It's within our grasp. This is the best side we've had for a long time and if we can stay clear of injuries, it's up to us.'

Seven points now separated fourth-placed Hammers from Liverpool, but West Ham still had two games in hand – both at home, against lowly Oxford United and then an eagerly awaited return against Chelsea.

Hammers overwhelmed Oxford 3–1 on 12 April, eight days before the struggling U's were due to face QPR in the Milk Cup final at Wembley. Gale maintained his ever-present record but, as he explains, only just: 'I got stuck in traffic in Canning Town. We didn't have mobile phones in those days and I ended up tearing three-quarters of a mile down Green Street to get to the ground while my dad, Peter, got out of his taxi and went to a phone box to let John Lyall know I was on my way. I more or less ran straight onto the pitch.' Gale was still catching his breath when Oxford took a shock 13th-minute lead through Ray Houghton, their diminutive, newly-capped Republic of Ireland international who had been discarded by Lyall just a couple of years earlier in favour of Alan Dickens.

Houghton admitted before the game that he had been dismayed to have been given a free transfer by West Ham, having made only one first-team appearance, as sub against Arsenal at Highbury in May 1982. The midfielder showed great character, however, by going to Fulham and impressing Oxford United enough to become their club record £125,000 signing in the summer of '85.

His opener stunned Hammers into life and the rest of the game was virtually one-way traffic, with Devonshire doing most of the damage in a second-half spree that produced three goals. There was an element of good fortune about the 49th-minute equaliser; defender John Trewick deflecting Cottee's cut-back past his own keeper, Alan Judge, who previously had made superb saves from Ward and Stewart.

And the U's were unhappy again when Steve Perryman, signed from Spurs and revelling in the role of sweeper, was booked for tripping Devonshire in the box. It led to a spot-kick but, with a rare misplacement, Stewart sliced his 71st penalty for the club wide of the goal. It was to be the last of his ten misses from his 86 attempts – a remarkable record.

Hammers' nerves were settled in the 65th minute. Pike, who was booked for a late challenge on Houghton, slotted through a perfect pass for McAvennie, who eased his frustration at seeing an earlier flying header hit a post by putting the home side ahead.

Stewart wrapped it up nine minutes from time. Showing his usual character and supreme confidence from the spot, the Scot ignored his earlier miss to make no mistake this time after Perryman had brought down Dickens with a carbon-copy lunge that brought about West Ham's first penalty.

The Hammers' fan club among opposing managers and players grew with each passing match. Perryman, whose Boxing Day winner for Spurs had ended that record-equalling run, said: 'There is a lot of pace up front and it is the most effective West Ham team I've played against. They resemble Liverpool in the relentless way they keep attacking you.'

Striker John Aldridge, who was later to become a prolific scorer at Anfield, added: 'Liverpool are the only other side who have played that well against us.'

Meanwhile, Dalglish's side had crushed Coventry City 5–0 at

BOYS OF '86

home, while Everton won by the only goal away to Arsenal, with the Merseysiders sharing top spot on 73 points. Manchester United's title hopes suffered a major blow when two Kerry Dixon goals gave Chelsea a shock 2–0 midweek victory at Old Trafford, to send the Blues leapfrogging over Hammers into fourth place, just a point behind United.

Chelsea had clearly recovered from their Easter drubbings – and were about to inflict a second devastating blow on another of their title rivals . . .

Chapter 12

CHAIN REACTION – Diana Ross

Chart Position: Number 1, April 1986

When people try to pinpoint the game, or the moment, when West Ham United's Championship dream was shattered, chances are they will reflect ruefully on the home game against Chelsea on Wednesday, 15 April.

A London club had not won the Football League since Arsenal's Double success in 1971, so the hopes of the capital rested with these two, who were separated by just a point among the elite's top five. Chelsea had won the coveted silverware only once before in their history, in 1955, whereas West Ham had never gone remotely close to winning the ultimate prize. Upton Park braced itself for a titanic thriller, a match that would inevitably have a critical bearing on the outcome of the title race that was hotting up. A point was useless to both sides – they both had to go for broke.

Although Chelsea had bounced back well following their four-goal Easter mauling by the Hammers just over a fortnight earlier, the suspension of striker David Speedie and injury to skipper Colin Pates left them weakened. A big plus for the Blues, however, was that nippy winger Pat Nevin was passed fit to play after a test on his injured knee shortly before kick-off. The skilful Scottish international had been well shackled by Ray Stewart and Mark Ward in Hammers' epic 4–0 victory at Stamford Bridge – but this was another day.

Queues had been forming outside the turnstiles on all four sides of the Boleyn Ground from mid-afternoon and by kick-off the biggest home crowd of the season to date – a 29,361 lock-out – had packed into Upton Park. Most were relieved when, after just five minutes,

121

Nevin spurned a fine chance to open the scoring as he shot wide of the advancing Phil Parkes.

The atmosphere was electric and the tension in the crowd briefly boiled over when a mini pitch invasion, chiefly caused by the sheer numbers crammed onto the terraces, forced referee Martin Bodenham to suspend play for 90 seconds.

West Ham went closest to breaking the deadlock in the first half when Alvin Martin nodded on Ward's corner but Alan Dickens' header was fingertipped onto the crossbar by stand-in keeper Tony Godden and Chelsea breathed again. Dicko turned provider, however, six minutes into the second half when his great run ended with a neat pass to Tony Cottee, who scored with a first-time shot from the edge of the box at the North Bank end. The crowd, chanting 'Johnny Lyall's Claret and Blue Army' were euphoric, sensing the title was within touching distance – but it was all to go horribly wrong just four minutes after Cottee's goal.

Tony Gale, who was in trouble long before half-time, finally limped off with a dead leg and the spotlight turned on his replacement, Neil Orr, who had been largely confined to the subs' bench after his Boxing Day injury coincided with the return of Geoff Pike. Orr had started only three of the previous 11 First Division matches and was understandably a little ring-rusty when he suddenly found himself in an unfamiliar position, alongside Alvin Martin in the back four.

Fifteen years on, Orr, at first, had difficulty remembering the events of the last 35 dramatic minutes of that night. But slowly, the pain of it all returned as he recalls the moment when his penalty-box slip allowed Nigel Spackman to net the simplest of equalisers.

'To be honest, I'd put it out of my mind but, talking about it now, it's all come flooding back to me,' he says from his North Berwick home.

'I remember the goal as if it was yesterday. The ball came over and it appeared that George Parris was going to clear it away. For some reason, though, he let it go. I was caught a bit off guard, and as I reacted to try and clear it myself, my standing leg just came away from under me and the ball went straight to Spackman. I remember thinking: "How the hell did the ball end up there?"

'The whole game was a nightmare for me. Nevin got behind me for the second goal to head the winner, too, and I also injured Geoff Pike's knee when I fell on him while clearing the ball.'

If it's any consolation, Neil, skipper Martin shouldered his share of the blame for the killer second goal, 12 minutes from time, that clinched Blues' 2–1 victory.

Martin admits: 'I remember feeling tired. I was thinking: "I've got to go to a World Cup and I'm knackered. I should be fresh."

'A lot of people blamed Neil for that defeat but I was at fault for their second goal when I got too tight on Kerry Dixon who turned me on the halfway line and crossed from the byline for Nevin to get in front of Neil at the far post. We played well but they hit us with two good finishes.'

With Chelsea keeper Steve Francis dropped after his 11-goal Easter battering, Godden was only wearing the keeper's shirt because first choice Eddie Niedzwiecki was still out injured. But Godden proved a hero when he somehow clawed away a stinging Alan Devonshire shot that was destined for the top corner.

Hammers left just three at the back as Martin moved up front to try and scramble a desperate equaliser. Ward blasted over from one of his fellow Scouser's nod-downs, while Dickens was a foot away from getting on the end of another. Chelsea conceded nine corners and many more free-kicks as Hammers attacked relentlessly, but to no avail.

Orr describes the mood in the home dressing–room afterwards: 'I just felt totally dejected but John wasn't the kind to crucify you individually if he knew that you were genuinely aware of your mistakes. I was disappointed for the other lads more than myself, but the team spirit at the time was such that we were all in it together, and there was never only one person to blame.'

Neil's fellow Scot Ray Stewart, who knew Orr better than anyone at West Ham, felt for his beleaguered teammate when he said: 'Neil got hate mail from fans after the Chelsea game and that's not nice for any player or his family. He obviously didn't deliberately fall over the ball. He's a strong-willed lad but I think it affected him to a certain degree because he seemed a bit jittery on the ball after that.'

But Stewart knew, too, the value of Orr's role in the team. Tonka adds: 'He was a great player's player. For example, he would always encourage me to get forward and he'd just fill in for me.'

Orr's collision with Pike ensured he kept his place as the latter re-entered hospital for a knee operation that would rule him out of all the remaining games. Orr himself tried desperately to put the Chelsea ordeal behind him. He says: 'When I look back at that Chelsea game, I admit, it did affect me. Talking about it now has brought it all flooding back to me and it wasn't a nice experience.

'It was one of those things, though, and luckily I didn't have much time to dwell on it then, because the games were coming thick and fast. It was important how we reacted after that and as it turned out we won the next six games. That showed the quality and character we had in the team, because it could quite easily have fallen apart after that Chelsea defeat. We just bounced straight back and kept going until the final Saturday of the season.'

Having proved himself fearless at Stamford Bridge, Ward was equally prepared for his rematch with the flame-haired Rougvie.

Says Mark: 'I remember Alvin saying to me when I first came down to West Ham: "That Chicken Run can destroy people, and they'll dig you out if they know you're not giving 100 per cent. So even if you're not the best player on the pitch, make sure you always give 100 per cent." It was a great piece of advice and I never forgot it.

'I came up against Rougvie and as far as I was concerned it was no contest, because he was a big centre-back playing at left-back. He wasn't a dirty player, he was clumsy and kept mistiming his challenges. I was getting one free-kick after another and in the end we went in for a tackle and as we both fell, with me on top of him, I put one hand on his forehead and stuck two fingers of my other hand straight up his nose! It was right in front of the Chicken Run – and Rougvie wanted to get up and kill me. If I was going to fail, it wasn't going to be through lack of commitment.'

Lyall disguised his disappointment after the 2–1 home defeat by Chelsea well. The manager said: 'Everton [who beat Watford the same night] have obviously got an advantage, but we must carry on and hope they slip up. We've had a great season and it is up to us to maintain it.'

The players heeded Lyall's words at Watford the following Saturday. With Gale restored to the defence, and Orr moving forward into his customary midfield role, it was West Ham who took early command and gave the *Match of the Day* cameras a treat.

Mark Ward gave left-back Paul Franklin, a centre-back standing in for the injured Wilf Rostron, a torrid afternoon and was at the heart of most of Hammers' best work. He and Devonshire linked up well on the edge of the Hornets' area after 59 minutes and following a low cross from Devonshire, Cottee nipped in front of John McClelland to fire high past Tony Coton. Ward was unfortunate not to score himself when he played a one-two with Cottee but saw his shot hit a post.

West Ham had to survive some late Watford pressure before putting the game beyond doubt. The move started at the back with Martin, who found McAvennie in acres of space and bearing down on Coton. The Hornets' keeper tried to haul down McAvennie, who brushed him aside before tapping home left-footed for his 26th goal of the season.

Watford manager Graham Taylor had nothing but admiration for the visitors. He said: 'West Ham put us in our place today with some marvellous attacking football. In midweek we were going all out to get a second when Everton scored. But Everton were never able to control us the way West Ham have today. West Ham were infinitely better.'

Lyall rated the performance 'as good as any we have turned in this season'. Journalist Martin Marks urged England manager Bobby Robson to have a very close look at Cottee. He wrote in the *Mail On Sunday*: 'How he has escaped full England recognition is becoming difficult to understand. He is already clearly ahead of Tony Woodcock and Trevor Francis and the 59th-minute goal he scored to sink Watford deserved a World Cup stage.'

Victory at Vicarage Road enabled Hammers to close the gap on Chelsea to two points as the Blues' own title hopes were effectively ended by a 1–1 home draw with Newcastle United. But Liverpool retained top spot with a 2–1 victory at basement club West Bromwich Albion, while Everton joined them on 79 points with a 1–0 home win over Ipswich Town. Manchester United's fading aspirations finally died in their goalless draw at Tottenham.

Newcastle United may have ruined Chelsea's dream but they were soon in a daze at Upton Park on Monday, 21 April, as Hammers romped to an 8–1 massacre – their biggest League win since an 8–0 defeat of Sunderland in 1968. Geoff Hurst wrote himself into Hammers' history books that day with six goals, but this night belonged to an unlikely hero in central defender Alvin Martin, who achieved the astonishing feat of scoring a hat-trick against three different goalkeepers – Martin Thomas, Chris Hedworth and Peter Beardsley.

The Magpies were forced to start with Thomas in goal even though their regular keeper was far from fit and had only appeared because his deputy, David McKellar, was injured at Stamford Bridge two days earlier.

The extent of Thomas's arm injury became obvious in the third minute when Martin set the claret-and-blue juggernaut rolling with

a close-range volley of which Hurst would have been proud. Thomas's mistakes in the 11th and 35th minutes gave Stewart and Orr long-range goals they would probably not have got against a fit keeper. Newcastle skipper Glenn Roeder back-heeled a chip intended for Cottee into his own goal in the 43rd minute and so it was no surprise when Thomas failed to start the second half.

Hedworth, a 21-year-old reserve defender, took over the number one jersey and made creditable saves from Dickens and Cottee before he, too, was injured in a tangle with the latter. He fell awkwardly and dislocated his right collarbone. He carried on after treatment and even managed to block a fierce Cottee shot with his chest before being beaten by Martin's header in the 64th minute following a Ward corner. Hedworth was immediately replaced by England striker Beardsley and eventually went off a few minutes later after playing on the left wing.

Beardsley proved himself to be the best of the three keepers, coming off his line with good judgement and making excellent saves from Martin and Cottee. Billy Whitehurst even pulled a goal back for Newcastle in the 76th minute before Beardsley also capitulated under an avalanche of West Ham pressure. Paul Goddard, who came on for Dickens ten minutes from the end, headed the sixth goal with his first touch in the 81st minute. McAvennie headed the seventh two minutes later and in the 84th minute Martin converted a penalty when Roeder was adjudged to have handled, although Newcastle's beleaguered defenders claimed Cottee was the offender.

It could easily have been 10–1, because Cottee headed against the bar near the end and Martin had earlier seen a shot turned against the post by Beardsley. Although Newcastle could justifiably point to their goalkeeping crisis as the obvious reason for such a heavy defeat, there were also rumours that a number of their players had spent rather too long enjoying themselves at Roeder's pub at Blackmoor between their excellent draw at Chelsea and that Upton Park massacre two days later.

Hammers' most emphatic win of the season lifted them into third place, seven points behind the top two, and ensured Alvin Martin's place in Upton Park folklore.

He still has the match ball among his collection of mementos at home and the first, and only, hat-trick of his 22-year playing career now forms part of his speech on the after-dinner circuit. (Incidentally, if you catch it, don't leave before the end or you will miss the hilarious Peter Beardsley punch-line!)

John Lyall was not laughing, however, when the dressing-room banter turned to Martin's unique goal feast. Martin explains: 'When we got the penalty, Ray picked the ball up because, as ever, he wanted to take it. It wasn't until the crowd started chanting my name that it became embarrassing for me not to take it. Until then it just hadn't occurred to me, I was just happy that it was another game we'd won. Afterwards, though, John said we should have been more professional and let Ray take the penalty. Everyone was saying: "C'mon John, it's his hat-trick." I think John went a bit too far that night.

'I recently met Martin Thomas on a veterans' tour to Russia and he told me it was now a pub-quiz question: "Who scored a hat-trick against three different keepers?" It was some night and no one associated with West Ham ever lets me forget it.'

Instead of heaping more praise on Martin, straight after the game Lyall singled out Goddard, who had become the forgotten man of Upton Park: 'The nice thing for me, on what was a memorable night, was to see Paul come on and score with his first touch. Paul has not been able to get in the side this season but has remained completely loyal – the sort of player managers dream about.'

The only Hammer not celebrating that night was Tony Cottee who, underlining his obsessive hunger for goals, says: 'I came away absolutely pissed off that I hadn't scored a goal. It was a good team performance but they had three keepers and I couldn't believe I hadn't scored. When the final whistle went I was absolutely gutted, but obviously pleased we'd won the game.' And not begrudging Martin his finest hour, Cottee adds: 'It had been an amazing game and all the players wanted Alvin to take the penalty – he had to.'

But Cottee never went long without scoring – as Coventry City soon found to their cost.

BOYS OF '86

Chapter 13

A KIND OF MAGIC – Queen

Chart Position: Number 3, April 1986

The matches came thick and fast for West Ham, who faced three at home in five hectic days. Before the visit of Coventry City on 26 April, Tony Cottee received the Hammer of the Year award. Frank McAvennie was voted runner-up, with Mark Ward third. It was worthy recognition for Cottee, who was about to forget his personal Newcastle nightmare by plundering his 24th goal of a magnificent season. Like all of the most feared strikers in the game, Cottee had to be single-minded and goals were his trademark. But reflecting on his best-ever season in football, he admits the fans' annual award for 1985–86 should have gone to his strike partner.

Cottee says: 'I won Hammer of the Year but I was absolutely staggered. I thought Frank should have got it. In my first full season I felt I'd had a good one but it was Trevor Brooking's last and I could understand why he took the honour. It was the same the next year when Paul Allen won it and I felt disappointed. Then in '85–86, I thought Frank had a better season than me. That's my honest opinion. I'd had spells when I was as good as him, and individual games where I'd done better, but, from the second game onwards, Frank had been so consistent. He made everything happen. I wasn't going to turn it down, of course, but for me Frank was our best player that season, without a doubt.

'There was a bit of banter between us after it was announced. I'd won the award but with me being a local lad, I think he understood the situation. Perhaps it had something to do with the fact that the fans saw I'd also been consistent over the previous two seasons, too. But as a fan, I'd have voted for Frank.'

BOYS OF '86

Hammers' player of the season became the man of the hour with a 61st-minute winner that kept them on course for the title. West Ham had struggled to break down Coventry City's solid defence which had been reinforced with a sweeper behind their back four. City were themselves fighting their perennial relegation battle but maybe it was a case of 'too many cooks' when four Sky Blues fell over themselves trying to clear a right-wing cross from McAvennie and Cottee popped up with a scrappy, though nonetheless vital, goal. It was only a momentary lapse by Coventry's well-organised defensive unit but Cottee had always feasted on scraps.

John Lyall admitted: 'It was the least creative goal we have scored this season. We're still in with a shout at the title. That was a tremendous result for us and things are very interesting. It will be tough playing four games in such a short time but when you are winning you feel you could play every day.'

By this stage of the season, 'training' at Chadwell Heath consisted of little more than rub-downs from physio Rob Jenkins, leisurely eight-a-side matches and rest, in readiness for the next critical battle that was always only hours away. West Ham were playing three crucial games a week for the last five weeks of the season – a gruelling schedule that would have many of the overpaid, overrated and overpampered 'stars' of today demanding an all-expenses paid chill-out period at The Priory rehab clinic.

And anyone who tries to argue that the Premiership in 2001–02 is a much faster spectacle than the stylish football served up by the likes of West Ham in the mid-'80s was obviously not at the highly charged home matches towards the end of this season, which were played at an electric pace.

Of course the players were fatigued – they were getting by on pure adrenalin, pumped up by the results they simply had to get to stay in touch with the Merseyside pace-setters. Says Cottee: 'We were knackered and playing it off the cuff towards the end of the season.'

Some of the sophisticated stuff that illuminated the majority of earlier victories had to be sacrificed as qualities of endurance and sheer will to win became increasingly important factors against teams who set out to make life as difficult as possible for the Hammers. So how did they manage to keep going? On the Continental-style diet of fresh fish, chicken and pasta, the favoured choice of modern footballers and coaches? Not likely. These were still the days when pre-match meals consisted of good, old-fashioned steak and chips. Billy Bonds, one of the fittest players ever, always swore by that dish

BOYS OF '86

before every game he played in a Hammers shirt. 'It never stopped me running everywhere during a game,' he argues. Bonzo sadly played no part in '85–86 but the players who did all subscribe to the same simplistic views as the all-time legend and find it hard to accept today's dietary habits as the key to success on the field.

Alan Devonshire, one of the most talented English midfielders of his generation, is unequivocal in his beliefs. In some ways Dev was a freak of nature. He was pale and thin, almost anaemic looking, when he first arrived at Upton Park from Southall for £5,000 in September 1976 and understandably struggled with the training until he gained the strength and stamina for top-flight football. Indeed, he famously collapsed in training during his first week with the club. He says: 'It pisses me off now when people talk about rigid diets and eating pasta and all that crap.

'I was always a big eater and I was lucky in that I could basically eat what I wanted,' continues the man who regularly used to enjoy a big Wimpy breakfast before training. 'On away trips, we used to have our steak or whatever on the Friday night at the hotel as soon as we got there in the early evening, but by 11.00 p.m. I was hungry again. I could never sleep in hotels anyway, so I'd tell John that I was going to have omelette and chips delivered to my room. He was fine about it but when I got into the England squad, he said to me: "You won't be able to have omelette and chips at 11 o'clock!"

'And I'll tell you what I used to do religiously on Sundays. I would go down to the shop and get myself three bottles of Coke and 15 bags of salt-and-vinegar crisps. And either side of eating my dinner, they all used to go! I just used to eat all day and that suited me. Everyone is different and that was what worked best for me.'

Cottee, who was still banging in the goals for Leicester City in the Premiership at the age of 35, adds: 'If you can't trap or pass a ball, it doesn't matter what you eat, it won't help you out on the field. At West Ham, we'd have steak and chips at the hotel on the Friday night. And then at around 11.30 on a Saturday morning we'd have fillet steak and beans before the game. I remember thinking to myself on my first-ever away trip to Old Trafford: "Cor, fillet steak, this is all right!" Nowadays it's chicken and pasta but I don't think it makes too much difference. There's more education, though, and players know they should have plenty of carbohydrates. They don't need to be told. In our day we just ate and drank what we wanted to. We didn't know any different.'

There couldn't have been much wrong with the eating habits at

Anfield either. On the same day Hammers stuttered past Coventry City, Kenny Dalglish's side made mincemeat of Birmingham City with a 5–0 pasting of the Blues, while Everton were held to a goalless draw at Nottingham Forest. If the Championship was going to come down to goal difference, Liverpool were firmly in the driving seat.

West Ham closed the gap on Everton to two points with a second successive 1–0 home win – this time over Manchester City who also employed a sweeper in Andy May. Hammers' laboured performance had not created a single chance until May made a shambles of an attempted dummy in his own penalty box and brought down Cottee. In a situation as tense as this, a cool head and assured touch was required and no one fitted the bill better than Ray Stewart, who thundered his penalty kick past the helpless Barry Siddall in front of the South Bank.

The loaned keeper from Stoke City then had to tip over a back-header from Tony Gale, push a fierce volley from Devonshire away for a corner and then distinguish himself again with a flying save from Ward's driven free-kick.

But it was far from one-way traffic. The red-and-black striped City shirts streamed forward in search of an equaliser and created several very good chances of their own. Dave Phillips fired wide, Mick McCarthy headed over from a Neil McNab cross and Northern Ireland international Sammy McIlroy volleyed straight at Phil Parkes.

The *Daily Mail*'s Jeff Powell noted the near state of exhaustion in the Hammers' camp when he wrote: 'For West Ham, this was the first of four games in eight days. It is hard to imagine how much they will have left to give if they do go to Everton next Monday needing victory to win the Championship.'

West Ham still had it all to do and remained third favourites to lift the crown, behind Liverpool, who were four points clear of Hammers – and Everton, who trailed their neighbours by two points.

Today, most top players at a third-placed club in April would wait until at least the outcome of the Championship before deciding their next move, regardless of whether they had previously signed a contract for the next five years or even five minutes. The complete lack of respect French stars Patrick Vieira and Nicolas Anelka showed Arsenal and their fans in recent seasons, for example, provides a good case for having the word 'loyalty' erased from the English Football Dictionary. There has been a constant stream of other less prominent players – and managers – sticking two

BOYS OF '86

metaphorical fingers up at the clubs who helped them to make their name in today's greed-ridden Premiership.

But in 1985–86, before Sky TV transformed the beautiful game with its seemingly endless pots of gold, loyalty was still a byword for most professional footballers. It certainly applied to West Ham skipper Alvin Martin, who, with the title race hotting up, committed himself to the club, 'for the rest of his career by signing a new five-year contract, keeping him at Upton Park until 1991'. This 'Alvin – a Hammer For Life' story was buried away on the local sports pages and made just four lines of copy. John Lyall said: 'It was typical of Alvin. I had not made any approach to him about it, but he just walked into my office one day and said that was what he would like to do if the club was agreeable – it was as simple as that.'

In hindsight, the report was a little off the mark. Martin in fact stayed at Upton Park until 1996 when, at the age of 38 and after 582 competitive matches, his aching limbs carried themselves the short distance to Leyton Orient.

Martin says: 'I was an England player but I'd never felt like leaving. It had never even occurred to me. Being captain, I felt I had a responsibility towards the club. It was only when John left that I found out how many clubs had come in for me over the years but, obviously, John wouldn't entertain them.'

But Martin was by no means the only loyal, long-serving player giving everything for the Hammers' cause. Of the title-chasing squad from that season, just look how many League and Cup appearances most of the players made in their Upton Park careers: Alan Devonshire (446), Phil Parkes (436), Ray Stewart (431), Geoff Pike (367), Tony Gale (358), George Parris (290). Tony Cottee, a lifelong West Ham fan, made 254 appearances in his first spell, while Alan Dickens (231), Mark Ward (203), Neil Orr (175) and Steve Walford (129) all spent at least four years with the club.

Following the advent of the radical Bosman freedom-of-contract ruling, combined with the rich rewards on offer to players of even the most limited ability, advised by voracious agents, clubs have long since lost the loyalty of their players. But Lyall did not need to motivate his men. They already had claret-and-blue blood pumping through their veins.

Two days after the 1–0 defeat of Manchester City, it was another full house as the biggest home crowd for 18 months – 31,121 – crammed into Upton Park on the evening of Wednesday, 30 April, to see the final make-or-break home game against struggling Ipswich

Town. It was yet another must-win match for Hammers, who also had one eye on the results of Liverpool and Everton, who were playing away to fourth-from-bottom Leicester City and third-from-bottom Oxford United respectively.

Before the game 27-goal Frank McAvennie, who had his personal sights set on the Golden Boot award for the First Division's leading scorer, said: 'Already the club are sure to finish higher than ever before in their history. Just one more point will guarantee us third place. But I still think we've got a great chance of winning the League. Even if Liverpool win at Leicester I've got a hunch that Chelsea will do us a favour by beating them on Saturday.'

Despite their perilous position, Ipswich were not expected to roll over and hand three points to Hammers on a plate. They needed one win from two away games to be certain of staying up and after four previous meetings with West Ham that season, they knew everything about their east London opponents.

The teams came out to a deafening roar as Hammers fans swayed in unison to the club's 'Bubbles' anthem. But the bubble was in dire danger of being burst when an uncharacteristic mistake by Martin let in Kevin Wilson who put the white-shirted visitors in front after 63 minutes. Their minds and bodies drained to breaking point, few expected West Ham to conjure a miraculous recovery.

Town keeper Paul Cooper tipped over a McAvennie strike and the dream was fading fast as McAvennie headed wide of the far post from a Ward cross. Ipswich defended heroically, led by the courageous Terry Butcher who made light of two stitches in a head wound that had to be heavily bandaged.

With news of Liverpool's interval lead at Filbert Street, a draw for Hammers would have virtually ended their title hopes, so Martin and Gale pushed further forward and Dickens became more adventurous in his running.

Hammers thought they were about to level as Gale nodded the ball down to Cottee but his shot hit the leg of a defender guarding the goal-line and bounced to safety. Upping the stakes, Lyall threw on Paul Goddard for Neil Orr with 20 minutes remaining and the experienced striker immediately showed his value by helping to set up the equaliser. Goddard linked well with Devonshire in the 72nd minute for Dickens to score with a delightfully flighted 20-yard shot over Cooper.

The stadium erupted. Now Hammers were pressing forward incessantly and, with just three minutes left, Ward's tenacity again

BOYS OF '86

paid handsome dividends. He headed for the byline in front of the North Bank, forcing his way between Ian Cranson and Nigel Gleghorn, and then went to ground. Referee Gerald Ashby did not hesitate to point to the spot, waving away furious protests from the Ipswich players, led by an apoplectic Butcher. Stewart had consistently and confidently dispatched his previous penalties with customary coolness, but he had never before taken one on which the club's first-ever Championship hopes rested – and with only three minutes left to play.

Once again, however, the canny Scot, who had previously scored from late spot-kicks in the 1981 League Cup final and the 1980 FA Cup quarter-final, displayed nerves of steel to drive the ball right-footed past Cooper. The sense of relief and excitement was embodied by 10,000 fans who covered the pitch after the final whistle to chant 'Bubbles' and 'We're Gonna Win The League'. They hugged and kissed each other, surging forward towards the tunnel area to try and catch the shirts, shinpads and tie-ups thrown down from the directors' box by their heroes. The following morning, groundsman Ron Pigram discovered that one fan had dug up the penalty spot to take home as a souvenir, causing staff to mount a filling-in operation before that day's reserve-team game! At the end of one of the most emotional nights in the club's history, a breathless Lyall declared: 'I've never seen scenes like this in 30 years.'

Hammers' two goalscoring heroes played down their own vital contributions. Ray Stewart said at the time: 'I'm used to taking penalties, it's my job. I don't practise against goalkeepers, I practise shooting against brick walls.' He still remains as modest as ever about his legendary 'Penalty King' status, saying: 'I loved taking the extra responsibility. It was quite near the end of the Ipswich game and I knew that if I'd missed, the fans would have put my windows in! By then, I'd had a lot of experience of taking penalties.'

Dickens had used his weaker left foot to score what everyone present remembers as a brilliantly executed goal from just outside the penalty area, but the unassuming, quietly spoken man of the team says: 'It was a fluke really. I think it was supposed to go in the bottom left-hand corner and ended up going in the top right or something. We needed to score, that was the main thing.

'The best goal I ever scored, which I have a great feeling for, was the one I got at Sheffield Wednesday – the first game after the Hillsborough Disaster – and that gave me a lot of satisfaction because I knew what I was doing.'

Given the opportunity, 15 years on, to confess that he hadn't been fouled for what everyone agreed was a dubious penalty decision, Mark Ward simply shrugs and says: 'It was given, that's all that matters.' He does, however, admit to some physical excesses in the heat of battle that night.

'I bit Terry Butcher on the back,' says Wardie with a mischievous look on his face. But the smirk is quickly replaced by a slight frown as he confesses: 'But I'm not proud of some of the things I've done on a football pitch. John never told me to fight hard for the ball, that was just the way I was. I was brought up to fight hard for everything in life. I remember John once asking my ex-wife Jane: "Is he like this at home?" She wouldn't speak to me on the way to games and, because we never went out much when I first came to the club, I never had much release. Football was my release.'

While Butcher, now staring relegation in the face, took out his pent-up frustration by booting a hole in the dressing-room door, there were only broad smiles in the room along the corridor. Gale recalls a slow drive down the Barking Road as fans continued their celebrations well into the night.

He says: 'The ground was rocking. When we went home the fans were watching the highlights on telly in the Boleyn and the pub was shaking. I said to my dad: "Look, they reckon we're gonna win the League." I thought that too.'

Lyall added: 'It's an incredible season for us and what a climax. Now we must win our last two matches and hope.'

Leaders Liverpool had duly completed a 2–0 victory at Leicester, with goals from Ian Rush and Ronnie Whelan, but Everton's shock 1–0 defeat to a Phillips goal at Oxford United's compact Manor Road ground proved fatal for their hopes and allowed West Ham to move a point above them into second place – four points behind the Anfield club, who had only one match to play.

BOYS OF '86

Chapter 14

SLEDGEHAMMER – Peter Gabriel

Chart Position: Number 1, May 1986

Leading scorer Frank McAvennie was literally dreaming of the Championship as he prepared for the penultimate match at West Bromwich Albion. After five consecutive victories in 11 days, the Scottish striker still had the strength, physically and mentally, to continue his wonderful goalscoring exploits in the last two matches of a momentous first season in England.

Frank said: 'I couldn't believe how fresh I felt before Wednesday's game against Ipswich, after feeling so tired after Monday's win over Manchester City. I felt I could have gone on forever – perhaps that was because I'd hardly done anything but sleep between the games. Now it doesn't matter how tired we feel because we can see the finishing line just two games away. We can go out at West Brom to bust a gut, not worrying about conserving our strength to face Everton on Monday. Any extra strength we might need up at Goodison would come from Chelsea taking points off Liverpool. That would give us just the chance we need to grab the title.'

West Brom had already been relegated to Division Two but, having been thrashed 5–1 at The Hawthorns exactly a year earlier, Hammers did not set off for the West Midlands with any hint of complacency.

Meanwhile, over at Stamford Bridge, Chelsea manager John Hollins was making all the right noises about the Blues doing all they could to facilitate a London League triumph for the first time in 15 years. 'We want West Ham to bring it to London,' he insisted.

Everton were at home to Southampton but, like the Hammers,

BOYS OF '86

could only hope that Liverpool lost at Chelsea if their title hopes were to stay alive.

After the best part of 48 hours asleep, McAvennie awoke from his slumber to head West Ham into a ninth-minute lead and he played a key part in the second goal, releasing Tony Cottee to score from a well-struck drive in the 24th minute. The players were given an even bigger lift when they saw the buzz of excitement among the travelling fans who, apparently, heard via a radio report that Chelsea were beating Liverpool.

McAvennie says: 'When we heard our supporters cheer we jumped to the same conclusion. I didn't even ask for the Stamford Bridge score at half-time. None of us did. We didn't want anything to disturb our concentration on this match.'

Tony Gale's pre-match cautionary warning that Albion were not to be treated lightly rang true as Craig Madden pulled one back in the 33rd minute. The Baggies threatened to spoil the party completely when, just after an hour, George Reilly was fouled in the penalty area by George Parris and then picked himself up to score the equaliser.

But Hammers, still believing that Chelsea were winning against Liverpool, somehow summoned the energy to surge forward again. Their reward came in the form of another penalty on 82 minutes after Mark Ward's cross hit the arm of the unlucky Derek Statham.

Ray Stewart thought he was scoring the goal to keep the Championship champagne on ice for another 48 hours but the mood after this 3–2 victory immediately turned sour when the players reached the dressing-room. There, they received the news no one associated with West Ham wanted to hear. Liverpool had won the title.

Whether the radio reporter had got it wrong, or a small group of fans had misheard the information filtering through from Stamford Bridge, we may never know for sure. The fact was, though, that Liverpool player-manager Kenny Dalglish had crowned his first season in charge at Anfield by scoring the only goal of the game in the 23rd minute – a well-taken volley that underlined his enduring class.

Stewart says: 'It's the first time I've ever cried after a football match.'

McAvennie adds: 'I've been beaten in five cup semi-finals in Scotland but I've never known a group of players as far down as we all were after that game. I was also crying.'

Lyall finally left his shell-shocked players to face a sympathetic media. The Hammers' boss had seen too much in his life and career to do anything but treat success and failure with equal magnanimity.

Said John: 'I found out Liverpool were winning during the second half. Of course it's hard. My players are dog-tired. They go out and force a win like that, then they come in and an official says: "Sorry lads. Liverpool won."

'Don't cry for the team. Instead, be proud of what has been achieved. Don't be too disappointed. Think of what progress this side has made to get up among the big boys and give them a shock or two. And think, too, of what we can achieve with these players over the next two or three years. The future looks marvellous.'

More on that later. In the meantime, the *Daily Mail*'s Patrick Collins posted a fitting epitaph to the best season in Hammers' history: 'His [Lyall's] pride is not misplaced. West Ham have proved that attractive football can also be effective football. They have grown into the most appealing side in England and they carry the confidence that their ultimate reward has merely been delayed.'

And what of the players? Neil Orr reveals that Lyall relayed the Stamford Bridge score to them during the half-time break. Neil says: 'At half-time, even John told us that Chelsea were 1–0 up, so we went out for the second half in confident mood. Whether John did that just to keep us fired up, I don't know, but when we came in after winning 3–2, he just said: "I'm so sorry lads, Liverpool won." There was nothing else to say really and I just remember the dressing-room feeling totally drained.'

And no one was more exhausted than the club captain. Martin told reporters after the West Brom game: 'I'm so shattered, I have had to force myself out on to the field in our last few games. Each match has been agony for me, and I never want to go through it again. I need a rest – but I know I'm not going to get one. I fly out with England on Tuesday night to prepare for Mexico with special training. So it's going to start all over again. Bobby Robson has warned us he's going to run our legs off in the first week. I can't wait!'

With Liverpool still celebrating their eighth League Championship in eleven years, the final day of the season, Monday, 5 May, proved a massive anti-climax for both West Ham and their hosts, Everton. While Hammers' fans wallowed in self-pity, spare a moment's thought for the blue half of Liverpool. Howard Kendall's team had absolutely slaughtered Southampton, 6–1, at Goodison Park the previous Saturday but, like West Ham, left the field heartbroken. At least Everton still had the first-ever all-Merseyside FA Cup final to look forward to the following Saturday, which meant the men in blue shirts were fighting for Wembley places.

A draw would have been enough for West Ham to have sealed the runners-up spot but the Toffees had more spark left in them and went on to complete a comfortable 3–1 win to ensure they finished two points behind Liverpool, with Hammers third on 84 points. This final points haul would have won West Ham the title two years earlier, when Liverpool reigned supreme on 80 points, and again in 1983, when the same Anfield machine won it with 82.

Consolations were conspicuously hard to find at West Ham but it's a measure of just what they were up against that Ian Rush, the Anfield goalscoring legend, subsequently declared in his autobiography (*Ian Rush: An Autobiography*) that 'this was the best Liverpool side I ever played in'. From a player who achieved so many great things in his illustrious Liverpool career, that's some statement.

As the final match at Goodison quickly slipped beyond Hammers' reach, the only statistic that still mattered to McAvennie at the time was winning the Golden Boot. But the award for the First Division's leading goalscorer was snatched from him by Everton's Gary Lineker, who followed his hat-trick against Southampton with two early second-half strikes to further deflate the battered Hammers. Trevor Steven extended Everton's lead from the penalty spot in the 72nd minute but only the woodwork stood between West Ham and what would have been a cruel rout.

Cottee headed his 20th League goal in the last move of the game at a ground that would later become his second home. Lineker's last match double took him to 30 League goals – four more than McAvennie – before both strikers jetted off to the World Cup finals. 'I was gutted,' says Frank.

The only consolation for Cottee and McAvennie is that they became the third strike partnership in Hammers' League history to net at least 20 League goals each in a season. Their 46-goal haul put them up there alongside illustrious former greats Johnny Dick (27) and Vic Keeble (20), who amassed 47 in 1958–59 – and the greatest West Ham goal-getters of all, Vic Watson (29) and Jimmy Ruffell (20), who ran riot in 1928–29.

And as a further personal reward for a brilliant season, Cottee received the Fiat Uno Young Player of the Year award from former West Ham boss Ron Greenwood. Tony had to collect his trophy on the pitch at Wembley prior to the FA Cup final, where he and 96,000

BOYS OF '86

others watched Liverpool complete their first Double with a 3–1 win over their arch rivals, while Lineker's consolation came by way of a 40th goal in his one and only season for Everton prior to his £2.75m move to Barcelona.

Two days after the Cup final, an Upton Park crowd of 4,127 saw Cottee net the last goal in a 5–1 win for a Hammers side over Spurs in a benefit match for Gerhardt Ampofo. The central defender's career had been cruelly cut short by a badly broken leg he suffered a year earlier when he accidentally tangled with Neil Orr in a supposedly harmless keep-ball training session. The young central defender had broken the same leg three years earlier but this time doctors told the distraught teenager there was no way back. The gate raised around £11,000 for the grateful Ampofo whose plight perhaps put the disappointment of missing out on the title into perspective.

The Upton Park trophy cabinet was not completely bare, however. The reserves visited Reading for their final match already confirmed as Combination League champions. They had rattled up 31 victories and 141 goals, including a 10–1 drubbing of Swansea City in their penultimate home fixture.

Skipper Steve Potts, Paul Ince, Kevin Keen and Stuart Slater, in particular, had plenty to look forward to but for the first-team regulars it was a time for reflection. Where did it go wrong? Did Liverpool win it, or did West Ham – and Everton – blow it? These are the key questions that occupied the minds of supporters and players alike and still do to this day.

McAvennie says unhesitatingly: 'We lost the title at Forest and at home to Chelsea.'

Orr, singled out for most blame from the fans after the 2–1 home defeat by Chelsea in mid-March, countered: 'People say that the Chelsea defeat was crucial but I think you have to look at the bigger picture. There were other defeats that season, against Luton at home early on, and at Nottingham Forest at the start of April, so it didn't come down to just one match. It did disappoint me when people said we lost the title that night against Chelsea. Another thing that some people might not remember is that Liverpool won something like 12 of their last 13 games. That is an amazing run and we did well to keep with them all the way.'

Alvin Martin absorbs the overall picture in his assessment that far from throwing away the title, West Ham did astonishingly well to even get that close and third place was instead cause for celebration.

He says: 'There were two factors that season: we had few injuries and we also signed Wardie and McAvennie, while getting Dev back was like another new signing. Although it went right through to the last two games, I don't think we blew our chance. I think that we just weren't quite good enough. Looking at things now, I'm not disappointed because no other West Ham side has ever come anywhere near to winning the title. We came close to topping Liverpool around the time when they were champions of Europe. We achieved something and we're proud of it.

'Realistically, I don't think we felt that we could have won the Championship – we were just hanging in there all the way throughout the run-in. We were always aware that we couldn't come out and say: "We can't win this." We just kept going and we kept winning. Once it got to the last three games we did start wondering whether Liverpool or Everton were going to slip up.

'There were two great eras for me at West Ham. One was between 1979 and 1981 and the other was in '85–86. Both times, we sustained continued success. In the early '80s we were in a lower division. We lost four games in our Second Division Championship season, and every week we were looking forward to playing knowing that we had a better chance of winning than the other team.

'To a certain degree 1986 was the same. We made an impact on the pitch but we also had a good bunch of lads. Wardie and McAvennie came in and added something to the dressing-room. They both helped to create something. It was a good time. The 1980 FA Cup final is my most memorable day, because we actually won something. But the 1985–86 season was on a par achievement-wise.'

Vice-captain Stewart subscribes to the Martin view, saying: 'Liverpool were as dominant throughout the '80s as any other club in the history of English football, so for a club of West Ham's size and resources to be challenging them for first spot right up to the last Saturday of the season was one hell of an honour. Everton were a very good side, too.'

Gale, who, along with Phil Parkes and Mark Ward, played in all 42 League matches, says: 'For a balanced side, quite honestly, we were the closest West Ham have ever come to winning the League. We'd never, ever looked like doing that before. Liverpool and Everton both had much stronger resources then. It was a year when one jumped out of the chasing pack and it happened to be us.

'It's the biggest regret of my career that we didn't win the Championship that year. We couldn't have done much else to have won it. It was good to be hanging in there until the end of the season,

BOYS OF '86

looking to win the title rather than worrying whether we might go down. My dad went to every home and away game and it was the best football he's ever seen. And it was also the best football I've ever played in.'

Gale takes exception to former Hammers' manager Harry Redknapp's previous assertion that the squad he assembled for the 2000–01 season – which finished as low as 15th place and resulted in his sacking – was the strongest the club had seen for two decades 'since Brooking and Devonshire in the early '80s'.

Gale continues: 'What would our side have been worth in the transfer market today? People talk about Harry Redknapp's wheeling and dealing but John worked miracles there. Harry may have put together a good squad but it's getting harder. Fourth or fifth is probably the best teams like West Ham can hope for these days but our Hammers side had a good chance in the '86 season and we blew it.

'It rankles with me when people – Harry included – say today's team is the best West Ham have had for 20 years. They don't remember the 1985–86 side. It's all about the team over the season. It's not a fluke over 42 games, is it? I know we were lucky with injuries but I thought we were the best team in the Division. We played the best football.'

UEFA's five-year ban on English clubs competing in Europe, imposed after rioting by Liverpool hooligans at the 1985 European Cup final against Juventus led to the death of 39 Juve fans, only compounded Hammers' disappointment. It cost them an automatic UEFA Cup place and a return to European competition for the first time since 1981.

Gale says: 'Third place would have got us Champions' League football today. Can you imagine that '86 side competing in Europe? An attacking side, home and away, we would've been brilliant.'

Yet of the Boys of '86, only Tony Cottee was still playing competitive football when Redknapp's West Ham finally re-entered Europe, via the Intertoto Cup, in 1999.

History tells us that West Ham United's highest-ever League placing was third in 1985–86 but the experienced Geoff Pike supports Redknapp's claim that he played in an even stronger Hammers side at the start of the '80s.

Pike says: 'From the point of view of results, obviously the '85–86 team did better than any other West Ham side. But, individually, man for man, I'd say the 1980–81 side I played in was better. I don't think there is any comparison. I know we were in the old Division Two at the time but we performed like a top side from the First. After beating Arsenal in the Cup final, we won the Second Division title the following season, reached the League Cup final and got as far as the quarter-finals of the European Cup Winners' cup. We went out to Dynamo Tbilisi but achieved something very few other clubs did then – we won in Russia. I think Tbilisi went on to win the trophy that season, so it shows just how well we were playing then.

'If you look at the following season after getting promotion, we were second in October and didn't slip out of the top six until the start of December. That side had the ability to do as well, if not better, than the team of '86.'

Pike was a member of the Cup final team that beat Arsenal 1–0 but another appearance under the famous Twin Towers was lost to the Boys of '86.

Alan Dickens raises an unusual point, made by none of his former teammates, when he says: 'Everyone was so deflated after the West Brom game but if we had either drawn or won that game at Goodison, we would have played in the Charity Shield at the start of the following season, against Liverpool. I don't think anybody in the West Ham camp realised that at the time. I think we kind of went out there thinking it was the last day of the season and we were going on holidays the next day.

'Looking back, I am still bitterly disappointed, because I never played at Wembley. No one discussed that possibility before the Everton game – I didn't realise it myself – but it was a big thing for me, and for West Ham. I know the Charity Shield doesn't mean much to some people, but it was a showcase occasion and we could have been there. In the end, Liverpool won the Double, so they had to play the League runners-up – Everton – at Wembley. I'm still gutted about that.'

Fellow midfielder Devonshire insists Hammers were already shot before they reached Goodison. He says: 'Quite simply, we were running on adrenalin at the end of the season. I still believe that if we'd needed to beat Everton on the Monday to win the League, we'd have done it. We were so deflated after hearing the news about Liverpool on the Saturday. The chance to finish second just didn't motivate us.'

Gale and McAvennie would both go on to win a League Championship medal on either side of the border in the seasons ahead. Tony, at the age of 35, with Blackburn Rovers in 1994–95;

Frank as the star of his beloved Celtic in their 1987–88 Centenary Double season.

Asked to compare the West Ham United teams with those in which they won the Championship, this is how Gale's combined 'Dream Team' would look: Phil Parkes, Ray Stewart, Tony Gale (naturally), Alvin Martin, Graeme Le Saux; Mark Ward, Tim Sherwood, Alan Dickens, Alan Devonshire; Alan Shearer, Frank McAvennie.

'John Lyall would be the team manager ahead of Kenny Dalglish – but I'd have Ray Harford as my defensive coach,' he adds. At least Lyall finally pipped Dalglish to one honour. Gale played in 15 of Rovers' Premiership matches on their way to the title and lost only once (to runners-up Manchester United, who were denied the title by West Ham for the second time in three years). Ironically, he lost his place in the second half of the season to Ian Pearce, who would later move to Upton Park. But how did the Boys of '86 compare to Rovers' last great side?

'That West Ham side was the better of the two. We were far more entertaining and it was a crime we weren't on the telly more that season,' says Gale.

McAvennie didn't select a combined line-up (which he says would comprise mainly Hammers) but adds: 'It would have been a good game, but West Ham were probably the more skilful side, whereas Celtic fought very hard for every ball.

'Paul McStay was world class and if I picked a combined team he would definitely get into my midfield. I was very fortunate in my career that my three main clubs – St Mirren, West Ham and Celtic – all played football the way it should be played: on the ground. It was a joy to play with those players and the crowd were really great to me – even though they couldn't pronounce my name right to start with, but I'll forgive them that! I had two great seasons in my career – one at West Ham and one at Celtic.'

McAvennie, and Scotland, did not have a great World Cup but at least he was going to Mexico. He and Alvin Martin could console themselves with the fact that they still had their first World Cup finals to look forward to, while their West Ham club-mates headed to all corners of the globe for their summer holidays. Okay, so not everyone was relaxing on sun-drenched beaches in exotic climes – Gale and Parkes would spend the last week of May near Chichester, coaching kids at the Sussex Beach Holiday Village owned by the future Hammers chairman Terry Brown.

While they were there, McAvennie nipped off to the Algarve for a brief holiday that was not all it was cracked up to be. Frank explains: 'Alvin had to join up with the England squad immediately but I had a week off before meeting up with the Scotland boys. Jack Petchey, one of the West Ham directors, owned a time-share in Portugal and invited me to go over there and enjoy myself at his penthouse. All the boys at West Ham were saying that Jack never did anything for nothing, but I just put it down to the fact that he must have liked me.

'When I got out there, everyone I bumped into – including the people who worked at the complex – all greeted me like a long-lost friend. I thought this was strange. It was only when I walked into the reception in the apartment block that I realised what had happened. Knowing I'd be going out there to his place for a few days, Jack had already arranged to display a giant poster of me, promoting the name of the apartment complex, with the words printed big and bold: "We wish Frank McAvennie good luck with Scotland's World Cup campaign". I'd been stitched up by Jack. He had used my name to drum up interest in his holiday villas! I wouldn't mind, but he even locked the room where he kept all his booze. I tried climbing over walls and all sorts, but just couldn't get in there no matter how hard I tried!'

According to Sir Alf Ramsey, who is still the only man to lead England to World Cup glory, Cottee should have joined Martin in Bobby Robson's 22-man squad for Mexico. In a rare newspaper exclusive, the triumphant manager in 1966 wrote: 'I've run the rule over 50 players since the turn of the year and I'd feel happier with the 22 I've selected, and the team I've picked from them. My party includes Tony Cottee. It would appear he's not in Robson's [the squad had still to be officially confirmed], even though he is the in-form striker at the moment. I've left out Mark Hateley and Chris Waddle. I've gone for Stewart Robson, and not Steve Hodge.'

In another exclusive tabloid interview, Nottingham Forest's outspoken boss Brian Clough strongly argued the case for the inclusion of three Hammers in the England party. In addition to Cottee, Cloughie urged Robson to take Phil Parkes as his third goalkeeper (behind Peter Shilton and Chris Woods) and Mark Ward.

Controversial Clough wrote: 'Parkes has the lot. Ability, experience and he's in peak form. He's also 35 but so what? Shilton's 36. Ray Clemence, another candidate, is 37. Ward's name will shock most people, just like his rapid rise has surprised me. You watch the young man, whether in the flesh or on television, and think: where the hell did he come from?

'I'll tell you what, Ward can play a bit. All credit to John Lyall for spotting that. Cottee is only 20, yet his goalscoring record over two or three years speaks for itself. I prefer strikers of his type to the traditional English centre-forward.'

Parkes still firmly believes that Gale should have won international recognition. Phil says: 'Galey and Alvin played so well together at club level, they had such a good understanding, and should have been tested together for England. Tony was definitely good enough at the time to be given his chance – he fully deserved it – but a succession of England managers only seemed interested in the big, aggressive type of centre-halves.'

Gale himself admits: 'When Alvin was sitting in the bath after the Everton game saying how knackered he was feeling, I still felt fresh and thought to myself I'd love the chance to go to the World Cup. To be honest, I think Bobby Robson would have looked at someone like myself and, the way I liked to play the game, he'd have considered me a bit of a risk – in the same way a lot of people in the game thought Rio Ferdinand was a bit of a risky player to have at the back before Sven-Goran Eriksson took over from Keegan.

'England had a lot of big centre-backs. The likes of Terry Fenwick, Russell Osman and Steve Foster got in in front of me. But I thought Alvin and I could have done well together, in the same way that Butcher and Osman took their club understanding at Ipswich into the England set-up.'

Despite Clough's recommendation, Ward modestly didn't consider himself a contender for an England place in his first season at West Ham. He says: 'Everton's Trevor Steven wore the England number seven shirt and, anyway, the national team was generally made up of players who were playing for the biggest clubs. Maybe if West Ham had done well again the following season, I might have got a look in.'

Clough and Ramsey's advice fell on deaf ears, however. Martin and McAvennie were the only two West Ham stars to go to Mexico '86, a tournament best remembered for Argentine hero Diego Maradona's infamous 'Hand of God' goal (and his sheer brilliance on the ball) that sunk England in the quarter-finals and the sudden, unexpected emergence of Lineker as a world-class performer.

England had been far from impressive in their opening group F matches, losing 1–0 to Portugal and sharing a goalless draw with

Morocco before scraping through with a Lineker-inspired 3–0 win over Poland. So enter Alvin at the second round phase. The West Ham skipper acquitted himself well in a 3–0 victory over Paraguay in the Azteca stadium, Mexico City, on 18 June, before Robson inexplicably dropped him in favour of Terry Fenwick for the 2–1 defeat by Argentina, who went on to beat West Germany 3–2 in the final.

Scotland, as usual, fared worse than England, although they had at least reached round one for the fourth consecutive finals tournament. But it was group E for exit as the Scots lost to Denmark (1–0) and West Germany (2–1) before a consolation goalless draw with Uruguay.

The First Division's second leading scorer had to settle for sub appearances in the first two matches and didn't feature at all in the final game, much to his dismay.

'I still can't understand why Fergie didn't give me more of a chance in Mexico,' says McAvennie. 'I didn't have a bust-up with him or anything like that but he knew I had the hump after only being sub for the first two matches, so he left me out of the third one completely. Charlie Nicholas and myself should have been the main strikers but I think he picked the likes of Paul Sturrock and Steve Archibald instead. It didn't make sense to most people and, after the season I'd had at West Ham, I was very disappointed.

'I don't know whether Fergie went off me after we played a non-contact friendly against Northern Ireland just before the World Cup. I could understand that he didn't want any players to sustain injuries but I can't play non-contact matches – I want to be able to put myself about. I couldn't trap a medicine ball in a phone box that day. I had roomed with Graeme Souness leading up to the World Cup and when Souness was also dropped for the last game in Mexico, against Uruguay, none of us could believe it.

'Fergie called me a "maniac" in his book, but what did he ever win?' jokes Frank. But he points out: 'I'm privileged that Fergie even took me to a World Cup. That's an experience great players like George Best and Ryan Giggs have never had.'

Still, there was always next season to look forward to. A renewed challenge for the League Championship was the prime target at Upton Park as the summer rolled on. West Ham fans had been filled with unprecedented optimism and they couldn't wait for next season to start.

After years of mediocrity, under-achievement and too many seasons spent fighting relegation battles, there was now so much more to look forward to. Or so we thought.

Chapter 15

SPIRIT IN THE SKY – Dr and the Medics

Chart Position: Number 1, June 1986

John Lyall had no reason whatsoever to suppose that the 1986–87 season would be any less successful or exciting than the previous best-ever League campaign.

His Boys of '86 were in their prime, a potent mix of vibrant youth and classy experience. Only Phil Parkes (35) and Geoff Pike (34) were over the age of 30 and the manager saw no reason to replace any of his existing first-team regulars or, crucially, to make any significant new signings.

There was brief speculation that Hammers were set to bid around £300,000 for Birmingham City keeper David Seaman but nothing came of it. He later joined QPR instead before becoming England's undisputed number one at Arsenal.

Lyall himself stated, six games before the end of the 1985–86 season, that he could see no need to enter the transfer market and spend big. He told the *Evening Standard*'s Michael Hart: 'We've had a tremendous season and at the moment I don't feel the need to make signings in the summer. Unless a player of exceptional quality was to become available I could envisage starting next season with a side very similar to the one playing at the moment.'

Entering his 13th managerial season as the longest-serving one-club manager in the Football League, the 46-year-old Lyall confirmed there was money available to spend but he repeated his intent to stick with what he already had. He said: 'There is no point in buying players of similar calibre to the ones we have already because that simply closes the avenues to our youths.'

Lyall was counting on the continued emergence of Tony Cottee,

Alan Dickens and George Parris who were among the brightest young prospects in the country, while also anticipating continued good progress from reserve-team starlets Steve Potts, Paul Ince and Kevin Keen.

He was, however, expecting his strike-force of Cottee and Frank McAvennie to face a tougher test against defences reinforced by a third central defender. Lyall observed: 'The policy of playing with three central defenders was popular during the World Cup and several teams tried to play that way against us in the First Division last season. A lot of managers think that the extra man strengthens the middle of the defence and is the answer to the long-ball game that teams are playing now.'

Lyall, however, would keep faith with Hammers' traditional flat back four in the 4–4–2 formation favoured by most teams. Whatever obstacles they might encounter from opposition in the months ahead, the West Ham boss didn't need a crystal ball when he declared: 'Liverpool will be the team to beat.'

Ah, Liverpool. They had dominated English and European football for a decade, during which time they won the European Cup four times (1977, 1978, 1981 and 1984) and finished runners-up once (1985), won the League Championship eight times (1976, 1977, 1979, 1980, 1982, 1983, 1984 and 1986) and twice finished runners-up (1978 and 1985).

Liverpool were the biggest club in the country – and one of the biggest in Europe – and had the resources to buy the best available players, although they were not quite rich enough to dissuade top scorer Ian Rush from accepting an irresistible deal from Lira-laden Juventus as soon as the Reds pipped Everton and West Ham for the title.

Everton, who had managed to stem the Red tide to win the Football League in 1985, had no answer either when Spanish giants Barcelona came calling for Gary Lineker. They then had £2m at their disposal and spent it wisely enough to regain the Championship, ahead of their fellow Merseysiders, in 1987.

But throughout their long reign of supremacy in the '70s and '80s, Liverpool always maintained their trusted policy of staying one step ahead of their closest rivals by buying while they were still at the top. They used their status to attract top players and, as a consequence, kept their existing players on their toes. There was never any complacency at Anfield as Bob Paisley, Joe Fagan and Kenny Dalglish worked their magic from the inner sanctum of the famed boot-room.

BOYS OF '86

And once Liverpool had decided that a player could no longer quite perform up to the standards he had set previously, he was invariably moved out well before he reached his sell-by date. This is how the well-oiled Anfield machine worked and it served the club famously well for the best part of two decades.

Not until Arsenal snatched the title from their grasp on the last, dramatic night of the season in 1989, when West Ham had just dropped into the Second Division, did Liverpool's grip on the English game slip. In all fairness (a favourite phrase often used by Lyall), however, much of Liverpool's relative decline had to do with the Hillsborough disaster that devastated the club and Dalglish especially. To be fair to Lyall, he had adopted Liverpool's buying policy when he followed the 1980 FA Cup triumph, and a narrowly failed Second Division promotion campaign, by splashing a club record £800,000 on Paul Goddard, whose capture ensured the Second Division Championship and a return to the top flight nine months later.

However, West Ham were inactive in the transfer market throughout the summer of '86. The only movement at Upton Park was through the exit gates: Steve Whitton ended four years as a Hammer with a £60,000 move to Birmingham City and third choice keeper Johnny Vaughan joined Fulham for £12,500 without having played a competitive first-team game. The club also released youth-teamers Dean Crumpton, Andy Parr, Alan Spiers and Trevor Lake.

Lyall's biggest dilemma one day during that close season was not about who he should or shouldn't sign, but whether he should stay as manager at all. His momentary threat to quit came during the pre-season tour to Holland, where six players – Cottee, McAvennie, Ward, Martin, Gale and Walford – had broken an 11 p.m. drinks curfew. Cottee desribes in detail in his autobiography how the 'West Ham Six' had sneaked out of the back door of their hotel in The Hague and returned to a local bar where they drank alcohol until past 3.00 a.m.

They naïvely believed their drinking exploits had gone undetected by the Hammers' management – until Lyall called a team meeting the next morning and delivered his shock ultimatum. He demanded that the six players involved each paid a £50 fine, or else he would quit. No one hesitated to cough up the cash.

It was a particularly eventful trip for Walford, who had to be restrained by horrified passengers on the return flight to London after he began to overheat and tried to open one of the exit doors in search of fresh air!

West Ham were in need of fresh blood but the early season results disguised the problems that lay ahead. An opening day home win over Coventry City, when Gale finally scored his first for the club with a curling free-kick, was followed by an impressive 3–2 win against Manchester United at Old Trafford on August Bank Holiday Monday.

But the bubble soon burst. A goalless draw at Oxford United was followed by successive home defeats, by Nottingham Forest and then Liverpool, who strolled out 5–2 winners. A thrilling 5–3 victory over Chelsea in October revived memories of the excitement generated the previous season but three away draws and a dismal 3–1 home defeat by newly promoted Charlton Athletic had brought Hammers back down to earth with a bang.

Cottee and McAvennie, and the tactics employed to help them regain the goalscoring touch, were becoming predictable but the most significant factor in this decline was a worsening injury situation.

Whereas West Ham had gone through their best-ever season with hardly a serious injury to speak of, this time they encountered a catalogue of blows. Alvin Martin and Alan Devonshire both missed more than half the League campaign; Ray Stewart made only 23 First Division appearances; while Gale was sidelined for a month just as Alvin made his abortive comeback from his long-term foot injury. The central defensive partnership which had won the admiration of all in 1985–86, played only ten League games in tandem the following season.

Young midfielder Paul Ince had made a promising start to his career, scoring with a diving header past Peter Shilton on his home début in the win over Southampton on 6 December, but he was one for the near future. A week earlier, Hammers had been well beaten, 4–0, at Newcastle in front of the live TV cameras. And to rub salt into West Ham wounds, the Magpies – so badly humiliated in that eight-goal drubbing at Upton Park in April – had signed 27-year-old England international Paul Goddard for £425,000.

Lyall could no longer keep his most experienced striker happy after a year of bench-warming duty, so he reluctantly allowed him to further himself at St James' Park. All very admirable but it left Cottee and McAvennie without competition for places, or adequate cover. Luckily, Cottee – the only ever-present – McAvennie and Wardie played more games than anyone, so Goddard's departure was not truly felt until soon after the start of the following season, when McAvennie left.

By then, however, the Scottish international had lost the scoring knack that made him such a big sensation in his first season, when all he touched seemed to turn to gold. McAvennie underlines the value of just what Hammers were losing in Goddard when he says: 'I've often wondered how things might have turned out if Sarge hadn't got injured at the start of our good season. Maybe we would have gone on and done even better. John bought me to play in the hole, behind the two main strikers, and I could have enjoyed that.'

When the manager did finally re-enter the transfer market early in 1987, his team was already going nowhere in mid-table. He signed 22-year-old Stewart Robson from Arsenal for £700,000 in January 1987 and followed it three months later by paying Ascoli £100,000 to bring former Gunners idol Liam Brady back from his seven-year Italian exile. The ageing Brady, 31, was no longer capable of reproducing the brilliance that made him such a star at Highbury, Juventus and Inter Milan but he still showed glimpses of magic and certainly offered more than Lyall's other two newcomers.

Aberdeen's Tommy McQueen (£150,000), 23, was not the new man the players – or the fans – had in mind to fill the left-back position, while rough-and-ready centre-back Gary Strodder (£100,000), 21, from Lincoln City, was merely a stop-gap as injuries continued to hit hard.

It was a clear sign of West Ham's plight that Billy Bonds, the legendary old warhorse, came back after more than a year out to play nine of the last ten league matches at the age of 40. Not only was Bonzo still worth his place in that side, the veteran even won the fans' vote for Hammer of the Year after playing just 17 League games.

Robson, who was still trying to shrug off a long-term pelvic injury when he signed, finally made his début in a 3–1 win at Coventry, where Cottee scored all three, but West Ham lost six and drew one of their next seven matches. They could not even turn to the Cups for salvation, exiting at the fifth-round replay stage in both competitions. The 5–0 Littlewoods Cup stuffing at Tottenham only added to the pain Hammers' fans felt after a 4–0 League defeat at White Hart Lane on Boxing Day.

After Sheffield Wednesday ended Hammers' FA Cup hopes for the second successive season, being gifted a 2–0 win at Upton Park, Alvin Martin stepped off the treatment table to declare: 'Teams have sussed us out – now we are paying for it. We were hitting long balls over the top of defences for Tony Cottee and Frank McAvennie to run on to. But our opponents seem to have worked that out and now we've had to change the way we approach goal – and that's proving hard. It's ridiculous that we're in trouble like this.'

So what went wrong?

Martin's comments only echoed the fears that Lyall himself hinted at even before the last season had finished – that opposing defences would adapt to counter the threat of West Ham's pacy strikers by either dropping deeper to deny them space to run into, and/or play with a sweeper.

The best teams have flexibility but while Cottee in fact improved on his previous goals tally by scoring 22 in the League and six in the Cups, McAvennie managed only seven First Division goals in his second season, three of which came in the first four of his 36 matches.

Long-term injuries to experienced players undoubtedly proved very costly. But injuries are part and parcel of football; all teams suffer them at some stage and the fact that Hammers used only 18 players throughout the previous season was an unrepeatable fluke. The squad lacked real strength in depth during the club's finest season, but this was camouflaged by the absence of any serious injuries to key players. But from the start of 1986–87 it was significantly further weakened by the sale of Goddard.

It was easy to appreciate Goddard's frustration and his desire for regular first-team football, but should Lyall have been more selfish and kept the England international at Upton Park longer? It's easy to say yes, but the squad rotation systems favoured by the top clubs today were unthinkable then, when a manager always fielded his strongest team.

Talking to the Boys of '86, the majority agree that the two positions in the team that needed strengthening most at the end of their greatest season were that of left-back and the central midfield anchor role. Although former England Under-21 skipper Robson was bought to provide the steel and power alongside the more subtle skills and youthful vision of Alan Dickens, a role for which Cottee recommended him to Lyall, 'Robbo' did not endear himself to teammates as much as he did those fans who rewarded his bravery and work-rate by voting him Hammer of the Year – ahead of Ward in 1988.

Gale pinpoints the problem created by the arrival of Robson when he says: 'When he came and started trying to play the one and two-touch stuff we'd been used to, you could see he didn't have a clue. He was a good player in his own right but he wanted to be Roy of the Rovers and he stopped the pattern. He was a strong personality, too, and sent Alan Dickens into his shell. So, in effect, what we felt was

BOYS OF '86

going to be one of the best signings after his performances for Arsenal, turned out to be one of John's worst. I don't mean that offensively but Robbo was the wrong player for West Ham.'

Dickens was also critical of Lyall: 'The feeling was so optimistic before the '86–87 season. We knew we were a good side. I walked into pre-season training that summer and I had a strong feeling that we were going to do well. We weren't frightened of anyone. We were going to places like Liverpool and thinking "we can win here". We had the same mentality Man United have today. We should have built on that and when I look back through my mum's scrapbooks, you can see how well we did at the start of '86–87.

'I got taken off a few times and felt that I was the easy option. I felt I was doing it for the team, but Incey and Stewart Robson came in and everything was disrupted. People were no longer playing for the team. We went from fourth and nearly ended up being relegated. It had all gone. The good team spirit we'd had for the previous 18 months had disappeared. I don't like having a go at anyone but if you're being ruthlessly honest, the manager has to take responsibility. He brought in the wrong players. I'm not being nasty but bringing back Billy Bonds – as fit as he still was at 40 – was not the thing to do and didn't send out the right message to our fans.'

Devonshire, although a staunch Lyall supporter, also believes Robson was the wrong choice to take over the midfield position previously shared by Neil Orr and Geoff Pike. Dev says: 'I don't like to say it, but I think John put his feet under the table a little bit after the '85–86 season. I expected him to go out and get two or three high quality players to take the squad on to that next level and I was very disappointed when it didn't happen. Even if it was another young left-sided player, I wouldn't have minded, because I knew we had to add to the squad with young, keen players. People will say it's easy speaking in hindsight but I knew at the time that we had to strengthen. It's like Ipswich Town now. They need to attract as many good players as they can while they've got the pull and the good reputation. If they don't, they could easily struggle.

'We needed another central midfielder but we didn't get one until Stewart Robson came along halfway through the next season – and he just wasn't a West Ham player. Playing for West Ham was all about one and two-touch passing but Robson couldn't play that way. We didn't need Robbo. He wanted to take all the corners and throw-ins and play against the style we were used to. The fans loved him because he ran about, but they didn't realise that when he was on his arse, not winning the ball, we were all suffering in midfield.

'Allen McKnight was the worst keeper I have ever seen at that level and David Kelly just didn't want to know. They were players who didn't understand how things worked at West Ham and weren't prepared to fit in, so in the end we suffered.'

Neil Orr adds: 'It was so disappointing that we didn't move on from there and when I look back now, it was obvious the squad needed strengthening. There was no way we were going to have another season without any major injuries and unfortunately that proved the case.

'Maybe John was happy with what he had, or he just couldn't get the players he wanted that summer. I don't know. But had we built on the success of the 1985–86 squad, I'm sure the club would have gone on to even greater things.'

Martin identified the players West Ham should have been trying to bring to Upton Park for a renewed title challenge. He says: 'When you looked around the dressing-room you'd think: "Yeah, this is all right." But can you imagine what it would've been like if two or three top-quality players had come in. Liverpool, for example, always went out and bought two new players even if they'd just won the Championship. West Ham never got to that stage.

'The following season (1986–87) I had a problem with my knee. If that had been Liverpool they would have gone out and bought a top-quality centre-half. If I'd got fit I might not have got back into the side – but that would have been my problem.

'Even if you'd taken Frank McAvennie's goals away from the '85–86 season, you'd see that we would have struggled. As it happened, we didn't get any injuries and we had a good run all the way through. The following year we needed a central midfielder, a left-back and, possibly, another striker. If we wanted to be the best we needed to sign the likes of Graeme Souness or Steve McMahon, Stuart Pearce and Mick Harford. We'd have been strong. Instead, we tried to get through the 1986–87 season with what we already had. Over 22 years at West Ham I had some ups and some downs . . . and downs . . . and downs. We'd always been two players short. Always. We were forever trying to make do. We always felt we had eight good players but we always seemed to accept the other three without trying to strengthen those particular positions.'

Stewart agrees: 'I'd go along with Alvin. Maybe we lacked the steel of a Souness in central midfield. Both Neil and Pikey did a great job but that was an area we should have improved on the following season.

'Georgie Parris also did well but he was still very young and lacked the experience of Frank Lampard or the calibre of an international down that left-hand side. It's all right looking back, but it wasn't for me to tell John his job.'

Mark Ward reflects ruefully on his four years as a Hammer and wonders what might have been: 'I played with some great individual players at different clubs but as a team, I've never got anywhere near what we had in 1985–86. I really thought we were the footballing team at that time. It's easy to see it now but we should have invested in the future and added to the squad. Apart from a central midfielder and left-back, we should also have signed a striker to put more pressure on Frank and Tony.

'I was amazed how far I'd come. I'd played in every game of the club's best-ever season and I thought it was the start of a great career at West Ham. But it wasn't to be.'

A year after celebrating their highest-ever League finish, no one was feeling the club's fall to 15th place 12 months later more acutely than the ambitious Tony Cottee. Despite attaining his best-ever individual goals tally at Upton Park and breaking into the senior England team, Cottee was becoming increasingly frustrated – and it showed. His pent-up frustration erupted in a training-ground bust-up with Stewart and Bonds that led to a written transfer request, which was subsequently withdrawn.

Cottee stayed, and hoped, as all Hammers fans did, that the lessons from failing to strengthen the previous summer would be learned and that 1986–87 was no more than a temporary setback. But it wasn't a blip. West Ham United were now in steady decline. McAvennie and Cottee both left, for Celtic and Everton respectively, the space of less than a year, while injuries continued to affect key players and the replacements were simply not good enough.

After slipping down another place to 16th in 1988, and staying up with only one game to play, Hammers left it too late the following season. They fell through the relegation trapdoor and with it ended John Lyall's 34-year love affair with the club.

The Boys of '86 should be immortalised at Upton Park, because no West Ham United team, either before or since, has even gone close to emulating their achievements. And as most of the millions provided by Sky TV gravitate ever increasingly towards the handful of elite clubs, it is now almost impossible to visualise another genuine Premiership title challenge emerging from east London in the foreseeable future.

Chapter 16

IF YOU WERE HERE TONIGHT –
Alexander O'Neal

Chart Position: Number 13, March 1986

Football has changed almost beyond all recognition since the Sky revolution that saw the birth of the FA Premiership in 1992 – but not all the changes have been for the better. For many purists football is no longer a sport, but a money-obsessed business in which greedy players – and managers – have very little or no loyalty to their clubs or their fans and will readily jump ship to feather their nests elsewhere.

In the course of writing this book, we, the authors, met and interviewed the majority of the West Ham squad from 1985–86. Without exception, all the players look back on that period of their careers with great pride and satisfaction. They had a genuine and obvious affinity with the supporters and the club who paid their wages. Their empathy with the fans shone through again when we organised for 12 of the squad, and Rob Jenkins, to attend the Boys of '86 reunion dinner at the Prince Regent Hotel, Woodford Bridge in Essex, in May 2001. Of the first-team regulars that season, only Phil Parkes, who was on a family holiday, couldn't make it. Despite all efforts to find a suitable route by road and rail from his remote countryside retreat in northern France, the big man was disappointed that he was finally unable to attend. Holidays and other prior commitments also prevented Geoff Pike, Ronnie Boyce, Mick McGiven and the fringe squad members from attending the function but the rest couldn't wait to be there.

Ray Stewart and Neil Orr arrived on the same flight from

BOYS OF '86

157

Edinburgh and Frank McAvennie flew down from Newcastle. The reception they received from guests – a sell-out crowd of 300 – evoked memories of that final home game against Ipswich Town when 100 times that number cheered their heroes to the rafters.

As Del Howard, reviewer on the unofficial West Ham Online website, so aptly put it: 'The first thing that struck me was the team spirit, which was such a factor in that great season. Many of them hadn't seen each other for over ten years but it was clear that they were still united in the true sense. How many of the current squad do you think would turn up to a reunion in 15 years' time? Or, come to think of it, one year?'

The Boys of '86 turned back time. Hair was thinning (Paul Hilton could easily have been mistaken for Fabien Barthez) and waistlines were thickening, but the good humour and banter were still there. They revelled in the atmosphere of a unique occasion.

Autograph hunters, who had not bought tickets to the dinner, came from as far afield as West Yorkshire to congregate in the car park, armed with an endless supply of old scrapbooks and pictures they wanted the players to sign. And showing the respect that simply does not exist between players and supporters today, the Vintage Clarets put down their beers in the hotel bar to go and chat and sign for their loyal followers.

Once they sat down to their meal, the players' attempts to eat were constantly interrupted as they obliged fans with an autograph here and a photograph there. All without a murmur of complaint. They willingly talked at length with their supporters and some of the debates continued well into the small hours.

Times may have changed drastically in football, but the enduring Frank McAvennie had not lost the qualities that made him an icon: his good looks, his charm, his wit – and the ability to drain the plentiful bar stocks of any establishment. Frankie still keeps laughing at life and himself. In a rare moment of introspection, he reflects on a turbulent life that has brought him moments of great exhilaration and others of utter despair. He claims he has settled down in the North-east with Karen, who fits Frank's luscious, leggy blonde template to a tee in all but one distinct area: she is as smart as she looks and seems to have the measure of her new husband.

Speaking before their wedding in August 2001, Frank revealed: 'We've been together two years now and we're gonna get married.'

His past experience of marriage had not tarnished his view of the female species because, in the next breath, Frank recalled how he had recently received his divorce settlement following his split from Laura.

'She [Laura] went to live in Spain with my five-year-old son and although I speak to Jake on the phone every other day, it's not the same as seeing him regularly. A lot has happened to me over the last two years, what with the court case and everything, and I felt like shit. But now I'm very happy.'

As the book neared completion, Frank phoned our office again to check if his appeal (through the pages of *Hammers News* magazine) for West Ham memorabilia during his two spells at the club had produced any response. A couple of emails from fans offering replica shirts were duly passed on and let's hope Frank can replace some of the cherished items he lost. 'My old West Ham and Celtic shirts went "missing" in storage before I came up here, and I'm really gutted about that because I wanted to hand them over to my boy when he gets older,' explains Frank.

Some of the speeches at the reunion were filled with heartfelt emotion. As the West Ham Board agonised over a replacement for the recently departed Redknapp, the Boys of '86 stood in turn and offered their honest opinions on who the new man should be. Not surprisingly, Glenn Roeder's name wasn't mentioned.

The players' passion for the West Ham they all once knew came shining through. The caring, family club that, once you were a part of, you rarely wanted to leave. To a man, the players were very disappointed that they were not joined at the top table by their manager, John Lyall, a father figure to some of them. The invite went out to John but the man who most deserves the title 'Mr West Ham' politely declined, citing the same reasons he'd earlier given for not agreeing to an interview for this book. Eminently decent man that he is, John responded to our written invite by phoning our office to say: 'Hello, thanks, but no thanks.' He seemed almost embarrassed to continue resisting all pleas for him to reconsider. 'I wish you the very best with it, it should be a great night and give my regards to all, but I'm very sorry, I really can't make it.'

John returned to tending his acreage in a quiet corner of deepest Suffolk and one immediately felt a sadness that a great man of his calibre no longer has a place in modern football. He would never dare admit it, but you get the feeling that, deep down, John feels a little sadness, too. John insists that his absence from the event was not a snub to West Ham. After all, this was not an official club function and, of the current Upton Park staff, only press officer Peter

Stewart (whom John knows well and likes) was in attendance.

Whatever feelings John may or may not still have for the club (and those emotional ties will surely take some breaking) he clearly still has a lot of feelings for the players who gave him his finest season as a top-flight manager. John attended Phil Parkes' 50th birthday bash at the big man's Berkshire home last year and, just a couple of weeks before the dinner, he visited Scotland to see Ray Stewart's Stirling Albion in action.

The main entertainment at the reunion was provided by guest speakers Alvin Martin and Tony Gale, who could both forge a fine reputation for themselves on the after-dinner circuit, in between their present radio commitments for TalkSPORT and Capital Radio respectively. The backbone of Hammers' defence works as smoothly and entertainingly on stage as it did towards the summit of the English First Division 15 years earlier. Their self-deprecating humour deserves a wider audience and if a radio or television producer hasn't got the vision to put them together again, then he's more foolish than the barman who tried to refuse McAvennie's polite but persistent requests for a late drink.

Months after imprisoned former London gangland killer Reggie Kray lost his battle against cancer, West Ham's old version of 'Reggie' showed he had lost none of his cutting edge. Asking Tony Cottee to nominate his next West Ham manager, Gale passed the microphone to TC and said: 'And don't say yourself!' When addressing little Wardie, Gale asked whether his matching yellow shirt and tie were acquired at the Liverpool branch of Mothercare.

Alan Devonshire introduced a serious note to the proceedings when he expressed disillusionment towards modern professional football. The successful Maidenhead United manager turned his back on the pro scene some years ago and it's very hard to disagree with his honest views.

Dev says: 'As far as I am concerned, the game isn't any better now than it used to be.

'People say it's quicker but if that's the case, why are there 39-year-olds playing in the Premiership now? They are playing on perfect pitches, with light balls and aero-dynamic boots, so they are entitled to look faster. Nowadays, players only care about themselves. It's a case of: "Well, I'm all right, sod the other ten." It wasn't like that when I was playing for West Ham. We won and lost together and if one player was having a bad time, we all got together to help him through. Team spirit – that's why we were successful. No one ever tried to break that spirit, because if they ever stepped out of line, the rest of us would be on them like a ton of bricks, because we knew it would affect us all in the long run. And that's what happened at West Ham. John bought a few bad buys, like Stewart Robson, Allen McKnight and David Kelly.'

Pride did not allow Devonshire to put himself forward for the vacant manager's position that Glenn Roeder eventually filled after several more likely candidates fell by the wayside – 'That's for others to do,' he says. But the greatest left-sided midfielder in Hammers' post-war history would enjoy the challenge of working with the youngster who has the ability to emulate him one day.

Devonshire says: 'I would relish the chance to work with and coach Joe Cole. I've watched him over the past couple of years and I don't feel he is learning or progressing as quickly as he should be. As someone who played a similar kind of game to him, in terms of dribbling and running with the ball, I feel that I would be able to pass on good tips. I think he does too much sometimes, shows tricks when he shouldn't and that kind of thing.

'I learned not to do that by getting kicked. I sat back one day and thought: hang on, something's wrong here, I'm getting whacked all the time. The defenders knew I was going to beat them, so they just resorted to fouling me. I gradually realised that it would be a better idea to just play a one-two with a teammate and pop the ball behind defenders that way. That saved me getting kicked and I learned that there were only certain times when I needed to dribble with the ball.

'Joe hasn't got a settled position, as many young players haven't, but I would play him on the left. He's only 19. A couple of years out there wouldn't do him any harm at all. Especially with someone like Nigel Winterburn behind him, who would talk to him and encourage him when to pass and when to go.

'For some reason, playing on the left just opened the pitch up for me. It was just so comfortable, I could stay outside and use the flank, or I could cut inside onto my favoured right foot. That's where the danger is, because defenders don't expect it, and, more often than not, you are playing on their weaker side.

'So I really think Joe Cole would be lethal out there. It would all open up for him and being naturally right-footed, he would enjoy being able to cut inside. He hasn't got a fantastic left foot, but I didn't have either, and it's not a big problem if you are getting in behind defenders and are only looking to slide a pass across the box for your striker. At the end of the day, Joe's got strengths and weaknesses but

the more you work on both, the better all-round player you will become.

'I believe in individual coaching – I take the more skilful players at Maidenhead on their own after sessions to work on their game – and I would do that with Joe. If I was coaching him, I would take him on his own for half an hour or 45 minutes after training every day, just to fine-tune his skills and decision-making when on the ball. He knows that the main point of his game is running at players with the ball and beating them with pace and skill, so the next job is to find him a position where he can express that to the maximum. He also needs to work on the other parts of his game, because there will be days when he can't do what he wants, so suddenly he might need to do another job for the team.'

Devonshire speaks a lot of sense and the precocious Cole could do a lot worse than listen to the advice of a former great who has been there, seen it, done it.

But the final word here on the future and past of West Ham United goes to Alvin Martin, a giant of the club whose loyalty and dedication to the claret and blue badge is an example to all those players at West Ham today.

'It would have been lovely for our side to have won the title in 1985–86. I look at Manchester United now and I can't see West Ham taking them to the wire on the last Saturday of the season, but we did that with Liverpool and Everton. We achieved something that year.

'After all the ups and downs, all the trials and tribulations, I look back on the 1980 Cup final and the 1985–86 season and it's something that all West Ham fans will remember. I was at West Ham for 22 years and there are some 19 or 20 lost years that we aren't going to talk about. But I might be sitting on the beach in years to come, and a West Ham fan could still come over and talk about that FA Cup final and the season when we nearly won the League. I was a part of that.'

WHERE ARE THEY NOW?

PLAYERS

Phil Parkes
Aged 51. Still lives at Wokingham, Berkshire. Runs his own building company but maintains his football links by commentating for BBC Radio Lancashire when their featured teams are playing away in London.

Ray Stewart
Age 42. Lives in Gleneagles, Scotland. Ray left Livingston to manage on a shoestring at Stirling Albion, who were unlucky to be relegated from the Scottish Second Division at the end of last season.

George Parris
Age 37. Lives at Rottingdean, near Brighton, Sussex. Still visits Upton Park regularly as a reporter for the Press Association. Recently quit playing local non-league football to concentrate on coaching football and cricket in schools.

Steve Walford
Age 43. Continues to own a house near Highgate, London, but is now based in Scotland for most of the year. Moved from Leicester City to become assistant to manager Martin O'Neill at Celtic where, in his first season, Steve helped the Glasgow giants to win the Scottish Premier League, League Cup and Scottish Cup treble.

BOYS OF '86

Tony Gale
Age 41. Still lives at Walton-on-Thames, Surrey. Now well established as one of the most widely respected football pundits on radio, working regularly for Capital Gold Sport, for whom he hosts a popular phone-in show, and also occasionally Sky TV.

Alvin Martin
Age 43. Still lives at Gidea Park, near Romford, Essex. Another successful and highly respected radio and TV pundit, Alvin appears regularly on TalkSPORT and Sky TV. He also runs an office furniture business with his wife, Maggie, while developing as a newcomer on the after-dinner circuit.

Mark Ward
Age 39. Back living in his native Liverpool, Mark is looking to continue his new career as a football coach after unfortunately being sacked as player/manager at non-league Altrincham during the second half of last season.

Alan Dickens
Age 37. Still lives at Barking, just a few miles from Upton Park. Passed The Knowledge four years ago and gets up at 5.30 a.m. each morning to drive his black cab into central London to pick up fares. Retains his football links by coaching local boys' and youth teams.

Neil Orr
Age 42. Lives at North Berwick, to the east of Edinburgh. Neil is full time head coach at Edinburgh University – one of the most successful university clubs in that sphere of football.

Geoff Pike
Age 45. Still living at Gidea Park, Essex. Geoff is a regional director for the Professional Footballers' Association in the south-east, where he organises and runs coaching courses for YTS players who are starting out with pro clubs.

Alan Devonshire
Age 45. Still lives at Ealing, west London. Alan is the successful manager of Ryman League club Maidenhead United, who have regularly won League and Cup honours since he took over four years ago.

Frank McAvennie

Age 40. Now living at Gateshead, near Newcastle, Tyne and Wear. Frank is unemployed but retains his passion for football and plays regularly in charity matches and for the Hammers' six-a-side Masters team. Hopes to take up a coaching position in the game before long.

Tony Cottee

Age 36. Lives at Chigwell, Essex. After finishing the 2000–01 season with a brief loan spell at Millwall, following his earlier dismissal as player-coach at Barnet, TC announced on his 36th birthday in July that he was finally hanging up his boots to pursue various media interests.

Paul Goddard

Age 42. Lives at East Bergholt, near Colchester, Essex. After coaching Ipswich Town's FA Premier Academy Under-19s squad Paul returned to West Ham in the summer of 2001 as assistant to new manager Glenn Roeder.

Greg Campbell

Age 36. Lives at Hemel Hempstead, Hertfordshire. Greg was recently made redundant from the job he held as a chauffeur for many years. Recently took his FA coaching badge.

Paul Hilton

Age 42. Lives at Great Dunmow, Essex. Paul coaches Ipswich Town's Under-15 squad.

MANAGER AND COACHES

John Lyall

Age 61. Retired and living with his family on his 35-acre farm near Ipswich, Suffolk.

Ronnie Boyce

Age 58. Works full time as a scout for Tottenham Hotspur.

Mick McGiven

Age 50. Reserve team manager and coach at Chelsea.

BOYS OF '86

1985–86 STATISTICS

CANON LEAGUE DIVISION ONE

17 August, 1985
BIRMINGHAM CITY – 1 (Hopkins 65)
WEST HAM UNITED – 0
Att: 11,164
Blues: Seaman, Ranson, Roberts, Wright, Armstrong (Kuhl 56), Daly, Bremner, Clarke, Jones, Geddis, Hopkins.
Hammers: Parkes, Stewart, Walford, Gale, Martin, Devonshire, Ward, McAvennie, Goddard (Dickens 42), Cottee, Orr.

20 August, 1985
WEST HAM UNITED – 3 (McAvennie 10, 66; Dickens 24)
QUEENS PARK RANGERS – 1 (Byrne 54)
Att: 15,530
Hammers: Parkes, Stewart, Walford, Gale, Martin, Devonshire, Ward, McAvennie, Dickens, Cottee, Orr. Sub: Campbell
Rangers: Hucker, Chivers, Dawes, Waddock, McDonald, Fenwick, Byrne, Robinson (James 45), Bannister, Fereday, Gregory.

24 August, 1985
WEST HAM UNITED – 0
LUTON TOWN – 1 (Harford 48, pen.)
Att: 14,104
Hammers: Parkes, Stewart, Walford, Gale, Martin, Devonshire, Ward, McAvennie, Dickens, Cottee (Campbell 82), Orr.
Hatters: Dibble, Johnson, Thomas, Nicholas, Elliott, Donaghy, Parker, B. Stein, Harford, Nwajiobi, Preece. Sub: North.

26 August, 1985
MANCHESTER UNITED – 2 (Hughes 55; Strachan 75)
WEST HAM UNITED – 0
Att: 50,773

Red Devils: Bailey, Duxbury, Albiston, Whiteside, McGrath, Hogg, Robson, Strachan, Hughes, Stapleton, Olsen.
Hammers: Parkes, Stewart, Walford, Gale, Martin, Devonshire, Ward, McAvennie, Dickens, Cottee (Campbell 78), Orr.

31 August, 1985
WEST HAM UNITED – 2 (McAvennie 21, 71)
LIVERPOOL – 2 (Johnston 52; Whelan 83)
Att: 19,762
Hammers: Parkes, Stewart, Walford, Gale, Martin, Devonshire, Ward, McAvennie, Dickens, Cottee, Orr. Sub: Campbell.
Reds: Grobbelaar, Neal, Kennedy, Lawrenson, Whelan, Hansen, Johnston, Nicol, Rush, Molby, Lee.

3 September, 1985
SOUTHAMPTON – 1 (Curtis 52)
WEST HAM UNITED – 1 (McAvennie 81)
Att: 14,477
Saints: Shilton, Golac, Dennis, Case, Wright, Bond, Townsend, Curtis, Jordan (Lawrence 75), Armstrong, Wallace.
Hammers: Parkes, Stewart, Walford, Gale, Martin, Devonshire, Ward, McAvennie, Dickens, Campbell (Cottee 69), Orr.

7 September, 1985
SHEFFIELD WEDNESDAY – 2 (Chapman 18; Thompson 58)
WEST HAM UNITED – 2 (McAvennie 9; Cottee 88)
Att: 19,287
Owls: Hodge, Morris, Worthington, Smith, Lyons, Madden, Marwood, Thompson (Stainrod), Chapman, Jonsson, Shelton.
Hammers: Parkes, Stewart, Walford, Gale, Martin, Parris, Ward, McAvennie (Barnes 73), Dickens, Cottee, Orr.

14 September, 1985
WEST HAM UNITED – 3 (McAvennie 31; Devonshire 46; Cottee 70)
LEICESTER CITY – 0
Att: 12,125
Hammers: Parkes, Stewart, Walford, Gale, Martin, Devonshire, Ward, McAvennie, Dickens, Cottee, Orr. Sub: Goddard.
Foxes: Andrews, Williams, R. Smith, Ramsey (Jones), Osman, O'Neill, Kelly, Bright, A. Smith, Mauchlen, Banks.

21 September, 1985

MANCHESTER CITY – 2 (Lillis 10; Melrose 49)

WEST HAM UNITED – 2 (Cottee 7; McCarthy 41 o.g.)

Att: 22,001

City: Nixon, May, Wilson, Clements, McCarthy, Phillips, Lillis, Power, Melrose, McIlroy, Simpson.

Hammers: Parkes, Stewart, Walford, Gale, Martin, Devonshire, Ward, McAvennie, Dickens, Cottee, Orr. Sub: Goddard.

28 September, 1985

WEST HAM UNITED – 4 (Cottee 6; McAvennie 12, 20; Dickens 59)

NOTTINGHAM FOREST – 2 (Metgod 61; Clough 70)

Att: 14,540

Hammers: Parkes, Stewart, Walford, Gale, Martin, Devonshire, Ward, McAvennie, Dickens, Cottee, Orr. Sub: Goddard.

Forest: Segers (Walsh 13), Walker, Pearce, Butterworth, Metgod, Bowyer, Mills, Campbell, Clough, Davenport, Webb.

5 October, 1985

NEWCASTLE UNITED – 1 (Reilly 84)

WEST HAM UNITED – 2 (McAvennie 12; Cottee 25)

Att: 26,709

Magpies: Thomas, Haddock, Anderson, Davies, Clarke, Roeder, McDonald, McCreery, Reilly, Beardsley, Stewart.

Hammers: Parkes, Stewart, Walford, Gale, Martin, Devonshire, Ward, McAvennie, Dickens, Cottee, Orr. Sub: Parris.

12 October, 1985

WEST HAM UNITED – 0

ARSENAL – 0

Att: 24,057

Hammers: Parkes, Stewart, Walford, Gale, Martin, Devonshire, Ward, McAvennie, Dickens (Parris 35), Cottee, Orr.

Gunners: Lukic, Anderson, Sansom, Davis, O'Leary (Rocastle), Caton, Whyte, Allinson, Nicholas, Woodcock, Rix.

19 October, 1985

WEST HAM UNITED – 4 (McAvennie 23, 79; Cottee 34, 57)

ASTON VILLA – 1 (Stainrod 6)

Att: 15,034

Hammers: Parkes, Stewart, Walford, Gale, Martin, Devonshire,

Ward, McAvennie, Parris, Cottee, Orr. Sub: Keen.
Villa: Spink, Williams (Bradley), Dorigo, Evans, Ormsby, Walker, Birch, Stainrod, Gray, Hodge, Walters.

26 October, 1985
IPSWICH TOWN – 0
WEST HAM UNITED – 1 (Cottee 26)
Att: 16,849
Town: Cooper, Yallop, McCall, Zondervan, Cranson, Atkins, Gleghorn (D'Avray 50), Brennan, Wilson, Cole, Dozzell.
Hammers: Parkes, Parris, Walford, Gale, Martin, Devonshire (Potts 64), Ward, McAvennie, Dickens, Cottee, Orr.

2 November, 1985
WEST HAM UNITED – 2 (McAvennie 74, 81)
EVERTON – 1 (Steven 60)
Att: 23,844
Hammers: Parkes, Stewart, Walford (Parris 68), Gale, Martin, Devonshire, Ward, McAvennie, Dickens, Cottee, Orr.
Toffees: Southall, Stevens, Harper, Ratcliffe, Van Den Hauwe, Heath, Steven, Lineker, Sharp, Bracewell, Sheedy.

9 November, 1985
OXFORD – 1 (Aldridge 21)
WEST HAM UNITED – 2 (Cottee 38; Ward 68)
Att: 13,140
U's: Hardwick, Langan, Slatter, Trewick, Briggs, Shotton, Houghton, Aldridge, Charles, Hebberd, R. Brown (Brock).
Hammers: Parkes, Stewart, Walford, Gale, Martin, Devonshire, Ward, McAvennie, Dickens, Cottee, Orr. Sub: Parris.

16 November, 1985
WEST HAM UNITED – 2 (McAvennie 27; Ward 56)
WATFORD – 1 (Sterling 66)
Att: 21,490
Hammers: Parkes, Stewart, Walford, Gale, Martin, Devonshire, Ward, McAvennie, Dickens, Cottee, Orr. Sub: Parris.
Hornets: Coton, Bardsley, Rostron, Talbot, Terry, Sinnott, Sterling, Allen, Barnes, Jackett, Porter (Smilie 75).

BOYS OF '86

23 November, 1985

COVENTRY CITY – 0

WEST HAM UNITED – 1 (McAvennie 55)

Att: 11,042

Sky Blues: Ogrizovic, Borrows, Downs, Bowman, Rodger, Peake, Adams, McGrath, Evans (Turner 68), Gibson, Bennett.

Hammers: Parkes, Stewart, Walford, Gale, Martin, Devonshire, Ward, McAvennie, Dickens, Cottee, Orr. Sub: Parris.

30 November, 1985

WEST HAM UNITED – 4 (Cottee 12; Parris 31; Devonshire 47; Orr 66)

WEST BROMWICH ALBION – 0

Att: 16,325

Hammers: Parkes, Stewart, Walford, Gale, Martin, Devonshire, Ward, Parris, Dickens, Cottee, Orr. Sub: Whitton.

Baggies: Bradshaw, Nicholl, Cowdrill, Hunt, Bennett, Robertson, Grealish, Whitehead (MacKenzie 63), Varadi, Thomas, Crooks.

7 December, 1985

QUEENS PARK RANGERS – 0

WEST HAM UNITED – 1 (McAvennie 73)

Att: 23,836

Rangers: Barron, McDonald, Dawes, Robinson, Wicks, Fenwick, Allen, Fillery, Bannister (Rosenior 44), Byrne, Fereday.

Hammers: Parkes, Stewart, Walford, Gale, Martin, Devonshire, Ward, McAvennie, Dickens, Cottee, Orr. Sub: Parris.

14 December, 1985

WEST HAM UNITED – 2 (McAvennie 37; Stewart 40 pen.)

BIRMINGHAM CITY – 0

Att: 17,481

Hammers: Parkes, Stewart, Walford (Parris 45), Gale, Martin, Devonshire, Ward, McAvennie, Dickens, Cottee, Orr

Blues: Seaman, Ranson, Roberts, Hagan, Kuhl, Wright, Bremner, Dicks, Rees, Geddis, Platnauer.

21 December, 1985

LUTON TOWN – 0

WEST HAM UNITED – 0

Att: 14,599

Hatters: Sealey, Breacker, Thomas, Nicholas, Foster, Donaghy, Hill, B. Stein, Harford, Daniel, Preece.
Hammers: Parkes, Stewart, Walford, Gale, Martin, Devonshire, Ward, McAvennie, Dickens, Cottee, Orr. Sub: Parris.

26 December, 1985
TOTTENHAM HOTSPUR – 1 (Perryman 85)
WEST HAM UNITED – 0
Att: 33,835
Spurs: Clemence, Thomas, Hughton, G. Stevens, Mabbutt, Perryman, Ardiles (P. Allen 70), Falco, C. Allen, Hoddle, Waddle.
Hammers: Parkes, Stewart, Walford, Gale, Martin, Devonshire, Ward, McAvennie, Dickens, Cottee, Orr. Sub: Parris.

11 January, 1986
LEICESTER CITY – 0
WEST HAM UNITED – 1 (McAvennie 54)
Att: 11,359
Foxes: Andrews, Feeley, Morgan, McAllister, Osman, O'Neil, Lynex, Bright (B. Smith 65), A. Smith, Mauchlen, Banks.
Hammers: Parkes, Stewart, Walford, Gale, Martin, Devonshire, Ward, McAvennie, Dickens, Cottee, Parris. Sub: Pike.

18 January, 1986
LIVERPOOL – 3 (Molby 58 pen.; Rush 67; Walsh 70)
WEST HAM UNITED – 1 (Dickens 82)
Att: 41,056
Reds: Grobbelaar, Nicol, Gillespie, Lawrenson, Whelan, Hansen, Walsh, Johnston, Rush, Molby, Wark.
Hammers: Parkes, Stewart, Walford, Gale, Martin, Devonshire, Ward, McAvennie, Dickens, Cottee, Parris. Sub: Pike.

2 February, 1986
WEST HAM UNITED – 2 (Ward 62; Cottee 76)
MANCHESTER UNITED – 1 (Robson 25)
Att: 20,170
Hammers: Parkes, Parris, Walford, Gale, Martin, Devonshire, Ward, McAvennie, Dickens, Cottee, Pike. Sub: Goddard.
Red Devils: Bailey, Gidman, Albiston, Whiteside, McGrath, Moran, Robson (T. Gibson 70), Olsen, Hughes, Stapleton, C. Gibson.

BOYS OF '86

15 March, 1986

ARSENAL – 1 (Woodcock 76)

WEST HAM UNITED – 0

Att: 31,240

Gunners: Lukic, Anderson, Sansom, Williams, O'Leary, Keown, Hayes, Rocastle, Nicholas, Woodcock, Rix. Sub: Orr.

Hammers: Parkes, Stewart, Parris, Gale, Martin, Devonshire, Ward, McAvennie, Dickens, Cottee, Pike.

19 March, 1986

ASTON VILLA – 2 (Hodge 38, 78)

WEST HAM UNITED – 1 (Hunt 2 o.g.)

Att: 11,579

Villa: Spink, Dorigo, Evans, Ormsby, Elliott, Hunt, Blair, Shaw, Gray, Hodge, Walters.

Hammers: Parkes, Parris, Walford, Gale, Martin, Orr, Ward, McAvennie, Dickens, Cottee (Goddard 76), Pike.

22 March, 1986

WEST HAM UNITED – 1 (McAvennie 6)

SHEFFIELD WEDNESDAY – 0

Att: 16,604

Hammers: Parkes, Stewart, Parris, Gale, Martin, Orr, Ward, McAvennie, Dickens, Cottee (Goddard 82), Pike.

Owls: Hodge, Sterland, Morris, Hart, Shirtliff, Worthington, Marwood, Megson, Thompson, Shutt, Snodin.

29 March, 1986

CHELSEA – 0

WEST HAM UNITED – 4 (Devonshire 23; Cottee 55, 64; McAvennie 68)

Att: 29,555

Blues: Godden, Wood, Rougvie, Pates, McLaughlin, Bumstead (Hazard 66), Nevin, Spackman, Lee, Speedie, McAllister.

Hammers: Parkes, Stewart, Parris, Gale, Hilton, Devonshire (Orr 77), Ward, McAvennie, Dickens, Cottee, Pike.

31 March, 1986

WEST HAM UNITED – 2 (Cottee 17, McAvennie 43)

TOTTENHAM HOTSPUR – 1 (Ardiles 22)

Att: 27,565

Hammers: Parkes, Stewart, Parris, Gale, Hilton, Devonshire (Orr 86),

Ward, McAvennie, Dickens, Cottee, Pike.
Spurs: Clemence, P. Allen, Thomas, Roberts, Miller, G. Stevens, Mabbutt, Falco, Galvin, Ardiles (C. Allen 72), Waddle.

2 April, 1986
NOTTINGHAM FOREST – 2 (Metgod 39, Rice 88)
WEST HAM UNITED – 1 (Cottee 69)
Att: 17,498
Forest: Sutton, Fleming, Pearce, Walker, Metgod, Bowyer, Carr, Webb, Clough, Campbell, Rice.
Hammers: Parkes, Stewart, Parris, Gale, Martin, Orr, Ward, McAvennie, Dickens, Cottee, Pike. Sub: Hilton.

8 April, 1986
WEST HAM UNITED – 1 (Martin 26)
SOUTHAMPTON – 0
Att: 22,459
Hammers: Parkes, Stewart, Parris, Gale, Martin, Devonshire, Ward, McAvennie, Dickens, Cottee, Pike. Sub: Orr.
Saints: Shilton, Forrest, Dennis, Case, Townsend, Bond, Holmes, Cockerill, Jordan, Armstrong, Puckett (Whitlock).

12 April, 1986
WEST HAM UNITED – 3 (Trewick 49 o.g.; McAvennie 65; Stewart 81 pen.)
OXFORD UNITED – 1 (Houghton 13)
Att: 23,956
Hammers: Parkes, Stewart, Parris, Gale, Martin, Devonshire, Ward, McAvennie, Dickens, Cottee, Pike. Sub: Orr.
U's: Judge, Langan, Trewick, Phillips, Briggs, Shotton, Houghton, Aldridge, Hamilton (Charles 68), Hebberd, Perryman.

15 April, 1986
WEST HAM UNITED – 1 (Cottee 51)
CHELSEA – 2 (Spackman 55; Nevin 78)
Att: 29,361
Hammers: Parkes, Stewart, Parris, Gale (Orr 45), Martin, Devonshire, Ward, McAvennie, Dickens, Cottee, Pike.
Blues: Godden, Wood, Millar, Rougvie, McLaughlin, Bumstead (McAllister), Nevin, Spackman, Dixon, Hazard, Murphy.

19 April, 1986
WATFORD – 0

BOYS OF '86

WEST HAM UNITED – 2 (Cottee 59; McAvennie 89)
Att: 16,651
Hornets: Coton, Gibbs, Franklin (Smilie 83), Talbot, Terry, McClelland, Sterling, Bardsley, West, Jackett, Barnes.
Hammers: Parkes, Stewart, Parris, Gale, Martin, Devonshire, Ward, McAvennie, Dickens, Cottee, Orr. Sub: Hilton.

21 April, 1986
WEST HAM UNITED – 8 (Martin 3, 64, 84 pen.; Stewart 11; Orr 35; Roeder 43 o.g.; Goddard 81; McAvennie 83)
NEWCASTLE UNITED – 1 (Whitehurst 76)
Att: 24,735
Hammers: Parkes, Stewart, Parris, Gale, Martin, Devonshire, Ward, McAvennie, Dickens (Goddard 80), Cottee, Orr.
Magpies: Thomas (Stewart 45), McDonald, Bailey, McCreery, Anderson, Roeder, Stephenson, Hedworth, Whitehurst, Beardsley, Cunningham.

26 April, 1986
WEST HAM UNITED – 1 (Cottee 61)
COVENTRY CITY – 0
Att: 27,251
Hammers: Parkes, Stewart, Parris, Gale, Martin, Devonshire, Ward, McAvennie, Dickens, Cottee, Orr. Sub: Goddard.
Sky Blues: Ogrizovic, Borrows, Downs, McGrath, Kilcline, Peake, Bennett, Brazil, Regis, Pickering, Adams.

28 April, 1986
WEST HAM UNITED – 1 (Stewart 19 pen)
MANCHESTER CITY – 0
Att: 27,153
Hammers: Parkes, Stewart, Parris, Gale, Martin, Devonshire, Ward, McAvennie, Dickens, Cottee, Orr. Sub: Goddard.
City: Siddall, Phillips, May, Reid, McCarthy, Wilson, Lillis, McIlroy, Davies, McNab, Simpson (Beckford).

30 April, 1986
WEST HAM UNITED – 2 (Dickens 72; Stewart 82 pen.)
IPSWICH TOWN – 1 (Wilson 63)
Att: 31,121
Hammers: Parkes, Stewart, Parris, Gale, Martin, Devonshire, Ward, McAvennie, Dickens, Cottee, Orr (Goddard 70).
Town: Cooper, Atkins (Yallop), McCall, Parkin, Cranson, Butcher, Gleghorn, Brennan, Dozzell, Wilson, Cole.

3 May, 1986
WEST BROMWICH ALBION – 2 (Madden 30; Reilly 64 pen.)
WEST HAM UNITED – 3 (McAvennie 6; Cottee 24; Stewart 82 pen.)
Att: 17,651
Baggies: Naylor, Whitehead, Statham, Cowdrill, Dyson, Palmer, Dickinson, MacKenzie (Robson 37), Reilly, Madden, Bradley.
Hammers: Parkes, Stewart, Parris, Gale, Martin, Devonshire, Ward, McAvennie, Dickens, Cottee, Orr. Sub: Goddard.

5 May, 1986
EVERTON – 3 (Lineker 42, 47; Steven 72 pen.)
WEST HAM UNITED – 1 (Cottee 89)
Att: 40,073
Toffees: Mimms, Stevens, Van Den Hauwe, Mountfield, Biling, Richardson, Steven, Lineker (Aspinall 75), Wilkinson, Heath, Sheedy.
Hammers: Parkes, Stewart, Parris, Gale, Martin, Devonshire, Ward, McAvennie, Dickens (Goddard 70), Cottee, Orr.

MILK CUP

24 September, 1985
Second Round, First Leg
WEST HAM UNITED – 3 (Cottee 49; McAvennie 56; Stewart 90 pen.)
SWANSEA CITY – 0
Att: 9,282
Hammers: Parkes, Stewart, Walford, Gale, Martin, Devonshire, Ward, McAvennie, Dickens, Cottee, Orr. Sub: Goddard.
Swans: Rimmer, Lewis, Sullivan, Price, Stevenson, Marustik, Hutchinson, Randell, Turner, Harrison, Pascoe.

BOYS OF '86

8 October, 1985
Second Round, Second Leg
SWANSEA CITY – 2 (Waddle 6; Randell 23)
WEST HAM UNITED – 3 (Stewart 11 pen., 43 pen.; Cottee 13)
Att: 3,584
Swans: Hughes, Sharpe, Sullivan, Price, McHale, Harrison, Hutchinson, Randell, Turner, Waddle (Stevenson), Pascoe.
Hammers: Parkes, Stewart, Walford, Gale, Martin, Devonshire, Ward, McAvennie (Parris 17), Dickens, Cottee, Orr.

24 October, 1986
Third Round
MANCHESTER UNITED – 1 (Whiteside 77)
WEST HAM UNITED – 0
Att: 32,057
Red Devils: Bailey, Duxbury (Brazil 35), Albiston, Whiteside, Moran, Hogg, McGrath, Olsen, Hughes, Stapleton, Barnes.
Hammers: Parkes, Stewart, Walford, Gale, Martin, Devonshire, Ward, McAvennie, Dickens (Parris 79), Cottee, Orr.

FA CUP

5 January, 1986
Third Round
CHARLTON ATHLETIC – 0
WEST HAM UNITED – 1 (Cottee 88)
Att: 13,037
Addicks: Johns, Humphrey, Reid, Curbishley, Thompson, Pender, Gritt, Lee, Pearson, Aizlewood, Flanagan.
Hammers: Parkes, Stewart, Walford, Gale, Devonshire, Ward, McAvennie, Dickens, Cottee, Parris. Sub: Pike.

25 January, 1986
Fourth Round
WEST HAM UNITED – 0
IPSWICH TOWN – 0
Att: 25,035
Hammers: Parkes, Stewart, Walford (Goddard 80), Gale, Martin, Devonshire, Ward, McAvennie, Dickens, Cottee, Parris.

Town: Cooper, Yallop, McCall, Stockwell (Zondervan 75), Cranson, Butcher, Putney, Brennan, D'Avray, Wilson, Dozzell.

4 February, 1986
Fourth Round Replay
IPSWICH TOWN – 1 (Dozzell 93)
WEST HAM UNITED – 1 (Cottee 106)
Att: 25,384
Town: Cooper, Yallop, McCall, Zondervan, Cranson, Butcher, Putney (Cole 62), Brennan, D'Avray, Wilson, Dozzell.
Hammers: Parkes, Parris, Walford (Orr 90), Gale, Martin, Devonshire, Ward, McAvennie, Dickens, Cottee, Pike.

6 February, 1986
Fourth Round, Second Replay
IPSWICH TOWN – 0
WEST HAM UNITED – 1 (Cottee 111)
Att: 14,515
Town: Cooper, Yallop, McCall, Zondervan, Cranson, Butcher, Putney (Stockwell 105), Brennan, D'Avray, Wilson, Dozzell.
Hammers: Parkes, Stewart, Parris, Gale, Martin, Orr, Ward, McAvennie, Dickens, Cottee, Pike. Sub: Goddard.

5 March, 1986
Fifth Round
WEST HAM UNITED – 1 (McAvennie 25)
MANCHESTER UNITED – 1 (Stapleton 73)
Att: 26,441
Hammers: Parkes, Stewart, Parris, Gale, Martin, Devonshire, Ward, McAvennie, Dickens, Cottee, Pike. Sub: Orr.
Red Devils: Turner, Duxbury, Albiston, Whiteside, McGrath, Moran, Robson (Olsen), Strachan, Hughes, Stapleton, C. Gibson.

9 March, 1986
Fifth Round Replay
MANCHESTER UNITED – 0
WEST HAM UNITED – 2 (Pike 18; Stewart 54 pen.)
Att: 30,441
Red Devils: Turner, Duxbury, Albiston, Whiteside, McGrath, Higgins, (Blackmore 76), Olsen, Strachan, Hughes, Stapleton, C.Gibson.

Hammers: Parkes, Stewart, Parris, Gale, Martin, Devonshire, Ward, McAvennie, Dickens, Cottee, Pike. Sub: Orr.

12 March, 1986
Sixth Round
SHEFFIELD WEDNESDAY – 2 (Worthington 16; Shutt 35)
WEST HAM UNITED – 1 (Cottee 48)
Att: 35,522
Owls: Hodge, Sterland, Morris, Smith, Shirtliff, Worthington, Marwood, (Chamberlain), Megson, Chapman, Shutt, Snodin.
Hammers: Parkes, Stewart, Parris, Gale, Martin, Devonshire, Ward, McAvennie, Dickens, Cottee, Pike. Sub: Orr.

APPEARANCE RECORD

Player	Appearances							
	LGE	SUB	LC	SUB	FAC	SUB	TOTAL	SUB
Barnes, Bobby		1						1
Campbell, Greg	1	2					1	2
Cottee, Tony	41	1	3		7		51	1
Devonshire, Alan	38		3		6		47	
Dickens, Alan	40	1	3		7		50	1
Gale, Tony	42		3		7		52	
Goddard, Paul	1	5		1		1	1	7
Hilton, Paul	2						2	
McAvennie, Frank	41		3		7		51	
Martin, Alvin	40		3		7		50	
Orr, Neil	33	3	3		1	1	37	4
Parkes, Phil	42		3		7		52	
Parris, George	23	3		2	7		30	5
Pike, Geoff	10				5		15	
Potts, Steve		1						1
Stewart, Ray	39		3		6		48	
Walford, Steve	27		3		3		33	
Ward, Mark	42		3		7		52	
(18 players used)								

BOYS OF '86

GOAL RECORD

Player	Goals			
	LGE	LC	FAC	TOTAL
Barnes, Bobby				
Campbell, Greg				
Cottee, Tony	20	2	4	26
Devonshire, Alan	3			3
Dickens, Alan		4		4
Gale, Tony				
Goddard, Paul	1			1
Hilton, Paul				
McAvennie, Frank	26	1	1	28
Martin, Alvin	4			4
Orr, Neil	2			2
Parkes, Phil				
Parris, George	1			1
Pike, Geoff			1	1
Potts, Steve				
Stewart, Ray	6	3	1	10
Walford, Steve				
Ward, Mark	3			3
(own goals)	4			4
Total	74	6	7	87

CANON LEAGUE DIVISION ONE FINAL TABLE

POS	TEAM	P	Home					Away					PTS
			W	D	L	F	A	W	D	L	F	A	
1	Liverpool	42	16	4	1	58	14	10	6	5	31	23	88
2	Everton	42	16	3	2	54	18	10	5	6	33	23	86
3	**West Ham**	42	17	2	2	48	16	9	4	8	26	24	84
4	Man Utd	42	12	5	4	35	12	10	5	6	35	24	76
5	Sheffield Wed	42	13	6	2	36	23	8	4	9	27	31	73
6	Chelsea	42	12	4	5	32	27	8	7	6	25	29	71
7	Arsenal	42	13	5	3	29	15	7	4	10	20	32	69
8	Nottm Forest	42	11	5	5	38	25	8	6	7	31	28	68
9	Luton	42	12	6	3	37	15	6	6	9	24	29	66
10	Tottenham	42	12	2	7	47	25	7	6	8	27	27	65
11	Newcastle	42	12	5	4	46	31	5	7	9	21	41	63
12	Watford	42	11	6	4	40	22	5	5	11	29	40	59
13	QPR	42	12	3	6	33	20	3	4	14	20	44	52
14	Southampton	42	10	6	5	32	18	2	4	15	19	44	46
15	Man City	42	7	7	7	25	26	4	5	12	18	31	45
16	Aston Villa	42	7	6	8	27	28	3	8	10	24	39	44
17	Coventry	42	6	5	10	31	35	5	5	11	17	36	43
18	Oxford	42	7	7	7	34	27	3	5	13	28	53	42
19	Leicester	42	7	8	6	35	35	3	4	14	19	41	42
20	Ipswich	42	8	5	8	20	24	3	3	15	12	31	41
21	Birmingham	42	5	2	14	13	25	3	3	15	17	48	29
22	West Brom	42	3	8	10	21	36	1	4	16	14	53	24

OTHER INFORMATION

Double wins: (8) – QPR, Leicester City, Newcastle United, Ipswich Town, Oxford United, Watford, Coventry City, West Bromwich Albion.

Double Losses: (0)

Won from behind: (7) – Aston Villa (h), Everton (h), Oxford United (h & a), Manchester United (h), Ipswich Town (h), Swansea City – LC (a).

Loss from in front: (2) Aston Villa (a), Chelsea (h).

Hammer of the Year: Tony Cottee.

Ever-presents: (3) – Tony Gale, Phil Parkes, Mark Ward.

Hat-tricks: (1) – Alvin Martin.

Leading scorer: (28) – Frank McAvennie.

SIGN OF THE TIMES

JULY 1985

4th – Thirteen-year-old Maths genius Ruth Lawrence wins a first-class degree at Oxford University.

7th – German tennis sensation Boris Becker becomes the youngest player to win the Men's Singles title at Wimbledon, at the age of 17.

8th – Southampton manager Lawrie McMenemy leaves The Dell to take over as boss at Sunderland.

9th – A tribunal decides that Spurs must pay Newcastle United £590,000 for the services of winger Chris Waddle.

10th – Scottish striker Andy Gray returns to Aston Villa from Everton for £150,000. Villa had sold Gray for £1.4 million to Wolves in 1979.

10th – Greenpeace ship the *Rainbow Warrior* is destroyed by explosions in Auckland Harbour, New Zealand.

13th – An estimated 70 million dollars is raised for the famine victims in Africa, thanks to the Live Aid concerts in London and Philadelphia, organised by Boomtown Rat, Bob Geldof.

15th – Spurs striker Garth Crooks joins West Bromwich Albion for £100,000.

22nd – It is reported that 250 of the PFA's 1,750 members are still without a club – the highest number of unemployed professional footballers since the war.

23rd – Everton pay Leicester City £800,000 for striker Gary Lineker and must also hand over a third of the profit if they sell him on within two years.

BOYS OF '86

25th – The Government's Bill to ban alcohol at sporting events is given the royal assent and becomes an Act of Parliament.

28th – England's 1966 World Cup winning team beat their old West German opponents 6–4 in a nostalgic game played at Leeds for the victims of the Bradford fire disaster. Geoff Hurst, 46, repeats his hat-trick of 19 years earlier.

29th – The FA fine Birmingham City £5,000 in connection with the riot at their game against Leeds United last season, when a teenage boy was killed by a falling wall.

30th – In a meeting at 10 Downing Street, football leaders agree to urge the clubs to introduce identity cards.

HIT SINGLES
'Frankie' Sister Sledge
'Suddenly' Billy Ocean
'Axel F' Harold Faltermeyer
'Cherish' Kool and the Gang
'Johnny Come Home' Fine Young Cannibals
'There Must Be An Angel' (Playing With My Heart) Eurythmics
'Into The Groove' Madonna

AUGUST 1985

4th – A crowd of 13,567 turn up at White Hart Lane for Glenn Hoddle's testimonial match between Spurs and Arsenal, earning the England midfielder around £50,000.

7th – Despite the deadlock over football on TV, an agreement is reached to show highlights of the FA Charity Shield match because part of the proceeds will go to the Bradford Disaster Fund.

8th – South African police kill 18 blacks.

8th – UEFA reject Liverpool's appeal against their ban in Europe.

10th – Everton secure a 2–0 victory over Manchester United in the FA Charity Shield at Wembley.

10th – Leicester City sign Motherwell midfielder Gary McAllister.

13th – Jack Charlton resigns as manager of Newcastle United.

23rd – Luton Town announce they are going ahead with their plan to ban all away supporters from Kenilworth Road.

27th – Former Hammers hero Bryan 'Pop' Robson takes over as manager at Carlisle United.

29th – Alcohol restrictions at football grounds lose Luton £5,000 sponsorship deal for their home game with Chelsea on 7 September.

HIT SINGLES
'We Don't Need Another Hero' Tina Turner
'Money For Nothing' Dire Straits
'Holiday' Madonna
'I Got You Babe' UB40/Chrissie Hynde
'White Wedding' Billy Idol

SEPTEMBER 1985

1st – The wreck of the *Titanic* is found off Newfoundland.

2nd – Khmer Rouge leader Pol Pot retires.

5th – More clubs drop out of the new Football League Competition – the Full Members' Cup – which is launched with only 27 First and Second Division clubs. Critics accuse the League of greed and cluttering fixtures in a critical World Cup season.

6th – Aston Villa midfielder Steve McMahon signs for Liverpool for £350,000, two years after turning down the Reds when moving from Everton to Villa Park.

10th – Although Scotland draw with Wales to earn a World Cup play-off against Australia, tragedy strikes as Scottish manager Jock Stein collapses and dies of a heart attack in the Cardiff dug-out, aged 62.

10th – Newcastle United appoint Willie McFaul as their new manager.

11th – England are held to a 1–1 draw by Romania in a World Cup qualifying match and still need one point to book their trip to Mexico.

17th – Fashion designer Laura Ashley dies in a fall.

19th – A massive earthquake devastates Mexico City, 20,000 die, just months before the country is due to stage the World Cup finals.

21st – Charlton Athletic play what may be their last game at the Valley, beating Stoke City 2–0. The ground is closed because many parts are extremely unsafe.

22nd – FIFA confirm that the recent earthquakes in Mexico will not prevent the 1986 World Cup finals from taking place there.

29th – West Brom manager Johnny Giles resigns after nine defeats in a row.

HIT SINGLES
'Dancing In The Street' Mick Jagger/David Bowie
'Drive' Cars
'Running Up That Hill' Kate Bush
'Tarzan Boy' Baltimora
'Holding Out For a Hero' Bonnie Tyler
'Part Time Lover' Stevie Wonder

OCTOBER 1985
2nd – Film actor Rock Hudson dies after a long fight against AIDS.
His death sparks a new worldwide awareness about the disease.

5th – Manchester United fail to equal Tottenham's 25-year record for
the most number of consecutive wins at the start of a season. After
winning ten on the spin, they can only manage a 1–1 draw at
Luton.

7th – Riots erupt in Tottenham after a black woman, Cherry Groce,
is shot during a police raid. The riots force the postponement of
two Spurs matches.

10th – Two massive names in the film world, Orson Welles and Yul
Brynner, die in the US.

15th – Aberdeen manager Alex Ferguson is confirmed as Scotland's
caretaker boss following the death of Jock Stein.

16th – England stuff Turkey 5–0 at Wembley to secure qualification
to the World Cup finals in Mexico.

27th – English clubs seek guidance from the Football League after
the Scottish FA ask them to release players for their World Cup
play-off against Australia next month.

30th – Brian Clough returns to his former club Derby County, as
Nottingham Forest face the Third Division Rams in the League
Cup third round and win 2–1.

HIT SINGLES
'If I Was' Midge Ure
'The Power of Love' Jennifer Rush
'The Power of Love' Huey Lewis and the News
'She's So Beautiful' Cliff Richard
'Take On Me' A-Ha
'Alive And Kicking' Simple Minds
'Miami Vice Theme' Jan Hammer

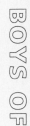

BOYS OF '86

NOVEMBER 1985

1st – Further talks between the League and TV companies end without agreement.

4th – Liverpool and Manchester United refuse to release their Scottish internationals for Scotland's trip to Australia.

8th – The first life sentence ever imposed on a football hooligan is given to a Chelsea 'fan' at the Old Bailey, following severe violence at a game between Chelsea and Manchester United last December.

9th – Russian Gary Kasparov, 22, becomes World Chess Champion.

11th – Twelve of the top clubs meet to finalise plans to be put before the Football League for a new Super League. They want a First Division of 20 clubs only.

13th – England draw 0–0 with Northern Ireland at Wembley, a result that guarantees the Irish qualification for Mexico.

14th – 25,000 people die in Colombia when Nevado del Ruiz volcano erupts, swamping the town of Armero.

15th – 40-year-old Pat Jennings, currently on a week-to-week contract as reserve goalkeeper at Arsenal, is told he can stay until the end of the season, when he will appear in the World Cup finals as Northern Ireland's number one.

19th – US President Ronald Reagan and his Russian opposite Mikhail Gorbachev meet in Geneva and issue a joint statement that a nuclear war could never be won and should never be fought.

22nd – Laurie Cunningham, sold six years ago by West Brom to Real Madrid for £900,000, returns to The Hawthorns on loan from Marseille.

28th – The Football League land a £2 million sponsorship of the League Cup by Littlewoods.

HIT SINGLES
'Nikita' Elton John
'Gambler' Madonna
'Something About You' Level 42
'Don't Break My Heart' UB40
'A Good Heart' Fergal Sharkey
'I'm Your Man' Wham!
'Road To Nowhere' Talking Heads

DECEMBER 1985

2nd – Aston Villa sign England Under-21 defender Paul Elliott from Luton Town for £400,000.

5th – The latest talks between the League and the TV negotiators last only five minutes. Prospects of live football on TV this season seem doomed.

13th – FIFA lift their ban on English clubs playing friendly matches in Europe.

15th – The World Cup draw is made in Mexico. England are drawn with Morocco, Portugal and Poland; Scotland will face West Germany, Denmark and Uruguay; while Northern Ireland will be grouped with Brazil, Spain and Algeria.

19th – Edward Kennedy says he will not run for President of the US.

20th – A deal worth £1.3m is at long last agreed which will bring live football back to TV, with West Ham United's FA Cup third-round tie against Charlton Athletic on 5 January pencilled in as the first match back on the box.

23rd – It is reported that the Football League's £1.2 million-a-season sponsorship deal with Canon, which ends in May, is in danger.

30th – President Zia of Pakistan ends martial law.

HIT SINGLES

'Do They Know It's Christmas?' Band Aid
'Saving All My Love For You' Whitney Houston
'Separate Lives' Phil Collins/Marilyn Martin
'Merry Christmas Everyone' Shakin Stevens
'West End Girls' Pet Shop Boys
'Walking In The Air' Aled Jones
'Last Christmas' Wham!

JANUARY 1986

1st – Spain and Portugal become the 11th and 12th members of the EEC.

6th – The famous fall-out between Margaret Thatcher and Michael Heseltine over the 'Westland Helicopter Crisis' becomes public.

7th – Canon confirm that they will not be renewing their sponsorship of the Football League at the end of the season.

8th – President Reagan freezes all Libyan government assets in the US.

14th – Birmingham City are knocked out of the FA Cup by non-league Altrincham.

16th – Not surprisingly, Birmingham City manager Ron Saunders resigns.

23rd – Birmingham appoint former Hammer John Bond as their new boss.

28th – US Space Shuttle Challenger explodes shortly after take-off, killing its seven astronauts, including civilian school teacher Christa McAuliffe.

28th – Coventry striker Terry Gibson joins Manchester United for £650,000, with Alan Brazil heading in the opposite direction.

29th – Coventry sign England international Nick Pickering from Sunderland for £120,000.

HIT SINGLES
'The Sun Always Shines on TV' A-Ha
'Hit That Perfect Beat' Bronski Beat
'Walk of Life' Dire Straits
'You Little Thief' Fergal Sharkey
'Girlie Girlie' Sophia George
'Dress You Up' Madonna
'We Built This City' Starship

FEBRUARY 1986
3rd – Nottingham Forest director Frank Allcock resigns, after manager Brian Clough reveals in the club programme that he and a former director were offering odds of 7–1 against Forest winning at Manchester United in a recent game (that Forest incidentally won 3–2).

7th – Haiti President Baby Doc Duvalier flees to France after demonstrations against his regime.

12th – The Channel Tunnel treaty between France and England is signed.

12th – The Football League Management Committee insist they will not give way to the big clubs who are seeking new voting procedures which would give them more power.

14th – In the draw for the European Championship qualifying section, England are grouped with Northern Ireland, Yugoslavia and Turkey.

14th – Ron Saunders is appointed the new West Brom manager – and becomes the first man to manage all three West Midlands clubs – Aston Villa, Birmingham and West Brom.

16th – Dr Mario Soares becomes President of Portugal.

18th – As fixtures continue to pile up, the Football League insist that the season must end by 3 May because of the World Cup.

26th – In a friendly match, England win 2–1 against Israel in Tel Aviv, with both goals coming from skipper Bryan Robson.

28th – PFA secretary Gordon Taylor warns clubs that they cannot go on receiving loans from his organisation to pay players' wages. As many as 12 clubs have already asked for help this season.

28th – Swedish Prime Minister Olaf Palme is assassinated in Stockholm.

HIT SINGLES

'When The Going Gets Tough, The Tough Get Going' Billy Ocean

'Borderline' Madonna

'Only Love' Nana Mouskouri

'System Addict' Five Star

'Living in America' James Brown

'The Phantom of The Opera' Sarah Brightman/Steve Harley

'Suspicious Minds' Fine Young Cannibals

'How Will I Know?' Whitney Houston

MARCH 1986

2nd – The Australia Bill formally severs Australia's constitutional ties with the UK.

5th – QPR secure a 2–2 draw at Liverpool in the League Cup semi-final second leg to take them through to Wembley 3–2 on aggregate.

10th – Manchester United sign Nottingham Forest striker Peter Davenport for £575,000.

12th – Oxford United set up a League Cup final against QPR with a 2–0 victory over Aston Villa in their semi-final second leg, after earning a 2–2 draw at Villa Park in the first leg.

13th – Figures published today show that over 40 Football League players were paid over £50,000 for a year's wages in 1985!

13th – Aston Villa sign West Brom's Steve Hunt and Sheffield Wednesday's Andy Blair for a combined fee of £250,000 in an effort to avoid relegation.

17th – The US dollar reaches its lowest post-war rate against the Japanese yen.

20th – Barcelona announce that coach Terry Venables will be leaving them on 30 June.

22nd – Arsenal manager Don Howe asks to be released from his contract after rumours that the Gunners have approached Terry Venables.

25th – Spurs legend Steve Perryman joins Oxford United on a free transfer after 19 years at White Hart Lane.

25th – Chief scout Steve Burtenshaw is put in charge of the Arsenal team.

26th – In another warm-up game, England beat Russia 1–0 in Tbilisi with a goal from Chris Waddle.

26th – Kenny Dalglish wins his 100th cap for Scotland in their 3–0 win over Romania.

30th – US actor James Cagney dies.

31st – Chelsea are beaten 6–0 at QPR, two days after losing 4–0 at home to the Hammers. That's 10 goals in 48 hours!

HIT SINGLES:
'Chain Reaction' Diana Ross
'Burning Heart' Survivor
'Manic Monday' Bangles
'Theme From New York, New York' Frank Sinatra
'Hi Ho Silver' Jim Diamond
'Kiss' Prince

APRIL 1986

2nd – A bomb explodes on TWA flight from Rome to Athens.

5th – In the FA Cup semi-finals, Liverpool beat Southampton 2–0 at White Hart Lane, while Everton beat Sheffield Wednesday 1–0. Both games are settled in extra time.

7th – Rangers sack manager Jock Wallace and appoint Scotland skipper Graeme Souness in his place. Souness will cost £4m to prise away from Sampdoria.

13th – Following eight games without a win, Coventry City manager Don Mackay resigns. Director George Curtis takes over as caretaker manager.

13th – Jack Nicklaus wins golf's US Masters, his 18th major.

14th – Gary Lineker is named as the Football Writers' Footballer of the Year.

15th – US bombers carry out air raids on targets around Libya in an attempt to wipe out terrorist bases.

18th – QPR skipper Terry Fenwick is banned from England's game against Scotland the following week and fined £200 after exceeding 41 disciplinary points this season.

20th – Oxford United beat the odds to lift the League Cup at Wembley, winning 3–0 against QPR with goals from Hebberd, Houghton and Charles.

23rd – England beat Scotland 2–1 in a typically thunderous battle at Wembley to leave Bobby Robson confident of World Cup glory in Mexico.

23rd – Former English cricketer turned BBC commentator Jim Laker dies.

24th – Chelsea sign Scottish striker Gordon Durie from Hibs for £350,000.

24th – Wallis Simpson, US-born Duchess of Windsor, dies.

25th – Hammers legend Bobby Moore resigns as manager of Southend United for 'personal reasons'.

26th – The biggest ever nuclear accident occurs at Chernobyl in the Ukraine.

28th – There are no real surprises as England boss Bobby Robson names his squad of 22 for Mexico, with Alvin Martin the only Hammer present.

HIT SINGLES
'Living Doll' Cliff Richard and The Young Ones
'Absolute Beginners' David Bowie
'Touch Me (I Want Your Body)' Samantha Fox
'You To Me Are Everything' Real Thing
'A Different Corner' George Michael
'Train of Thought' A-Ha

MAY 1986
1st – One and a half million blacks go on strike in South Africa.

3rd – Liverpool clinch the First Division title with a 1–0 win at Chelsea.

4th – Merseyside fans are rumoured to be paying £1,000 for a terrace ticket at next week's FA Cup final.

7th – Romanian club Steaua Bucharest surprisingly beat Barcelona on penalties in the European Cup final in Seville.

9th – UEFA announce that their ban on English clubs in Europe will remain in force.

BOYS OF '86

10th – The red half of Merseyside are celebrating as Liverpool lift the FA Cup to secure the double with a 3–1 victory over Everton. Lineker gives the Toffees the lead, but goals from Rush (2) and Johnston win it for the Reds.

13th – Tottenham Hotspur manager Peter Shreeves is sacked.

14th – Millwall manager George Graham is announced as the new Arsenal boss.

14th – Russian president Gorbachev reveals the true extent of the Chernobyl disaster.

16th – David Pleat takes over at Spurs.

17th – England beat Mexico 3–0 in a friendly to put themselves among the favourites for the tournament.

24th – England win their final warm-up game, 1–0 against Canada. Gary Lineker badly sprains a wrist, but is thought to be okay for the finals.

31st – In the opening game of the World Cup finals, Italy can only manage a 1–1 draw against Bulgaria, in front of 105,000 fans in the Azteca Stadium.

HIT SINGLES

'Rock Me Amadeus' Falco
'A Kind of Magic' Queen
'What Have You Done For Me Lately?' Janet Jackson
'Live To Tell' Madonna
'Just Say No' Grange Hill Cast
'Lessons in Love' Level 42
'The Greatest Love of All' Whitney Houston
'I Heard it Through the Grapevine' Marvin Gaye
'The Chicken Song' Spitting Image
'On My Own' Patti Labelle/Michael McDonald
'Spirit In the Sky' Dr and The Medics